DISSECT

A L I E N S

TERROR IN SPACE

JOHN L. FLYNN

DISSECTING ALIENS

TERROR IN SPACE

JOHN L. FLYNN

B📖XTREE

First published in the UK in 1995 by
BOXTREE LIMITED
Broadwall House
21 Broadwall
London SE1 9PL.

First published in the USA by Image Publishing

10 9 8 7 6 5 4 3 2 1

This publication is not licensed by, nor is Boxtree or Image Publishing affiliated with, Twentieth Century Fox Corporation. This is a scholarly work intended to document the evolution of a film series

NO photos appearing in this book are copyright Twentieth Century Fox Corporation

Book design: Paul Nicosia
Cover photo: Annie Peel
Model by: Chris Fitzgerald

Printed and bound in Great Britain by The Bath Press, Avon

ISBN: 0 7522 0863 2

A CIP catalogue record for this book is available from the British Library

"In space no one can hear you scream."
—*Alien* (1979)

"This time it's war."
—*Aliens* (1986)

"The bitch is back."
—*Alien 3* (1992)

TABLE OF CONTENTS

AUTHOR'S FOREWORD AND ACKNOWLEDGMENTS

This book is about Ridley Scott's ground-breaking ALIEN (1979), James Cameron's rousing sequel ALIENS (1986), David Fincher's grimly seductive ALIEN 3 (1992) and the still to be produced ALIEN 4. I am not only concerned with the films themselves but also their origins and precursors, their licensing agreements and the impact these motion pictures have had on the industry as a whole. Nowhere else can this material be found in a single volume. For each chapter and film, I provide the title and credits, release information, a plot synopsis, and background of production information as it relates to the project, concluding with an appraisal of the film's overall impact as well as its importance today.

Back in July 1979, less than six weeks after the first motion picture had premiered, I met both Dan O'Bannon and Ron Cobb for the first time at a small science fiction gathering (then known as Uni-Con) in Washington, D.C.. They were busy making the rounds at the various conventions to promote their new film, and I was a fledging writer trying to get an exclusive interview to sell to one of the numerous science fiction magazines. Dan's enthusiasm for the project was contagious. Even though I was never able to place my article with a major publication, I began collecting and researching material about ALIEN and its inevitable sequels with the hopes of one day returning to the source. Now, fifteen years later, after having written and published dozens of articles, short stories and five books, my enthusiasm to write about ALIEN was still there. I was no longer a new writer looking for a scoop but an established author being sought after by a publisher to produce a work about the ALIEN films. The book you are now holding is the end result of that fifteen-year period of collecting and research.

Without the kind assistance of many friends in both science fiction fandom and the motion picture industry, this book could never have been written. Especially helpful have been the public relations staff at 20th Century-Fox, which may have changed faces over the last fifteen years but never their willingness to answer questions about the ALIEN series. I am particularly grateful to Terry Erdmann, of Pros and Cons Publicity, for your continued assistance and friendship over the years. I am also thankful to the handful of devoted ALIEN fans who shared their invaluable time in hunting down precious leads and rare information.

John L. Flynn

November 1994

INTRODUCTION
THE PRECURSORS TO "ALIEN"

From "The Thing (from Another World, 1951)" to "The Parasite Murders"(1974)

The original ALIEN (1979) and its three sequels are considered by many as the precursors of science fiction's new wave, alternately known as Cyberpunk or Heavy Metal, style literature and film. William Gibson, the Hugo and Nebula award-winning author of Neuromancer (1985), which first popularized this new wave, credits the first film as a major influence on his writing (and those of his peers), singling out its "dirty spaceship, lived-in future" look as something that immediately appealed to him. The pioneering efforts of Dan O'Bannon, Ronald Shusett, Walter Hill, David Giler, Ridley Scott, James Cameron and David Fincher do, in fact, deserve recognition for providing a valuable link between science fiction and gothic horror. Even though the audi-

ence imagines itself to be secure in the comfortable, well-illuminated world of technology, another world—filled with darkness, danger and primitive terror—awaits on the other side. But just as the ALIEN films have inspired a whole new generation of writers and filmmakers, including the countless parodies, pastiches and rip-offs, they too were inspired by earlier works. In fact, the roots of the first film go back nearly one hundred years.

The struggle between humans and their otherworldly counterparts is so archetypal that it can be traced back to the earliest works of modern science fiction. H(erbert) G(eorge) Wells, recognized as one of the genre's founding fathers, envisioned the first confrontation between humans and aliens in his classic tale of science fiction, THE WAR OF THE WORLDS (1898). Ever since his superior Martians first invaded the English countryside, the idea of two highly successful species competing for resources and survival has fascinated science fiction

These covers from Amazing Stories *are examples of early alien invasion stories (copyright ©1927 Experimenter Publishing Co.)*

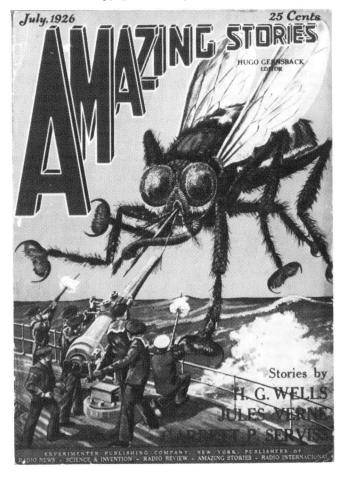

writers. Frederic Brown's classic story "Arena" (1944) finds the fate of a human-alien conflict being decided by single combatants on an equally-alien world. The aliens in Arthur Clarke's CHILDHOOD'S END (1953) and Clifford Simak's "Kindergarten" (1953) remain totally indifferent to man's existence as though humans are mere ants beneath their feet. Similarly, the man-eating plants in John Wyndham's DAY OF THE TRIFFIDS (1951), the monster wasps of Keith Roberts' THE FURIES (1966), or the aquatic demons of Brian Aldiss' "The Saliva Tree" (1966) view humans as simply a means to propagate their own species. These stories, and countless others like them, have all told the same, familiar tale. Humans have been threatened by alien creatures in pulp fiction as often as helpless heroines have been threatened by mustached villains in melodrama. Sometimes the stories are allegories of racism and xenophobia, reflections of cold war paranoia or metaphors for incurable diseases; but more often than not, they are simple adventure tales which force humans to confront their worst nightmares.

ALIEN and its sequels fit that classic mold perfectly, recalling not only the best pulp adventure stories of the thirties and forties but also the best from the science fiction films of the fifties and sixties. Thus, when the intrepid crew of the Nostromo first encounter the remains of an extraterrestrial culture in the form of a derelict spacecraft, it should surprise no one that other, earlier explorers have been that way before. One of the earliest journeys in pulp fiction, before the notion became such a heavy cliché, took place during The Voyage of the Space Beagle (serialized in Astounding Science Fiction between 1939-1943) by A(lfred) E(lton) Van Vogt. His series of short stories, later collected into novel form (1950), followed the adventures of the crew and technicians of an exploratory survey ship. Their discovery of a great alien derelict and the psychic presence that haunts it evokes an encounter of the deadliest kind.

By the late forties and early fifties, that plotline had become so commonplace in pulp fiction that it was rarely invoked by science fiction writers. But since Hollywood often fails to keep up with literary trends, period science fiction films involving a derelict spaceship and its deadly cargo appeared somewhat unique. The

most direct influence on ALIEN came be seen in THE THING (FROM ANOTHER WORLD, 1951), IT! THE TERROR FROM BEYOND SPACE (1958), PLANET OF THE VAMPIRES (1965), QUEEN OF BLOOD (1966) and other motion pictures.

1951 - THE THING (FROM ANOTHER WORLD) - RKO/Winchester Pictures, b/w, 86 min. Director: Christian Nyby (and Howard Hawks). Producer: Howard Hawks. Screenwriter: Charles Lederer based on the novella "Who Goes There?" by John W. Campbell. Starring: Kenneth Tobey, Margaret Sheridan, Robert Cornthwaite, Dewey Martin, Bill Self, Douglas Spencer, and James Arness.

The thing (in THE THING FROM ANOTHER WORLD, 1951) was not the metamorphosing creature of its source, John W. Campbell's 1938 novella "Who Goes There?," but a blood-drinking carrot man. If the one line description sounds a trifle corny, the creature evoked by James Arness was quite terrifying. Howard Hawks' superb science fiction classic provides a wonderful departure from the overworked clichés of pulp literature. The roots of Gothic terror - along with its staples of walking dead, dismemberment, and mutation - have been transformed into a "real" horror from beyond the solar system.

The movie opens with the discovery of a flying saucer embedded in the ice at the Arctic circle. Members of an army research station (including Kenneth Tobey, Robert Cornthwaite, Dewey Martin, Margaret Sheridan, Douglas Spencer and Bill Self) have been alerted of UFO sightings, but are confounded when they come upon the derelict craft. Instinctively, they recover the only survivor of the crew - a "vegoid" (played by GUNSMOKE'S James Arness) - and bring his frozen body to the safety of their encampment. When one of the soldiers accidentally unthaws the creature, it begins to run amok, killing and draining men of blood. The station's resident mad doctor (Cornthwaite) urges the others to capture the "thing" alive, while leader Tobey believes that a "dead monster is a good monster." Ultimately, they trap the "thing" in the greenhouse and cook it to death. Journalist Spencer's final warning to "keep watching the skies" reminds audiences of their Cold War paranoia by suggesting that other "things" may be coming.

Rigorous pacing, thanks to the superior editing

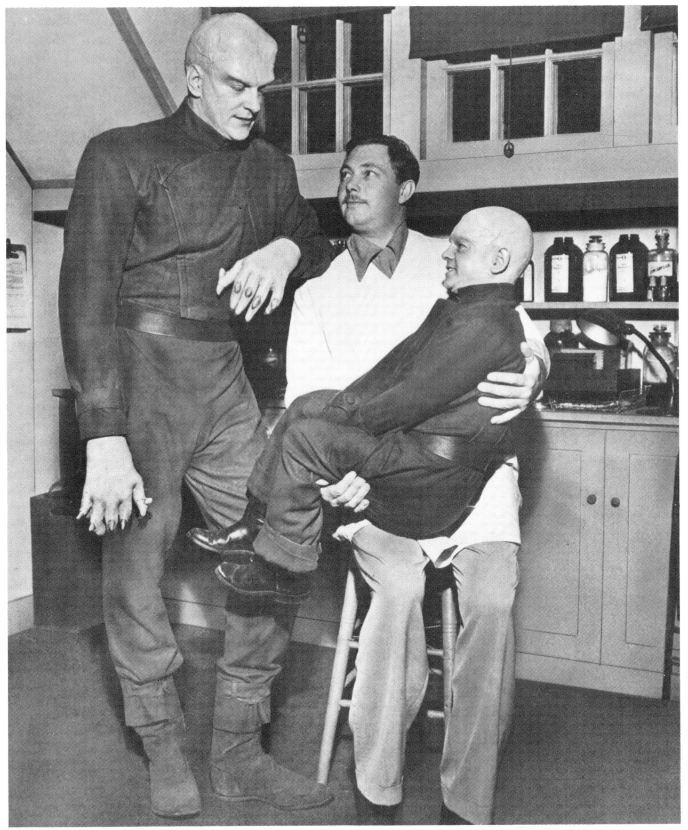

A rare behind the scenes shot from The Thing (From Another World) *(photo copyright © RKO Radio Pictures)*

of Roland Gross, helped make THE THING (FROM ANOTHER WORLD) one of the top moneymakers for 1951. Although some of the edge has been lost in light of the ALIEN films, the motion picture is still a tight suspense thriller. It also has the distinction of having launched the whole sub-genre of invasions from space as the first science fiction monster film. [John Carpenter remade THE THING in 1982 as one of the many ALIEN rip-offs, eliminating the "vegoid" monster, and returning to the original source material.]

Even though the action in THE THING (FROM ANOTHER WORLD) takes place entirely on earth, the structure and general plotting of the film anticipates the screen story of ALIEN by Dan O'Bannon. Both films open with a small, isolated group of explorers discovering the remains of an alien spacecraft. By accident, they introduce an alien lifeform into their environment, which matures and later destroys their fellow members. Each creature follows a peculiar life-cycle, beginning as a rooted organism, a small pulsating plant in THE THING and an egg-like pod in ALIEN. Both creatures undergo an unusual transformation which changes their cellular structure and form. Though ultimately man-like in form, the aliens are both inhumanly strong, deadly, and virtually invulnerable to conventional means of attack. Both groups try every means possible to destroy the creature, and eventually succeed when their basic instinct for survival leads them to solutions their rational minds have somehow overlooked.

The two films also share a number of other striking similarities. Both feature a collection of rugged individualists (both male and female) who are in conflict not only with the monster but also each other. Those battle lines are drawn between the no-nonsense commander and the inhumane, knowledge-hungry scientist. In each, it is the lone scientist (or science officer), who continually protects the alien from harm for whatever misguided reason. Ultimately, he is destroyed by the creature (or his companions) as a repayment for his perverse efforts. The claustrophobic environments of the Arctic Station—with its collection of cramped underground passageways, control center and convenient airducts—are also strangely reconstructed in the twisting corridors of the Nostromo's

three levels. In fact, the alien creature instinctively knows the best routes through the maze of corridors, and times each attack appropriately when only one human is present. The plots, though similar in nature, are like most murder mysteries, exercises in mounting terror, beginning with the initial discovery and moving carefully through each murder to the bitter end.

Prior to its release in 1979, ALIEN was blasted by the press (notably Rolling Stone, Cinefantastique and American Film) for its derivative nature. Most film critics seemed ready to dismiss the motion picture as simply a big-budget remake of THE THING (FROM ANOTHER WORLD), but the notable similarities went far beyond Howard Hawks' film to the very archetypal nature of science fiction. Those similarities were inherent in another motion picture as well . . .

1955 - THE QUATERMASS XPERIMENT (a.k.a. THE CREEPING UNKNOWN) - Hammer Films, b/w, 82 min. Director: Val Guest. Producer: Anthony Hinds. Screenwriters: Guest and Richard Landau. Starring: Brian Donlevy, Margia Dean, Jack Warner, Richard Wordsworth, David King Wood, Harold Lang, and Lionel Jeffries.

Based on a popular British teleseries, THE QUATERMASS XPERIMENT (released in the United States as THE CREEPING UNKNOWN, 1955) introduced another familiar, science fiction formula into the cinematic mainstream. The sole survivor (Richard Wordsworth) of a doomed space expedition returns to earth with an alien organism growing within his body. Even though he has

Although known in America as The Creeping Unknown, *this film is better known in England as* The Quatermass Experiment *(photo copyright ©1956 United Artists)*

somehow survived the crash of his rocketship, he begins acting strangely as a fungus-like growth appears on his hand. That growth creeps over his entire body and ultimately consumes him until he is nothing but a living fungus. Professor Quatermass (Brian Donlevy) is called upon to confront the octopus-blob creature, and manages to electrocute the organism before it can spread over the entire London area. The alien spore, which infects the astronaut's body, anticipates the egg-like pods in ALIEN, and the "creeping unknown" foreshadows the complex life-cycle which begins with the alien parasite growing within a human host. But this idea was certainly not a new one when Val Guest first began sketching plans for his big screen remake of Nigel Kneale's popular Quatermass. Pulp science fiction adventures had relied on this familiar formula for years.

1956 - FORBIDDEN PLANET - M-G-M, 98 min. Director: Fred M. Wilcox. Producer: Nicholas Nayfack. Screenwriter: Cyril Hume. Starring: Walter Pidgeon, Anne Francis, Leslie Nielsen, Warren Stevens, Jack Kelly, Richard Anderson, Earl Holliman, and James Drury.

Loosely based on Shakespeare's The Tempest, FORBIDDEN PLANET (1956) introduced audiences to a futuristic Prospero who unleashes the terrors of some lost, extraterrestrial culture upon the unsuspecting crew of a starship. While much has been written over the years, praising its special effects or discussing the parallels to the Bard's last play, the film is nothing less than remarkable. Created on a studio sound stage by director Fred Wilcox and scenarist Cyril Hume, it represents the best of Fifties' science fiction. The film was also a further extension of the genre's pulp adventure plot which, in literature, had long since become a cliché.

After traveling for more than a year in hyperspace, the United Planets Cruiser C57-D arrives at the forbidden world of Altair IV. Commander J.J. Adams (Leslie Nielsen) and crew have been dispatched by Earth base to investigate the fate of a colony planted there years before. They find only one survivor, a reclusive philologist named Morbius (Walter Pidgeon), and his innocent daughter Altaira (Anne Francis). (Apparently, when the recall notice came, Morbius decided to remain behind with his wife, who has since passed away. The other members of his party were vaporized when their

Earl Holliman and Robby the Robot in **Forbidden Planet *(photo copyright ©1994 Turner Pictures)***

ship blasted off.) They also discover an amazing robot named Robby, which the mad doctor claims he "tinkered together." Morbius insists that Adams and his crew leave immediately, refusing to take any responsibility for their lives. The starship commander declines, and orders his men to make camp.

Later that night, several men are murdered by some strange invisible force, which literally rends and tears the astronauts apart. The ship's doctor (Warren Stevens) suspects Morbius sent his robot on a rampage to frighten them away, but when the cook (Earl Holliman) comes forward to clear Robby, the mystery deepens. Eventually, they discover the remains of a buried civilization, abandoned millions of years before by its builders, the Krell, but still maintained by automation. Morbius has somehow tapped into their secret power supply, and his bestial side (known as the Id), jealous of the commander's affection for his daughter Altaira, has produced an unstoppable monster. The mad doctor dies fighting his own creation, thus leaving the others free to take off in their ship.

The evil Caliban in FORBIDDEN PLANET is the synthesis of Morbius' petty jealousies and unspeakable desires all bound together in one monster. Like the "veg-oid" monster in THE THING (FROM ANOTHER WORLD, 1951) and its lineal descendant in ALIEN, the invisible, monstrous biped acts totally on instinct. It grows and mutates, becoming larger and more terrible, with each attack. Despite the best efforts of the starship crew, they are unable to destroy the alien menace. And like the other scientists, who have protected their monsters for inexplicable reasons, Morbius cannot transcend his desires to play God, and the evil force (which is himself) destroys him.

On the other hand, it is the mad doctor's other creation, Robby the Robot, that represents both benevolence and goodwill, the dreams of science made whole in synthetic form. Robby, like his lineal descendant Bishop in ALIENS, reminds audiences of his basic programming (by reciting Isaac Asimov's three rules of robots), then attempts to protect his human masters when the monster attacks. Both Robby and Bishop are destroyed by the alien menace, but later resurrected to once again serve humans.

The similarities between FORBIDDEN PLANET and the ALIEN films do not simply end there. Dan O'Bannon's original descriptions of his all-male crew are strangely drawn like those members of the C57-D. His sterile, button-down, duty conscious "heroes" remind script readers of Commander J.J. Addams, Doctor Astrow and crew. When they are first confronted with the remains of the Krell civilization (and later the invisible monster), they react in ways that tend to echo those of another expedition to a forbidden world. Ultimately, through the great sacrifice of their comrades, they are able to finally destroy the monster. FORBIDDEN PLANET was very well received in its day, and continues to delight audiences nearly forty years later in spite of its derivative origins.

1958 - IT! THE TERROR FROM BEYOND SPACE

(a.k.a. IT! THE VAMPIRE FROM BEYOND SPACE) - United Artists, b/w, 69 min. Director: Edward L Cahn. Producer: Robert E. Kent. Writer: Jerome Bixby. Starring: Marshall Thompson, Shawn Smith, Kim Spalding, Ann Doran, Ray "Crash" Corrigan, and Dabbs Greer.

Director Edward Cahn teamed with noted science fiction writer Jerome Bixby to create the first, intergalactic vampire stowaway in United Artists' IT! THE TERROR FROM BEYOND SPACE (1958). Although this low budget shocker owes much to A.E. Van Vogt's 1950 novel THE VOYAGE OF THE SPACE BEAGLE, THE THING (FROM ANOTHER WORLD, 1951) and FORBIDDEN PLANET (1956), the plotline is a direct descendent of the monster in the haunted house story. Returning from Mars, a space expedition discovers it has inadvertently taken a blood-drinking monster (Ray "Crash" Corrigan) on board. Relentlessly, the vampire stalks members of the male and female crew and drains them of blood one-by-one. (As

Generally considered to be one of the biggest influences on Alien — though you couldn't tell from this photo — was It! The Terror from Beyond Space

usual in films like this, the crew behaves rather stupidly, and make easy prey for the creature.) Captain Marshall Thompson and the remaining survivors attempt to contain the monster in the lower section of the ship, but "it" soon breaks free and pursues them section by section to the bridge. Backed up against the bulkhead, the crew is forced to decompress the ship and blast the monster into deep space. The special effects are laughable, and the rubber- suited monster is less than credible; but IT! THE TERROR FROM BEYOND SPACE is a lively precursor to QUEEN OF BLOOD (1966) and ALIEN (1979).

ALIEN perhaps shares more in common with IT! THE TERROR FROM BEYOND SPACE than any of the other motion pictures which came before it. The plotline is an almost scene by scene remake, beginning with the first discovery that the monster is aboard and climaxing with the decompression of the spacecraft. Those analogous scenes are complimented by similarities in the make-up of the crew and the set design of the space ships. Even the alien creatures share a common link. Both are man-like in form, though inhumanly strong and nearly inde-structible; both have razor-sharp teeth and claws for rending and tearing victims, and both seem to instinctive-ly play a complex game of hide-and-seek with their human quarry. The singular difference in terms of plot, which sets ALIEN apart from this film, appears to be its creature's complex life-cycle, which begins as a rooted organism, grows and mutates within the human host, then emerges and matures on its own. A similar life-cycle was, however, first exploited by two other films which debuted in that same year.

1958 - FIEND WITHOUT A FACE - Eros, 75 min. Director: Arthur Crabtree. Producer: John Croydon. Screenwriter: Herbert J. Leder. Starring: Kyanston Reeves, Marshall Thompson, Terry Kilburn, Kim Parker, Peter Madden, and Michael Balfour.

The creatures in Arthur Crabtree's FIEND WITH-OUT A FACE (1958) were disembodied brains which wrapped themselves around a victim's head (with the help of a spinal cord-like tail) and sucked the victims dry. Unleashed by a mad scientist (Marshall Thompson) who has learned to transform thoughts into physical form, these organic parasites scramble around much like ALIEN's face hugger, propelled by the whip of their multi-

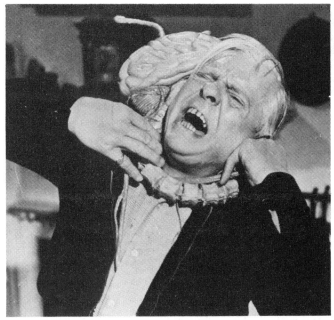

Could this be the face-hugger's first appearance in **Fiend Without a Face***? (photo copyright ©1962 Metro-Goldwyn-Mayer, Inc.)*

jointed tails. They depend on human hosts to provide them with greater mobility as they struggle to take con-trol of a remote army base (near the Canadian frontier), and are very difficult to kill. While the idea may be bor-rowed from Robert Heinlein's THE PUPPET MASTERS (1951), the climax is clearly inspired by THE THING (FROM ANOTHER WORLD) as the soldiers of the isolated base fight an all-out war with the parasites. Similar plot developments can be found not only in the original ALIEN but also James Cameron's ALIENS.

1958 - NIGHT OF THE BLOOD BEAST - American International Pictures, b/w, 65 min. Director: Bernard Kowalski. Producer: Roger Corman. Writer: Martin Varno. Based on a story by Gene Corman. Starring: Michael Emmet, Angela Greene, John Baer and Ed Nelson.

Like THE QUATERMASS XPERIMENT (1955), NIGHT OF THE BLOOD BEAST (1958) introduced yet another astronaut who has returned from space with alien embryos growing within his body. Apparently, dur-ing his deep space mission, some alien intelligence took control of his rocketship and mind, and implanted fertil-ized eggs with the astronaut's chest cavity. The astronaut returns to earth dead, but later revives under the control of his extraterrestrial hosts. A single "blood beast" even-tually hatches and turns deadly, destroying everything in its path. This low-budgeter does not strive for the same

Man versus man in a rubber suit in **Night of the Blood Beast**

epic proportions of ALIEN, and is cinematically unremarkable; but its use of this familiar science fiction plot does foretell the shape of stranger things to come.

1965 - PLANET OF THE VAMPIRES (TERRORE NELLO SPAZIO, a.k.a. DEMON PLANET) - Italian/Spanish, 85 min. Director: Mario Bava. Producer: Fulvio Luciana. Writers: I.B. Melchoir, Callisto Casulich, Antonio Roman, and Bava. Starring: Barry Sullivan, Norma Bengell, Evi Marandi, Angel Aranda, Fernando Villena, and Franco Andrei.

Director Mario Bava's TERRORE NELLO SPAZIO (PLANET OF THE VAMPIRES, 1965) combined elements from not only pulp science fiction but also gothic horror to produce a visually intense motion picture. Bava had been Italy's leading cinematographer in the Fifties and became a producer of a series of fine, low budget horror films in the Sixties. His first foray into the field of science fiction has the visual pace and styling of a classic horror film, even though the alien sets are made from cardboard and the plot is derivative of IT! THE TERROR FROM BEYOND SPACE (1958) and a half of dozen other films.

While surveying the planet Aura, the lead rocketship of a two-ship expedition mysteriously vanishes, and the second (led by Barry Sullivan) sets out to investigate. Later, it too is pulled off course and forced to land by a strange gravitational field. Once on the planet's surface, the crew discovers the ruins of their sister craft as well as the bodies of her crew. Sullivan orders his men to bury the dead astronauts; but, shortly after burial, their bodies begin to rise from the grave and attack the others for blood. Eventually, Sullivan learns that the disembod-

ied inhabitants of the planet have lured the two rocketships there in order to possess their bodies and thus leave their world. Sullivan must quickly decide whether to destroy his own ship or allow these "space vampires" to roam the galaxy unchecked.

Bava's film anticipates the original ALIEN (1979) with his novel blending of gothic horror and science fiction. The crew's discovery of a derelict ship and their ultimate conflict with some alien, predatory force, determined to possess them in order to propagate its species, are familiar staples of the genre. And even though the script is innocuous, Bava's direction is somewhat compelling with his ever-moving camera creating an atmosphere of tension and menace. (Both Ridley Scott and James Cameron must have studied his technique before embarking on their classic efforts.) Other elements in the film are strangely familiar, not the least of which is the alien landscape easily recognizable in H.R. Giger's designs for the storm-swept planetoid in ALIEN. These elements, and a hundred or so like them, can be traced directly to other films, like THE THING (FROM ANOTHER WORLD, 1951), FORBIDDEN PLANET (1956) and IT! THE TERROR FROM BEYOND SPACE (1958). But then the same thing can be said of a number of other horror fantasies of the period; interesting approaches, like that of

"Get away from her, you bitch!" Well, maybe not. Actually it's **Planet of the Vampires** *(photo copyright ©1965 American International Pictures)*

director Bava, make the material seem somehow fresh. American International Pictures followed, one year later, with their own version of the familiar story, QUEEN OF BLOOD (a.k.a. PLANET OF BLOOD, 1966).

1966 - QUEEN OF BLOOD (a.k.a. PLANET OF BLOOD) - George Edwards Productions/AIP, 88 min. Director: Curtis Harrington. Producer: George Edwards. Screenwriter: Curtis Harrington. Based on the novel by Charles Nuetzel. Starring: John Saxon, Basil Rathbone, Judi Meredith, Dennis Hopper, Florence Marley, and Forrest J. Ackerman.

Dark, smoothly shot in shadowy interiors that recall the claustrophobic paranoia of Howard Hawks' THE THING (FROM ANOTHER WORLD) and evoke the work of Ridley Scott's ALIEN, QUEEN OF BLOOD was yet one more remake of IT! THE TERROR FROM BEYOND SPACE. Director Curtis Harrington (under the guidance of Roger Corman) cannibalized the superior Russian film NIEBO ZOWIET (THE HEAVENS CALL, 1959) for stock footage, and shot the balance of the motion picture in eight days with a budget of less than fifty thousand dollars. Yet QUEEN OF BLOOD manages to transcend those humble origins to be a compelling atmospheric piece of horror fantasy.

In 1990, an expedition is sent to Mars to investi-

Famous Monster Forest J Ackerman carrying alien eggs in **Queen of Blood** *(photo copyright ©1966 American International Pictures)*

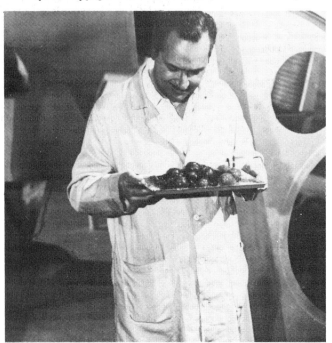

gate a mysterious transmission of unknown origin. When the first expedition fails to report back, earth scientists dispatch a second ship. Three astronauts (John Saxon, Judi Meredith, and Dennis Hopper) discover a derelict spacecraft (at the point of transmission) and its sole survivor, a green-tinted alien (Florence Marley). After they take her aboard their spaceship, crew members begin to die, one by one, their bodies completely drained of blood. Marley is really a hemophiliac vampire, the sole survivor of her race, who has come aboard their ship to breed a new race. Finally, during the climactic struggle with Meredith, the vampire is cut and bleeds to death. However, her nest of eggs is uncovered by the mission commander (Basil Rathbone in his last role) and his assistant (Forrest J. Ackerman, the famous SF collector and editor of Famous Monsters of Filmland, in a cameo role.], and removed from the ship for study on earth.

The film's rudimentary plot aside, QUEEN OF BLOOD was an effective thriller. Harrington follows the creature as she stalks her prey in the narrow, claustrophobic corridors of the spaceship, suggesting a similar collection of scenes thirteen years later. Her nest of eggs which, when carelessly removed from the ship, may someday threaten all life on earth evokes an equally chilling premise in ALIEN: Ash has been sent by the Company to collect specimens for study by the bioweapons. Characterization and dialogue are uniformly bad, but the director's tight camera angles generate a real sense of terror.

1974 - DARK STAR - Jack H. Harris Enterprises, 83 min. Director and Producer: John Carpenter. Executive Producer: Jack H. Harris. Screenwriters: Carpenter and Dan O'Bannon. Starring: Brian Narelle, Andre Pahich, Cal Kuniholm, Dan O'Bannon, Joe Saunders, and Miles Watkins.

More than any other science fiction film, DARK STAR (1974), John Carpenter's feature film debut, inspired co-writer Dan O'Bannon to begin working on his script for ALIEN. Made with the ridiculously low budget of $60,000 over a three-year period by the two University of Southern California cinema students, the film anticipates several of O'Bannon's key themes, including paranoia, the breakdown of technology and the metaphysical boredom of astronauts on a deep-space voyage. Even

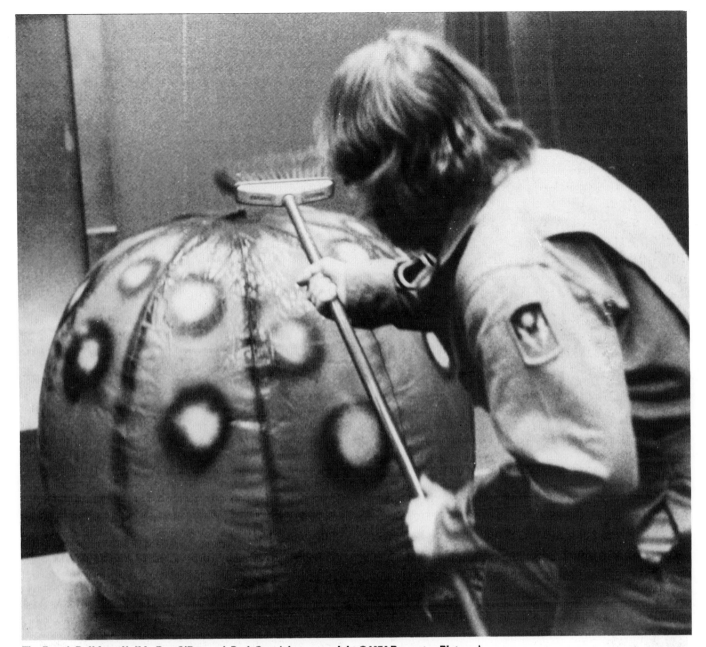

The Beach Ball from Hell in Dan O'Bannon's Dark Star *(photo copyright ©1974 Bryanston Pictures)*

though the motion picture is often dismissed as a simple cult comedy (by film students for film students), it is a sly satire of Stanley Kubrick's 2001: A SPACE ODYSSEY, among others.

The crew of the spaceship Dark Star, whose Commander Powell (Joe Saunders) is dead but kept alive and animated in a cryogenic freezer, have grown complacent over the last few months in deep space, and that boredom has begun to affect every aspect of their mission to destroy planets and stars which are unstable.

Doolittle (Brian Narelle), Talby (Andre Pahich), Boiler (Cal Kuniholm), and Pinback (Dan O'Bannon) are, in fact, slowly going insane. When the ship is threatened by the crew's pet alien (which resembles nothing more than a beachball with claws), Pinback madly chases it throughout the ship, and ends up getting caught in a liftshaft with the lift in motion. Boiler loses his temper during an insane conversation with one of the ship's talking bombs, and blasts it with a ray-gun, effectively destroying the ship. The other two are thrown free of the blast, but can't survive in their spacesuits beyond a few hours. Doolittle attempts to surf down to the planet below and becomes a shooting star; Talby gets trapped in the gravitational pull of the Phoenix asteroids and spends the rest of eternity cruising the stars.

DARK STAR's delicious mix of polished realism and bleak, despairing satire expertly builds one conceit upon the next to produce a black comedy of epic proportions. The film is clearly funny, but in retrospect the comedy does seem strained at times and certain aspects are dated. The classic conflict between tired astronauts and an alien predator aboard a starship not only receives a comic twist but also establishes the dramatic formula which O'Bannon would later rely upon for ALIEN. Perhaps the strongest element in the work details the deteriorating conditions aboard the ship, how the crew members (in various stages of psychosis) are slowly being driven crazy by the close quarters of the ship. This element of discontentment and complacency would also later surface to provide the crew of the Nostromo with a slight edge. Pinback and the others transcend the buttoned-down space voyagers (commonplace in science fiction films), observe no real dress code and act like hippies who despise conformity. Dallas, Ripley and the others demonstrate a similar irreverence.

Technically brilliant, considering its limited budget, cast and crew, DARK STAR is also highly sophisticated work of science fiction and farce.

1974 - THE PARASITE MURDERS (THEY CAME FROM WITHIN) - Cinepix/Canadian Development Corporation, 87 min. Director and Screenwriter: David Cronenberg. Producer: Ivan Reitman. Starring: Paul Hampton, Joe Silver, Lynn Lowry, Barbara Steele, Allan Migicovsky, and Susan Petrie.

David Cronenberg's THE PARASITE MURDERS (a.k.a. THEY CAME FROM WITHIN, 1974) also introduced a parasitic creature which takes root in the human host and eventually turns monstrous, like the one in ALIEN. In an attempt to produce a species of animal that will develop a special symbiotic bond with humanity (by reducing sexual tension), a research scientist (Fred Doerderllein) creates, then implants a parasite in place of the organ transplants his patients have requested. The organism acts like an aphrodisiac, and gives the patients a false

sense of euphoria as they turn into sexual fiends. Eventually, the vaguely phallic parasites emerge from their human hosts and attach themselves to other victims. A young doctor (Paul Hampton) and his wife (Lynn Lowry) fight a losing battle against the creatures in the isolated Starliner complex as their companions are taken over one by one. The film's structure is remarkably similar to Don Siegel's INVASION OF THE BODY SNATCHERS (1956), but Director Cronenberg's analogy of rapidly spreading sexual disease is far more disturbing and real. This analogy is further intensified in light of the government's recent revelations about its own genetic experiments in the Fifties and Sixties. The parasitic creatures, with their phallic bodies, are lineal ancestors of H.R. Giger's alien.

*****

The original ALIEN (1979) and its three sequels are clearly derivative. These motion pictures follow in the same footsteps of various predecessors which have invoked the familiar, archetypal struggle of humans with their otherworldly counterparts. Human beings have been threatened by alien creatures in pulp fiction for nearly a hundred years, and in the cinema for less than half that time. But just as each of these films have attempted to add some new twist to the well-worn story, others come along (every few years) with fancier special effects or even more visually-shocking material. ALIEN succeeds not simply as an adventure tale, in which humans are forced to confront their worst nightmares, but also because of its complex milieu, its unusual production design, its rigorous pacing and a dozen other exemplary features. Over and above all these, ALIEN's evocation of past works—like Shakespeare's reworking of a chestnut to create his own unique vision—makes it somehow classic and contemporary at the same time. ALIEN and its sequels fit the classic mold perfectly, recalling the best from the past, while offering audiences a dark glimpse into the future of science fiction and gothic horror.

CHAPTER ONE:
"ALIEN" (1979) - THE FIRST ENCOUNTER

1979 - ALIEN - 20th Century Fox, in association with Brandywine Productions, 124 min, Panavision (released in 70mm, Dolby Stereo). Director: Ridley Scott. Producers: Gordon Carroll, Walter Hill and David Giler. Executive Producer: Ronald Shusett. Screenwriter: Dan O'Bannon. Based on a story by Dan O'Bannon and Ronald Shusett. Music Composer: Jerry Goldsmith. Director of Photography: Derek Vanlint. Film Editor: Terry Rawlings. Special Effects Supervisors: Brian Johnson and Nick Allder. Visual Design Consultant: Dan O'Bannon. Conceptual Artist: Ron Cobb. Additional Conceptual Artists: Jean "Moebius" Girard, Chris Foss and H.R. Giger. Art Directors: Les Dilley and Roger Christian. Starring: Tom Skerritt, Sigourney Weaver, Veronica Cartwright, Harry Dean Stanton, John Hurt, Ian Holm, Yaphet Kotto, and Helen Horton as the voice of Mother. Released on May 25, 1979

In some distant region of uncharted space, the battered commercial starship Nostromo, with its vast cargo of oil and precious minerals in tow, receives a message of unknown origin from a planetoid in the vicinity. Its crew of seven astronauts—five men and two women—are awakened from their "hypersleep," a kind of suspended animation, to investigate the transmission. Setting down upon the barren world, they discover an awesome galactic horror—an indestructible alien which threatens to destroy each of them. Those few, tantalizing details of plot, revealed by publicist Charles Lippincott during a slide presentation at the 1978 World Science Fiction Convention held in Phoenix, Arizona, first introduced audiences to an upcoming, major motion picture from Twentieth Century-Fox. At first glance, the storyline

may have seemed to most fans of science fiction and horror films as a grisly hybrid of the most lurid elements from IT! THE TERROR FROM BEYOND SPACE (1958), FIEND WITHOUT A FACE (1958) and NIGHT OF THE BLOOD BEAST (1958). But ALIEN was far more than just a "B" movie with a multi-million dollar budget and ad campaign. And even though Fox's decision to commit production funding was based not on its "original" storyline but rather the enthusiastic response to THE OMEN (1976) and STAR WARS (1977), two previous summer blockbusters, the film was also much more than just a cinematic commodity.

"ALIEN is like a gothic horror film in space," author Dan O'Bannon first explained his original concept for the motion picture nearly seventeen years ago. "I was fascinated and excited with the notion of having some form of uncontrollable monstrosity loose on board a space vessel. The thing is breaking down every barrier the crew puts up, and nothing can kill it. There's nowhere to run, once they reach the opposite end of the ship. I like the concept of a newly discovered planet where the human explorers (read invaders) uncover a form of life which is different. Their misinterpretation of this alien leads to most of the problems."

The relentless death-struggle between a small crew and a cosmic creature in ALIEN, though clearly derivative of numerous science fiction and horror films and the pulp adventure stories of the thirties and forties, was exactly the kind of motion picture Twentieth Century-Fox wanted to make into a summer blockbuster. Produced by Gordon Carroll, David Giler and Walter Hill with breathtaking imagination, and utilizing some of the most innovative and spectacular special effects ever filmed, the familiar story was carefully engineered to plunge audiences into a maelstrom of terror and suspense. But somewhere between that original story by O'Bannon and its debut in 1979, the motion picture developed into something very special.

THE RON SHUSETT-DAN O'BANNON COLLABORATION

The story for ALIEN (1979) was originally conceived by Dan O'Bannon in the summer of 1972 as two separate script ideas, and only later evolved, after numerous revisions and rewrites, into the blueprint for the highly successful film. O'Bannon was the talented, University of Southern California film student who had not only co-written the science fiction satire DARK STAR (1974), with John Carpenter, but also produced the visual effects for the film and starred as the character Pinback. While still working on the cult parody, he decided to write yet another screenplay, similar in theme to DARK STAR but totally different in tone. Entitled "Memory," the story provided the backbone of what would eventually become the first half of ALIEN—a crew of astronauts discover a dormant creature on an alien planet. Before he could work out the complex second half, however, the screenplay was set aside so that O'Bannon (and the others) could complete the painstaking work of piecing together of the independent film project for general distribution.

The cult success of DARK STAR brought O'Bannon to the attention of George Lucas and the special effects wizards of Industrial Light & Magic. Lucas was working on a film called STAR WARS (1977), and he hired O'Bannon to provide some of the computer animation and graphic effects for his project. Early in 1975, once he had completed his work for Lucas, O'Bannon was hired by European surrealist filmmaker Aléxandro Jodorowsky to engineer some of the visual effects for his proposed multimillion-dollar adaptation of Frank Herbert's DUNE. Dan O'Bannon traveled to Europe and met with Jodorowsky and three of the best fantasy artists in the world, including surrealist painter Hans Rudi Giger of Switzerland, Heavy Metal artist Jean "Moebius" Girard of France, and Chris Foss of England. After less than six months of preproduction in Paris, however, the film project folded under heavy financial problems. O'Bannon had not been paid by Jodorowsky, and used the remainder of his savings for a one-way ticket home. Broke and depressed, he found himself back at square one. "DUNE collapsed so badly," Dan later revealed, "that I ended up in Los Angeles without any money, without an apartment, without a car, with half of my belongings back in Paris and the other half in storage."

O'Bannon accepted the invitation of a friend, producer and screenwriter Ron Shusett, to camp out on his couch for a few weeks "to get his act together." He struggled for more than a week to put the demons behind him, then turned to the one thing he felt confident in. Anxious to write again, Dan retrieved his portable typewriter from storage and began revising his science fiction thriller. "It was only about twenty pages long, and pretty sketchy; but I remember thinking it was one of the best beginnings I'd ever had—I just didn't know where the hell to go with it. At that time, it started with the alien transmission and the awakening from hypersleep, and went through the discovery of the dead space captain inside the derelict. Beyond that, my ideas were kind of nebulous," O'Bannon explained some years later. He realized that, after all these years, he still couldn't solve the second half, and turned back to his files.

Both he and Shusett spent weeks, working through the stacks and stacks of notes and partially completed story ideas. Finally, after nearly a month, Shusett suggested that the two of them work collaboratively on one project, and try to sell the story idea to one of the big studios. Dan O'Bannon accepted his proposition and began discussing possible story concepts. Ron had been toying with an adaptation of Philip K. Dick's short story "We Can Remember It for You Wholesale," and offered his idea for TOTAL RECALL. O'Bannon was still not satisfied with "Memory," but nonetheless offered his concept. While Dan liked Shusett's idea, the latter did not think much of his thriller. "I thought it was just a good B-movie," said Ron Shusett long after the fact, "which showed a lack of vision on my part." The two writers turned their attention to an early draft of what would eventually become TOTAL RECALL, but failed to get beyond the first third. They turned back to "Memory," and struggled for weeks to figure out the rest of the story.

During one of their frequent brainstorming sessions, Shusett recalled another story idea O'Bannon had started to write in the early seventies and later abandoned. The story was titled "Gremlins" (no relation to the Joe Dante- Steven Spielberg film), and dealt with the little monsters which harass a B-17 bomber crew on a night raid over Tokyo during World War II. Ron suggested that they combine plot lines, and use the premise for the second half of an alien stalking the crewmen aboard their own ship. Dan O'Bannon liked the synthesis of ideas.

Within a few days, he was hard at work on the script for STAR BEAST, the working title of the film.

O'Bannon's first screen treatment for STAR BEAST was, unfortunately, little more than a retread of IT! THE TERROR FROM BEYOND SPACE (1958) and QUEEN OF BLOOD (1966). Set in the year 2087 A.D., the script began aboard the commercial starship Snark with the interception of a radio transmission of unknown origin. Awakened from hypersleep, the crew diverts to the source of the signal, a storm-swept planetoid, and discovers the remains of a downed spacecraft and its sole inhabitant, a skeletonized pilot. The crew takes a number of scientific readings, and return to their ship with a misshapen skull as proof of their findings. The skull carries the host of an alien creature inside, which quickly matures to full size and begins terrorizing the crew once they have set course for home. Evading capture by the beast, the crew eventually joins forces to blast the creature into space. O'Bannon was not at all pleased with his first draft, and explained his frustration to Shusett: "STAR BEAST is just a simple monster movie which needs some brand new inspirational idea. It will fall right into place, if we can come up with a simple way of making the monster amazing...." But neither could think of a way of making their "star beast" unique.

While he and Shusett were trying to devise a brilliant, nightmarish creature for the core of the story, O'Bannon found it difficult to shake the images of H.R. Giger's early conceptual designs for the failed DUNE. His designs and the handful of paintings, which were later gathered into the art book NERONOMICON, had a profound effect on O'Bannon's work. "I had never seen anything that was quite as horrible and at the same time as beautiful as his work. And so I ended up writing a script with Giger's monster at the center," he explained. But though the design of the monster itself was unique, the story remained derivative of most B-movies. Finally, after having discussed H.R. Giger's work with Shusett, Ron had an inspirational nightmare of his own. He woke O'Bannon up in the middle of the night and said, "Dan, I have the idea. I know what the monster does. The monster screws the human being. It plants the seed, grows and emerges from the body of the human—a hybrid monster. It's in

THE FINAL WORD ON DR. WHO • GEORGE PAL'S PUPPETOONS

FANTASTIC FILMS

The Magazine of Visual Fantasy and Science Fiction

$2.00
OCTOBER/1979

ALIEN

DIRECTOR RIDLEY SCOTT INTERVIEWED

The 8th Annual Paris Science Fiction and Fantasy Film Festival • The Quatermass Films (Five Million Miles To Earth, The Creeping Unknown, The Enemy Within)

there, and we don't know until it comes out and escapes in the ship, and all during the movie, it's chasing them and changing into different forms." Shusett's idea, which no one had ever thought of before, broke the block, and just that quickly, the story fell right into place.

Within three weeks, they had worked out the whole story outline to the project now called ALIEN. Their original intent was to produce a low-budget feature that they could package and sell independently. Shusett began searching for the financing, while O'Bannon sequestered himself in solitude for three months to write the complete script. Dan emerged from that solitude only a few times, first to argue over the greater potential of the story (if sold to a major studio) with his partner, and to hire Ron Cobb, a former political cartoonist and illustrator, to complete several preliminary sketches. O'Bannon was determined to direct ALIEN himself. He felt qualified, having substituted for Carpenter during the DARK STAR shoot, and didn't want his project lost in development hell. However, after several rejections from the major studios, Dan relented, agreeing to circulate their modest little script (and some Cobb illustrations) without his name attached as director. A mutual friend of theirs, Mark Haggard, passed the script to writer-director Walter Hill who had only months before founded Brandywine Productions with producer Gordon Carroll and writer David Giler. Their independent production company had reviewed over three hundred script submissions, and despite the fact O'Bannon's screenplay needed work, Hill felt ALIEN was the most commercially viable of all the works they had read. After several weeks of negotiations, Brandywine optioned the script in October 1976. "From that point on," Dan remembered, "it just sort of exploded in all directions."

THE ORIGINAL SCRIPT

The preface to the original script, which O'Bannon and Shusett sold to Brandywine Productions, begins with a variation of the epigram, a definition: "Alien, adjective- strange, foreign, distant, remote, hostile, repugnant...."

O'Bannon's subsequent narrative generally parallels the finished film, scene for scene, with the exception of several critical differences. Set in the year 2087 A.D., the story opens aboard the starship Snark with the interception of an indecipherable radio transmission. Awakened from hypersleep by the ship's talking computer (reminiscent of HAL-9000), the six-man crew of astronauts diverts the ship to a small asteroid and sets down on its storm-swept, hostile surface. Standard, Broussard and Melkonis leave the ship (with simple breathing masks) to search for the source of the transmission, and discover a derelict spacecraft. Gaining entry through several gaping holes, perforated in the ship's fuselage, they find a cavernous chamber containing an array of dead machinery. Further investigation leads them to a dead pilot, his lone skeletonized, extraterrestrial body lying in repose at the controls. (Apparently, the console in front of him is the source of the strange transmission.) Next to the dead pilot, the astronauts find an empty alien egg (but no egg chamber, as in the finished film). Broussard also notices that the pilot has scratched out what appears to be the image of a triangle on the panel in front of him. They take the skull of the fossilized alien (referring to him as "Poor Yurick") back with them to the ship, as proof of their findings.

Upon return to the Snark, their companions (Hunter, Roby and Faust) reveal that they've discovered an ancient stone pyramid - suggestive of the scrawled triangle - on the horizon. After reviewing the data they've collected from the derelict in holographic form, the crew speculates on the origin of the craft and structure. The astronauts suspect the pyramid may be either a mass grave or the remains of the alien crew frozen in suspended animation. Even their talkative computer can't seem to offer a valid explanation. They decide to mount a second expedition in order to get some answers.

Broussard, Melkonis and Standard fight their way through a dust storm, and eventually reach the base of the pyramid. They search for an entrance, and discover a dark, narrow tunnel at the top. Once inside the towering structure, Broussard finds strange hieroglyphics, which have a primitive, religious significance, telling some ancient, epic history. Spaced at intervals are stone statues depicting grotesque monsters, half anthropoid and half octopus. He stumbles upon a secret room, containing a pedestal with rows of leathery urns—just like the one in the derelict ship. The light from his "data-stick" causes one of the urns to come to life. When Broussard leans over its spongy, almost organic surface, a small alien creature springs out, attaching itself to his face, wrapping its tentacles around his head. Melkonis and Standard come quickly to his aide, and carry him back to their starship's infirmary.

Though efforts to break its grasp fail, the alien parasite soon drops off as strangely as it once held onto the astronaut's face. The crew breathes a collective sigh of relief, while speculating on its origins. Humanity has apparently not discovered any other lifeforms in its exploration of the galaxy, and questions about the alien creature's life cycle and indigenous nature consume the crew. Broussard is simply happy to be rid of the parasite, and anxious to leave the planetoid far behind. His fellow crewmembers set course for earth, totally unaware that he is now playing host to some deadly predator. Shortly after lift-off, as they prepare to return to hypersleep, the alien rips a massive hole in Broussard's chest and escapes, during the ensuing pandemonium, into the lower decks of the starship.

Roby panics, while the remainder of the crew organize a "hunt and destroy" mission. But the creature still manages to evade capture, moving through the airducts, rapidly maturing into a six-foot tall, multi-tentacled monstrosity with razor-sharp teeth. The alien not only grows larger but also gains a ferocious appetite, ransacking the ship's food lockers to feed itself. When it finally re-emerges, the alien swoops down, like an oversized bird, and grabs Melkonis for food. The creature then begins stalking the other members of the crew, mysteriously vanishing after each attack.

Working feverishly against time with the data collected from the pyramid, Roby and Standard manage to unscramble some of the hieroglyphics. The tomb was once a fertility temple where the aliens stored their eggs and had mating rituals. The creature, itself, has four distinct life stages—from egg to face-hugger, then adult warrior to cocoon. It doesn't simply eat all of its victims, but rather transforms some of them into spores to foster a new generation of creatures. When attempts to poison the alien with gas fail, and Standard is captured, Roby discovers a room in the lower decks of the ship where the creature has cocooned several of the others. Still conscious, Standard begs his companion to kill him, and Roby obliges by torching him with a flame-thrower. Alone, and near the point of collapse, Roby sets the ship to self-destructs before escaping in a lifepod.

Dan O'Bannon's original script for ALIEN is both highly original and derivative, interesting and remarkably unsophisticated, unusual and clearly the result of a neophyte talent hitting upon a concept unable or unprepared to develop fully. Whereas O'Bannon's nightmarish creature is brilliantly realized, his plotline seems borrowed from a handful of classic science fiction films, including THE THING (FROM ANOTHER WORLD, 1951), FORBIDDEN PLANET (1956), IT! THE TERROR FROM BEYOND SPACE (1958), and QUEEN OF BLOOD (1966). By having his characters discover a derelict spacecraft and its fossilized pilot, Dan's plot structure provides an eerie introduction to the story; but their subsequent journeys on the planetoid's surface needlessly complicates the plot. The characters themselves are not particularly interesting; their personalities (beyond perhaps Roby) are largely interchangeable. In fact, the notion of an all-male crew must have been a miscalculation on the part of O'Bannon, considering he and his partner Shusett's intent was to produce something commercially viable. The dialogue is equally weak, relying too much on tense, artificial machismo or the "Jesus, gadzooks" quality of bad B-movies. O'Bannon does manage to heighten suspense by keeping the mystery of the pyramid (and its strange occupants) locked safely away in its hieroglyphics; but, by the time the astronauts finally figure out the puzzle, there's really only one thing left to do: DESTROY THE ALIEN!! The ending then turns on a somewhat predictable countdown to destruction, like dozens of other motion pictures before it. But the screenplay was imaginative enough to attract Walter Hill and his partners in Brandywine Productions.

"The O'Bannon-Shusett script was, in any kind of literary sense, unsophisticated," Hill explained. "It had not even B-picture merit. That was its problem. Nobody could take it seriously. It wasn't a professional job. It was poorly written. But there was no question in my mind that they wanted to do a science fiction version of JAWS. They had also worked out a very interesting problem. How do you destroy a creature you can't kill without destroying your own life support system? I thought this was a good notion . . ."

BRANDYWINE PRODUCTIONS

Months before O'Bannon had finished his original script for ALIEN, writer-director Walter Hill, producer Gordon Carroll and writer David Giler joined forces to create Brandywine Productions. Carroll, who had worked as a line producer for more than fifteen years, had known both Hill and Giler for some time, and when he finally introduced his mutual friends, the three began talking casually about the formation of their own company. (Hill and Giler worked right down the hall from one another in offices on the Twentieth Century-Fox lot.) When executives at Fox agreed to provide them with offices in exchange for a first- refusal production agreement,

Carroll, Hill and Giler became independent producers.

Walter Hill had begun his career in the late sixties as assistant director on several low-budget thrillers, and soon turned to writing such screenplays as HICKEY AND BOGGS (1972) for Robert Culp and Bill Cosby, THE GETAWAY (1973) for Sam Peckinpah, THE MACINTOSH MAN (1973) and THE DROWNING POOL (1976) for Paul Newman, and THE THIEF WHO CAME TO DINNER (1973) for Ryan O'Neal and Jacqueline Bisset. When the original director left HARD TIMES (1975), Hill was given the chance to make his directorial debut (based on the strength of his screenplay for the film). Subsequent turns at THE DRIVER (1978), THE WARRIORS (1979), STREETS OF FIRE (1984), and EXTREME PREJUDICE (1987) helped establish his reputation for white-knuckle thrillers and pulsating violence. The explosive, high-action premise of 48 HOURS (1982), and its sequel, made him one of the most sought-after directors of the eighties.

Unlike Hill, David Giler spent nearly ten years writing scripts for television, and eventually turned to filmmaking as both a screenwriter and director. Giler's first sales were to the war drama, THE GALLANT MEN (1962, ABC), and the anthology series, THE KRAFT THEATRE (1963, NBC). Subsequent sales to BURKE'S LAW (1963, ABC), THE MAN FROM U.N.C.L.E. (1964, NBC), its spin-off, THE GIRL FROM U.N.C.L.E. (1966, NBC), and others helped establish his reputation as an important television writer. He made the transition to the big screen with successful scripts for MYRA BRECKINRIDGE (1970), THE PARALLAX VIEW (1974) and FUN WITH DICK AND JANE (1977). He directed his first feature, THE BLACK BIRD (1975), from his own script.

Brandywine Productions reviewed over three hundred script submissions before taking a six-month option on O'Bannon's screenplay for $1000. Walter Hill was not only interested in the project from a production point of view but he also expressed an interest in directing the film as well. Unable to attract a single studio, Hill rewrote significant passages and punched up most of the dialogue. Their six-month option was quickly running out, and they had to move fast in order to salvage their first project. Since Brandywine had a first-refusal production agreement with Twentieth Century-Fox, the rewrite was submitted first to Fox executives. Even though the studio had previously turned down the O'Bannon script, they agreed to commit development money to the project based on the revisions made by Hill.

THE WALTER HILL-DAVID GILER REWRITES

When Twentieth Century-Fox finally agreed to develop ALIEN as a project, late in March 1977, the decision was based entirely upon Walter Hill's rewrite. Completed over a three-day period, his rewrite maintained much of Dan O'Bannon's original material, including the discovery of the derelict spacecraft, the sighting of the pyramid, and the invasion of the alien parasite. But since Hill had always been concerned with the script's one-dimensional characterization, he tried to add an element of discord, suggesting that the astronauts didn't really like one another. Descriptions of action and dialogue were either shortened or tightened, and some scenes were completely rewritten from scratch. Several names were also changed to add a more contemporary feel. Broussard became Dallas, Roby became Ripley, and Faust became Faraday.

The single, most important change in Hill's rewrite was the addition of subplot that would function as a catalyst for action when the Alien was offscreen. Walter relied on O'Bannon's talking computer to provide that subplot by making the machine (now named "Mother") indifferent to the survival of its crew. Thus, when Ripley goes to "pull the plug," he learns that the computer has been conducting its own experiment in Darwinian evolution: "Two highly successful species in immediate competition for resources and survival. In the interests of pure scientific research I removed myself from the struggle." This exchange added dimension to the story, and gave the classic B-movie plot a sense of purpose and theme.

Overall, Hill had revised about 30% of Dan O'Bannon's original script, enough to garner a development deal with Fox but not enough to "green light" the project. Still more changes were needed before the script could go before the camera, and Hill called upon his writing counterpart at Brandywine. "Basically, it was a pastiche of Fifties movies," David Giler explained his first impression of the script. "Really terrible. Just awful. It was amateurishly written, although the central idea was sound. We took it and rewrote it completely, added Ash and the robot subplot. We added the cat, Jones. We also changed the characters around. We fleshed it out, basically. If we had shot the original O'Bannon script, we would have had a remake of IT! THE TERROR FROM BEYOND SPACE."

The first collaborative efforts of Walter Hill and David Giler on ALIEN took place at the former's home in the Hollywood Hills in the fall of 1977. Giler's first concern addressed the issue of the talking computer. Although he liked the added dimension Hill had given the script, he felt the concept of the ship's computer was far too close to HAL 9000 in Stanley Kubrick's 2001: A SPACE ODYSSEY (1968). Hill, on the other hand, felt the conflict between man and machine was a necessary subplot. The two writers tossed around many ideas before settling on a compromise: the introduction of Ash, a robotic science officer who has been placed aboard to both study and protect the alien parasite. "Mother" was retained as the ship's computer, but much of the material written for its character was now shifted to Ash. (Like O'Bannon's version, the talking computer functions in the limited capacity of answering questions and, at the climax, counting down the minutes to the starship's destruction.)

Hill and Giler next revised the cast of characters by replacing O'Bannon's West Point cadets with "space-going truck drivers." In addition to the mysterious Ash, they made two of the characters female, one black and created a realistic hierarchy of command. Captain, first officer, warrant officer, science officer and engineer were titles substituted for the buttoned-down heroes in the original script. Their seven characters - Ripley, Dallas, Kane, Ash, Lambert, Parker and Brett - are far more complicated individuals than those first envisioned in Broussard, Roby, Standard, Melkonis, Hunter and Faust. The writers even went as far as dealing with the crew's sexuality, by including an intimate moment between Ripley and Dallas (later deleted during the actual production).

To further streamline the plot, only one excursion outside the ship was made. Hill found O'Bannon's pyra-

mid to be a fascinating concept, and even expanded the sequence to include an entire city in his initial rewrite. However, Giler was convinced the second expedition merely delayed the meeting with the alien unnecessarily, adding texture but little substance to the overall work. The egg chamber was then moved aboard the ship. Regrettably, they also had to cut the dead, indigenous society and the discovery of the strange hieroglyphics.

Other changes to the original script were merely cosmetic in nature. Hill and Giler renamed the Snark Leviathan, then Nostromo. "Poor Yurick's skull" was dropped in place of having the astronauts return with an undisturbed egg (later discarded). The attempt to poison the creature with gas was changed to blasting it out the airlock (also discarded). These simple changes (and dozens of others like them) continued throughout preproduction in London, in New York just prior to Hill's departure to work on another film, and during post-production. In fact, one of the most controversial changes was discussed during the final editing on the film. Gordon Carroll wondered if most audience members would see the distinction between the dead fossilized pilot and the alien. Hill's solution was to cut it from the final film, but the sanity of cooler production heads prevailed.

By the time he had finished his final rewrite on the film, Hill had simply tired of the project. "Even though I was intrigued by ALIEN," he revealed, "I'd grown out of love with the idea of doing it." Hill had also committed to do a western, the still unproduced LAST GUN, and later made THE WARRIORS instead. His herculean efforts as well as the contributions of David Giler are clearly evident in the final shooting script.

THE FINAL SHOOTING SCRIPT

The commercial towing vehicle, Nostromo, with its crew of seven astronauts (and one cat) and its cargo of 20 million tons of mineral ore, is returning to earth. Less than ten months away, the ship's master computer (nicknamed "Mother") receives a message to divert its course in order to investigate a mysterious transmission of unknown origin. Awakened from hypersleep the crew is less than enthusiastic with the news. But Captain Dallas (Tom Skerritt) explains to the others that its one of their mission requirements to investigate any intelligent signals, or risk total forfeiture of shares. Engineers Parker (Yaphet Kotto) and Brett (Harry Dean Stanton) concede to the captain's wishes, and prepare the ship for landing.

Descending upon the storm-swept planetoid (of LV-421, later named Archeron), the Nostromo experiences a great deal of turbulence, and actually shatters one of its landing gear on the violent, almost primordial surface. The external damage is severe but not enough to keep them from eventually taking off. The source of the radio signal is less then 2,000 meters away.

The Captain, first officer Kane (John Hurt) and Lambert (Veronica Cartwright) don pressure suits, and trace the cyclic signal to the remains of a downed spacecraft, which looks like its structure is organic. They enter the ship through several gaping holes, perforated in its fuselage, of an indeterminate origin. Once inside, the astronauts find a huge, elephantine creature, fossilized, growing literally out of its command chair. The creature has been dead for a long time, and there is evidence that something has exploded, outward, from its ribs. Before they can speculate further, Kane discovers an organic chamber filled with hundreds of eggs below the pilot, and descends for a closer examination.

Meanwhile, back aboard the Nostromo, Warrant Officer Ripley (Sigourney Weaver) has begun to translate the alien transmission. She believes the signal is more of a warning than a distress call. But Ash (Ian Holm), the ship's coldly rational science officer, convinces her to ignore the findings as it is far too late to warn their shipmates. They must already know of the possible danger.

Once Kane has reached the base of the chamber, he exceeds the bounds of good judgment by peering into the maw of one of the newly-opened eggs. An octopus-like creature (referred to as a "face hugger") explodes outward, smashing through his space helmet and attaching itself unyieldingly to his face. Dallas and Lambert rush their comrade back to the ship for immediate medical attention, but are refused entry by Ripley (who is now in command) insisting they spend the requisite twenty-four hours in quarantine for decontamination. Ash violates her direct orders, and takes the three astronauts to

the infirmary. Only after Kane has been placed on the examination table and the remains of his helmet cut away, do the crew members realize what has they are dealing with. Clamped squarely over his face is a gruesome alien organism, held firmly in place by eight spindly fingers and secured by a long tail which constricts tightly around Kane's neck at the slightest hint of an attempt to dislodge it.

When efforts to prey the tenacious beast from Kane's face prove unsuccessful, Ash and Dallas mount a more direct assault by attempting to amputate one of its digits. At the first incision, however, a yellowish fluid oozes from the wound. Incredibly corrosive, it eats through the floor within seconds, penetrating two decks of the ship and threatening to eat through the hull before suddenly dissipating on its own. The creature has a wonderful defense mechanism; because its sprouts acid for blood, they dare not attempt to kill it. The "face-hugger" has also implanted something down Kane's throat, apparently feeding him air and keeping him alive, and any further attempts to remove it might also kill Kane. The crew agrees to freeze him, once they are underway, and let earth scientists deal with the problem.

Ash seems enthralled with the creature, declaring it the "perfect organism for life in outer space" and begins running a series of scientific tests on it. Ripley, on the other hand, remains indifferent to the creature, but pissed off enough with Ash to question his loyalty to the mission with the Captain. Ash was apparently a late substitute, according to Dallas, placed aboard their ship just before they left earth. The Captain doesn't trust him, nor does he trust anyone else (including Ripley). But before they can continue their discussion, the ship's two key officers learn that Kane is feeling better.

Even though efforts to break its grip have previously failed, the alien assailant has dropped off and died of its own accord, leaving Kane weak but seemingly healthy. Anxious to leave the planetoid far behind, the crew blasts off for earth, unaware than Kane now harbors an embryonic creature in his belly. Shortly after lift-off, while the crew is eating their final meal before hibernation, the alien parasite rips a hole in Kane's chest, struggles free and escapes unchecked during the confusion.

After "burying" Kane's body in space, the crew, armed simply with cattle prods and flame-throwers, sets after the "little" creature. But the Alien manages to evade capture, rapidly maturing into an eight-foot tall monstrosity. (The monster is part-insect, part-human, and part-serpentine, with an obscene, elongated head, dark bulbous eyes, and a vile array of teeth.) It first kills Brett, while he is looking for the ship's cat Jones, and then Captain Dallas, as he searches the narrow air shafts. At one point, Parker manages to lure the creature into the airlock but fails to blast it into space. (Note: this last scene was later cut from the final film.)

Ripley assumes command of the Nostromo, and tries to contact "Mother" for instructions. But according to the computer, the rest of her crew is expendable; the only thing that remains an important priority is the return of the creature to the Company's bio-weapons division. Ash attempts to prevent the Warrant Officer from telling the others, by trying to silence her; but Parker and Lambert's timely arrival free Ripley from her assailant. During the ensuing conflict, Ash suffers several near-fatal wounds. Those subsequent injuries reveal that he is, in fact, an android, placed aboard the ship by the Company in order to protect the creature from harm. He further reveals that their chances are not very good, since the Alien adapts perfectly to each hostile environment it encounters. It is the ultimate bio-weapon—the perfect killing machine—and that it will not stop until they are all dead.

With their choices very limited, Ripley decides to abandon ship in the shuttlecraft Snark (later called Narcissus), and set the Nostromo for self-destruct. She assigns Parker and Lambert the task of acquiring coolant for their air support, while she readies the shuttle for take-off. But before they can complete the task, Parker and Lambert are both attacked by the creature. Ripley hears their helpless cries over the intercom and instinctively sets the ship for self-destruct. During the ten-minute countdown, she discovers the cocooned bodies of Brett and Captain Dallas in the lower decks of the ship. Dallas is barely

alive but harboring a parasite within him; he begs Ripley to kill him, and she reluctantly obliges. (These scenes were also cut from the final film.) Ripley then struggles toward the shuttle, with the ship's cat in tow, but the Alien has cut off her escape route to the Snark. Trapped on the doomed ship, she begins to panic and, with time working against her, races back to prevent detonation.

Backtracking to the command center, the Warrant Officer knows that she has less than a few seconds left to turn off the fail-safe device. But before Ripley can execute the proper commands, the option to override self-destruct passes; she now has less than five minutes to reach a safe distance from the explosion. Her only chance for escape is to get to the shuttlecraft.

Ripley works her way to the shuttle and blasts off moments before the Nostromo (and its cargo of 20 million tons of mineral ore) self-destructs. Seemingly secure aboard the Snark, she begins preparation for the ten-month journey in hypersleep by safely securing her

cat, then discovers the Alien has found its way onto the shuttle. Ripley quickly climbs into a spacesuit and immediately decompresses the ship, blasting the creature out the airlock door. With survival its primary instinct, the Alien tries to climb back into the shuttle through the engine exhaust; but Ripley wisely turns on the powerful rockets and watches, almost in disbelief, as the last vestige of the Alien disappears into space.

Later, Ripley records her last log entry: "Final report of the Commercial Starship Nostromo. Third Officer Reporting. The other members of the crew—Kane, Lambert, Parker, Brett, Ash and Captain Dallas—are dead, the cargo and ship destroyed. I should reach the outer frontier in about six weeks. With a little luck, the network should pick me up. This is Ripley, last survivor of the Nostromo, signing off." She retires to hypersleep with her cat, and awaits rescue...

*****

Because the final shooting script, with substantial amounts of new material added by Walter Hill and

David Giler, had significantly changed the original screenplay by Dan O'Bannon, 20th Century-Fox recommended to the Writers Guild of America that the partners at Brandywine receive sole credit. O'Bannon (along with Ronald Shusett) would be credited with the story idea but nothing more. This request triggered an arbitration hearing by the WGA in which both sides were required to submit their original material for an independent evaluation. Experts reviewed both scripts and their subsequent rewrites, and ultimately declined Fox's request. Even though three people were probably responsible for the final shooting script, O'Bannon was awarded sole screenplay credit. The Guild felt that producers often "tinker" with a writer's words (prior to putting them before the camera), but that there would have been no words (or idea, for that matter) had O'Bannon not first written them. Unfair as the ruling may have seemed, it did cause a number of terse moments (before and after filming) between Hill & Giler and O'Bannon.

THE DIRECTOR—RIDLEY SCOTT

After Walter Hill had decided not to direct ALIEN, the three partners at Brandywine Productions began looking for the right candidate for the job. They discussed both Steven Spielberg and Brian DePalma, but neither of them were available. (Spielberg had just completed CLOSE ENCOUNTERS OF THE THIRD KIND, and was set to begin 1941, while DePalma had just finished CARRIE, and was starting work on THE FURY.) Searching for a suitable director who was, at the same time available, Hill, Giler and Gordon Carroll each made list of possible candidates, which included Tobe Hooper and Ridley Scott. David Giler recalled having seen Scott's THE DUELLISTS (1976) at the Cannes Film festival, and arranged to have Sandy Leiberson, a Twentieth Century-Fox executive in London, deliver a copy of the ALIEN script to him.

THE DUELLISTS, an adaptation of Joseph Conrad's short story "The Duel," had begun as an hour-long drama for French Television. But it eventually developed into a major motion picture, produced by David Puttnam and starring Keith Carradine and Harvey Keitel. When executives first saw a rough cut of the richly textured and visually elegant film, they suggested Scott

Alien *director Ridley Scott, seen here directing Harrison Ford in* Blade Runner *(photo copyright ©1992 The Ladd Company)*

enter the piece in the 1977 Cannes Film Festival. The motion picture eventually won a Special Jury Prize, and firmly established Ridley Scott as a new filmmaker of the first rank. But Scott was no stranger to the industry. He had already directed thousands of highly successful and acclaimed television commercials in England.

Scott was born in 1939, in South Shields, Tyne and Wear, England, and was later brought up in London, Cumbria, Wales and Germany. He completed his education in Stockton on Tees, in the Northeast. As a child, he showed little aptitude for any school subject other than art, and his parents urged him to study at the West Hartlepool College of Art, then later at the Royal College of Art in London. It was while at the Royal College, in the newly-formed Film School, that he first discovered a natural aptitude for filmmaking. With a single Bolex movie camera, and less than 100 British pounds, he made his first film, a 16mm short titled BOY ON A BICYCLE, about a young boy playing truant from school and meeting a madman. His younger brother Tony (who would also become a noted filmmaker) played the boy, and his father the crazed stranger. The British Film Institute was so impressed that Scott received a grant to expand and elaborate on the short. For Ridley, it was only the beginning . . .

Upon graduation from the Royal College of Art, Scott won a traveling design scholarship which took him to New York, where he worked with Bob Drew Associates, took photographs, and watched theatre and documentary film directors at work. A job as a set designer with BBC-TV followed shortly thereafter. He made a half-hour, 16mm version of PATHS OF GLORY, as part of a BBC production course, which netted him work as a director and designer on several popular series, including Z-CARS and THE INFORMER. After three years of dramatic television, he formed Ridley Scott Associates (with his brother) and began producing and directing commercials. His London-based company was so popular that he soon won assignments in the United States from Levi-Strauss Jeans, Strongbow Cider, and the Hovis Bread Company.

After THE DUELLISTS, Ridley Scott was trying to find financing for TRISTAN AND ISEULT, an Arthurian tale about knights and sorcery, when the script arrived from Sandy Leiberson. ALIEN bypassed a whole pile of scripts he had been reading, but since he was so committed to the other film, Ridley did not immediately agree to make ALIEN. "I was never very involved with science fiction beyond knowing that someday, at some point, I wanted to make a film in that genre," Scott explained his initial reaction. "ALIEN came right out of the blue; it was really terrific." He passed on the opportunity, but two months later, after his Arthurian film had fallen through, he contacted Hill and Giler to find out if it was still available. They said "yes" and, within two days, Ridley Scott was in Los Angeles to discuss his vision of the project.

No sooner had Scott agreed to make the film than he found himself confronted with the most difficult and complex problem of the shoot: how to make the alien creature look otherworldly enough to satisfy contemporary audiences weaned on STAR WARS (1977) and CLOSE ENCOUNTERS OF THE THIRD KIND (1977). Most previous attempts by fellow filmmakers to depict extraterrestrial lifeforms had come down to men in rubber suits (like Ray "Crash" Corrigan in IT! THE TERROR

FROM BEYOND SPACE, 1958) or elaborate mechanical contrivances that rarely (if ever) produced a convincing alien. Stanley Kubrick, the director Ridley Scott most admired, had decided not to introduce his extraterrestrials in 2001: A SPACE ODYSSEY (1968) after months of costly experimentation failed to render the monolith-builders believable. Douglas Trumbull had run into a similar problem during production of SILENT RUNNING (1971), and ended up dropping the alien-subplot from the final shooting script by Deric Washburn, Michael Cimino and Steven Bochco. Ridley knew he did not have that luxury—the alien was central to his story, and he had not one but three different creatures to imagine.

"When you take on a subject like this," Scott explained, "after the initial flush of excitement, the problem of what the hell it's going to look like suddenly starts hanging over you like a thundercloud. How do we do the beast in its various forms? One had to see it at some point or other. So I arrived in Hollywood with that misgiving and ended up going through about seven months worth of preproduction drawings without finding anything I really like. There was the usual blob and clawed creature and all that sort of stuff, which wouldn't have been right even if we'd done them well. I think I would have been embarrassed by them rather than proud; and it was desperately important for me to be proud of them. I had visions of screwing around with this for months; but as it happened, it worked out very quickly. Just after I got to Hollywood, Dan O'Bannon came in with a copy of Giger's Necronomicon and said, 'What do you think of this?' I started leafing through it until I came to this one half-page painting, and I just stopped and said: 'Good God, I don't believe it! That's it!'"

Ridley Scott had settled upon Giger's "Necronom IV," a startling and nightmarish creature that was part-insect, part-human and part-serpentine. He didn't have to see any more paintings or sketches to know that H.R. Giger was essential to the project. In early February 1978, Scott, Gordon Carroll and David Giler flew to Zurich, and met with the Swiss surrealist painter at his home. They discussed the film at length, and ultimately agreed to Giger's very modest terms.

GIGER AND THE "ALIEN" DESIGNS

The roots of Hans Rudi Giger's futile imagination can be traced back to other surrealistic artists of the twentieth century whose metaphoric language of dreams has translated their work into modern masterpieces. Many of Hans Giger's landscapes resemble those of Max Ernst, particularly the textual designs in Ernst's "Day and Night" (1943) and "The Eye of Silence" (1944). His backgrounds recall the dream-like architecture of Ferdinand Cheval's "Dream Palace" or Antonio Gaudi's "Church of the Holy Father," while his penchant for "bio-mechanical" artifices seems drawn from Marcel Duchamp. Other subtle nuances in his work evoke the best of artists Bocklin, Escher, Bosch, Dali and Matta. Giger's meticulously crafted art also reveals a hidden language of its own, totally dissimilar from those who have come before.

Born in Chur, Switzerland, on February 5, 1940, the famous painter and surrealist was plagued by nightmares and bizarre waking dreams as a child. At about age five, a photographic essay in Life Magazine for Jean Cocteau's BEAUTY AND THE BEAST (1946) exposed Giger to the potentials of artistic expression and inspired him to begin drawing. He soon discovered an affinity for illustrating pornographic fantasies. His father strongly disapproved; because he owned a small pharmacy, he hoped his son would one day run it. But Giger had little interest in school or learning, just drawing.

At eighteen, the artist was employed as a draftsman by the Meissen architectural firm where he learned much about composition and symmetry. Following his mandatory one-year service in the military, Hans enrolled in art school. He spent nearly four years studying interior and industrial design at the College of Arts and Crafts in Zurich, and landed a high-profile position with the firm of Andreas Christen's upon graduation. That same year, Giger met Li Tobler, an actress with whom he carried on a turbulent love affair, until she killed herself in 1975. It was during this time that he began utilizing his talents to create a personal visual world now called "bio-mechanical" by the artist. Inspired by the writings of Edgar Allan Poe and H.P. Lovecraft, Giger's surreal paintings and sketches combined the real world with the technological to produce horrifying nightmare images. But because his

work was so unlike any of his contemporaries he found only limited success. In fact, many galleries were so offended by his pencil sketches and air-brushed paintings that they refused to display them.

Giger's nightmare images did finally attract the attention of Swiss moviemaker F.M. Murer who, in 1969, hired him to produce designs for his 45-minute science fiction short, SWISS MADE 2069 (1970). His unique designs for an extraterrestrial visitor and his pet won critical acclaim for the film, and subsequently led to his work on Alexandro Jodorowsky's DUNE. While working in Paris on the doomed project, H.R. Giger met Dan O'Bannon once, briefly, but left a major impression. (The screenwriter was, in fact, inspired by Giger's work, and envisioned his alien like one of the nightmarish creatures.) Hans became disillusioned with the world of filmmaking, after the DUNE project collapsed, and went back to producing artwork in his studio in Zurich.

In August 1977, nearly a year after Brandywine had optioned the script for ALIEN, Dan O'Bannon (as design consultant) called Giger at his home in Zurich to discuss his designing the alien. Giger was somewhat hesitant to commit himself to the project, as he had never been paid for his work on DUNE. He finally agreed, upon receipt of a small retainer (authorized by Carroll), and produced a number of preliminary sketches of the face hugger and the alien egg. But Hill dismissed his work as "sick," and insisted that O'Bannon's original artist Ron Cobb be turned loose on the problem. H.R. Giger was again released from his retainer, and returned to his painting. Thankfully, O'Bannon kept pressing Carroll and Giler to use Giger's designs. When copies of the newly-published Necronomicon arrived in the production office, Dan found an ally in Ridley Scott, who loved the surrealist's work. Giger was hired to produce the alien, and later asked to design the alien planet, the landscape, the derelict ship, and the egg silo (later discarded).

The Alien itself was the film's most important design and greatest technical achievement. Conceived and designed by the surrealist as a "bio-mechanical," the Alien evolves through several distinctive phases. Giger worked closely with Ridley Scott throughout the entire production, designing the creature in its various forms. The "face-hugger," which attaches to Kane's head, was clearly sexual in appearance, with a long, tightly-coiled tail for launching itself, two finger-like protrusions for holding onto its victim and an inseminating organ which it thrusts down the victim's throat. The "chest-buster," inspired from a painting by Francis Bacon, was envisioned as a mouth and small body, as this second alien had to literally eat its way out of the victim. And finally the Alien creature in its final state—the key to the whole production—had to be tall, graceful and menacing, thoroughly convincing and totally alien in appearance.

H. R. Giger's designs for the final creature were, in fact, an extension of the "Necronom IV" upon which Ridley Scott had first lighted. Though part insectoid and part serpentine, the alien was still essentially man-like in appearance. To distract from its human shape, the Swiss surrealist endowed the creature with a long, phallic head, seemingly life-less eyes, a vile array of teeth, and an elongated tail. In addition to designing the three aliens, Giger sculpted and constructed the Alien suit, while Carlo Rambaldi worked on articulating the Alien head (through cables and remotes).

The suit, consisting of fifteen separate pieces, was made by Giger at a cost of $250,000 to fit over the 6'10" frame of twenty-six year-old Nigerian Bolaji Badejo. Badejo had been a graphic arts student in London when a twist of fate brought him to the attention of Ridley Scott. The director had been looking for basketball players, and had tested Peter Mayhew (Chewbacca in STAR WARS), but it was Badejo's combination of height and slimness that convinced Scott he was right for the role. Bolaji was signed in May, and Giger was given four months to build the suit around him. Each of the parts were, therefore, customized to fit over the tall, slim Nigerian. Over a one-piece black body suit, the rib cage was pulled on like a sweater and the legs were put on like a pair of pants (zipped up the side). The arms were pulled on separately like sleeves, fitted over with gloves, and the feet were worn like shoes. The head and tail were placed on last, with cables and wires securely hidden. (Various body parts and a full second suit were also constructed for the stunt man.)

By the time Giger had finished with the Alien suit, he had created a fully-realized monster. But the final problem was how to make it look both menacing and totally convincing on screen. "I never liked horror films before," Ridley Scott commented, "because in the end it's always been a man in a rubber suit. Well, there's no way to deal with that. The most important thing in a film of this type is not what you see, but the effect of what you think you saw. It's like a sort of after-burn—that's the reason I decided to limit the creature's appearances." Because the alien is only glimpsed but never fully seen, it sustains an atmosphere of mystery and terror.

That atmosphere of mystery and terror was also carried forward in Giger's designs for the alien landscape, the derelict and the space jockey. Originally hired for just the alien designs, Hans soon found himself prevailed upon by Scott, Carroll and Giler to produce additional work for the movie. The alien world, as described in the original script, was a planetoid, approximately 1200 kilometers in diameter with a gravity level equivalent to .86 of Earth gravity, orbiting a large ringed world. Its freezing atmosphere was made up of zenite, nitrogen, carbon

dioxide, and methane with a surface structure of rock on top of a lava base. Although never mentioned in the final film, the planetoid was named "Acheron." Translating those concepts into a convincingly foreign landscape

required the talents of the noted artist and surrealist.

At first, H.R. Giger merely provided some sketches of the landscape which, like the alien creature, reflected his personal "bio-mechanical" vision. But when he arrived on the set during preproduction, he dismayed to learn that his unique "vision" (of the alien world) had been translated into easily recognizable human structures and patterns. He then took charge of the project. Along with his assistant Mia Bonzanigo and a handful of technicians, he resculpted the landscape using real bones, bits of motors, pipes and wires, and Plasticine. The planetoid set—with its twisted shapes and structures resembling large skeletal fragments—was constructed full scale on an entire soundstage over a three-week period.

Giger also designed the exteriors and interiors for the derelict ship, including the space jockey. When the crew of the Nostromo respond to the extraterrestrial signal, they had to discover a spaceship totally alien to their own technology. The design of the derelict was typical Giger in its suggestion of an organic machinery; most remarkably, at a single glance, the ship appeared not the product of human builders. His sketches were then translated to an eight-foot prototype by model-builder Peter Boysey and a full-scale set (most notably, the entrance to the derelict) by art-director Les Dilley. The curved walls—both interior and exterior—were built of lumber, covered with lathe and webbing, and built up with pre-cast plaster forms. The final layers of plaster were added by Giger himself, and then the surfaces were painted.

Inside the derelict, the crew of the Nostromo find the decaying body of a large alien creature. It reclines in something like an acceleration couch at the controls of something resembling a cannon. Even though Ron Cobb had completed dozens of sketches of the space jockey for Dan O'Bannon, Ridley Scott was not satisfied. He wanted something that would look totally alien but again different enough from the titular character. One day, while thumbing through Giger's Necronomicon, he lighted on one of the paintings. While not of a space jockey, it was indeed similar to what Scott had in mind. He showed the page to Giger and asked him to reproduce it in full scale. Hans first sculpted the space jockey in clay, then cast it in polyester, and painted it himself with latex to give it an outerworldly appearance. The result was one of the most terrifying and unsettling in the film.

THE PRODUCTION STAFF

Once Ridley Scott was satisfied with Giger's work on various preproduction aspects of the film, the director realized that his selection of the right production team was the only other critical element to the success of the film. Based upon the recommendations of his associate producer Ivor Powell, he chose Michael Seymour, a man he had worked with on television commercials for over two years, as the production designer. Seymour, a graduate of the Royal College of Art, had begun his career as a production assistant for Thames Television, and soon turned to commercials and feature films. His first credit as an assistant art director came from Richard Lester's THE KNACK (1965). He worked in preproduction on Tony Richardson's THE CHARGE OF THE LIGHT BRIGADE (1968), followed by THE BEDSITTING ROOM (1969), THE LOVES OF ISADORA (1968), GUMSHOE (1972) and Vincent Price's excellent THEATRE OF BLOOD (1973). He had just begun work for director Claude Chabrol on THE ST. PETERSBURG-CANNES EXPRESS when the film developed financial trouble and was subsequently canceled. That film's cancellation freed him to begin work on ALIEN.

Since political cartoonist Ron Cobb and futuristic designer Chris Foss had already been hired by Dan O'Bannon to produce certain designs for the ship Nostromo, Scott added Jean "Moebius" Giraud to his art department to work on the costumes and spacesuits. "As the film involved three specific aspects—the planet, everything to do with the alien and the Earth ship—we decided that any one of those elements should be a full-time job for a designer," Scott explained. Their fully-functional, realistic hardware provided an excellent contrast with Giger's otherworldly concepts for the planet and the two alien cultures. Michael Seymour also hired Roger Christian and Les Dilley, both of whom had won an Academy Award for STAR WARS (1977), as art directors, with Ian Whittaker being retained as the set decorator. ALIEN had one of the strongest art departments of any motion picture.

John Mollo, who had just won an Academy Award for the costumes in STAR WARS (1977), was also brought aboard to design the costumes for the Nostromo crew. Scott wanted the crew to wear costumes that had a lived-in

From the new Twentieth-Century Fox film

THE BOOK OF ALIEN

by Paul Scanlon and Michael Gross

look, indicating the nature of the work they do aboard the ship, and suggested fatigues of some nature. (Moebius had worked briefly on the designs but had produced uniforms which were far too militaristic.) Mollo created a series of casual jumpsuits, similar to the ones engineers and mechanics might wear, and Ron Cobb provided the insignias. Later, once Moebius had finished the designs for the spacesuits, which resembled Japanese medieval armor, Mollo adapted those into practical suits. His contributions to the film added much to its believability.

*****

For reasons of economy, Gordon Carroll, David Giler and Ridley Scott decided to make the film at Shepperton Studios, just outside London. The original budget of $4.5 million quickly escalated to $13 million, which was totally unacceptable to Twentieth Century-Fox. Carroll and Giler tried negotiating with the executives, asking for $9.5 but finally settling for $9 million. Since STAR WARS had cost about $9 million to make, Fox expected Brandywine to see that ALIEN didn't cost any more. The Producers also had to negotiate for time. Twentieth Century-Fox wanted to release the motion picture on May 25, 1979, two years to the day after STAR WARS had debuted, and insisted upon a tight production schedule. They started talking about 17 weeks of shooting, and finally settled upon 16 weeks, with less than four months of post-production. With time of the essence, Scott took the script and drew storyboards for every key sequence in the film. Ridley knew he could maintain a tight shooting schedule if he simply followed his storyboards. He would also have to oversee the set construction and the special effects.

One of the most remarkable, complex and ingenious sets ever designed for a motion picture—that of the gigantic commercial space-tug Nostromo—was built over several large sound stages. Since the script called for a well-used, slightly battered spacecraft, they had to make the sets look lived-in. "We started by building model sets, then an actual section of a space-tug corridor of part of the operational bridge," Michael Seymour recalled. "Then, after further discussions, we began building the sets in earnest." The Nostromo was first envisioned by Cobb with three levels or decks. The

designers toyed with the notion of building a huge three-story set, but it was decided that this would prove impractical for filming purposes. So the "A" (or top) level was constructed first, filling much of the giant "C" soundstage at Shepperton.

The "A" level comprised the astronauts' living areas, mess room, computer annex, infirmary, many linking corridors and the bridge. Here, amidst a veritable technological wonderland, the seven astronauts sat at their own stations to navigate or operate the ship, surrounded by forty television screens. The monitors, ranging in size from five-inch to twenty-two-inch, displayed various pictures of computer readouts, technological and navigational information, maps, and views of space outside. Masses of other technical equipment were there, plus hundreds of switches and literally thousands of flashing indicator lights. The many television monitors were fed pictures and films from a special video center situated on the side, headed by Dick Hewitt, the video coordinator. The numerous banks of circuits and electronic equipment were prepared by the props and construction departments, and were made up ingeniously from old aircraft, automobile and radio/television sets.

"We must have spent thousands of pounds on scrap from old jet-aircraft engines particularly," said Les Dilley. "And it all paid off handsomely because the set looked so authentic."

In another section of "A" level, the "hypersleep" chamber was comprised of a flower-pedal-like arrangement of perspex-enclosed beds. The mess room was an actual working kitchen with sink and disposal units, cabinets, microwave and various foods in powder or tablet form. The infirmary was equipped with an operating table, medicines and drugs, and an over-head suspended array of surgical instruments. Each area was connected by padded and illuminated corridors which were fully operational.

Later sequences for the film were staged on the lower levels of the ship, built separately on other soundstages. "B" level, the general maintenance area, and "C" level, containing the vast engine rooms plus a seemingly endless network of complex machinery-filled corridors and the landing gear, were painstakingly constructed by

Les Dilley, Roger Christian and crew. "One of the basic ideas of all these complicated interior sets was that you could actually walk from corridor to corridor, from bridge to mess, from mess to infirmary, and so on, thus giving both the actors and the audience the feeling of being inside a vast spacecraft—both huge and claustrophobic at one and the same time," Seymour commented. "We wanted people to have the impression that it's a real place, that it's more science-fact than science fiction, and also that the whole place is well used, lived in and slightly battered after years of service."

THE SPECIAL EFFECTS

While all the interior and planet surface sequences for ALIEN were filmed at Shepperton Studios, the six months of special effects and model photography were completed at the Bray Studios, in Windsor, about fifteen miles away. Once the home of Hammer Films, the Bray Studios had once played host to hundreds of motion picture productions. Now, the studios were wit-

nessing a most unusual production, with dozens of complex visuals. Most of the visual effects were completed under the direction of Brian Johnson, who was working simultaneously on the effects for THE EMPIRE STRIKES BACK (1980), and the supervision of Nick Allder. Their highly-complex and technical wizardry contributed to many of the breathtaking sequences that took place in space and on the planet surface.

Nick Allder, thirty-six when the production began, always knew that he wanted to be involved in the movie business in some way, since the age of nine. His father was a camera engineer and nine-year-old Nick could "lace up" a Mitchell movie camera like an expert. When he finished school, he started a small commercials company and worked on numerous television and theatrical projects. In the early 1960's, he joined Les Bowie's special effects company, and worked on a several Hammer films. He later completed the special effects for GORDON OF KHARTOUM (1966), THE LONG DUEL (1967), BATTLE OF BRITTAIN (1969), THE MEDUSA TOUCH (1978) and THE WILD GEESE (1978). He is best known for his work on SPACE 1999 (1972). His partner, Brian Johnson, was also an alumnus of SPACE 1999 and numerous other projects.

Most of the special effects and model work centered around the space-tug Nostromo and the vast oil refinery it tows. Although the space-tug was supposed to be eight hundred feet in length, the model of the Nostromo was actually eight feet long. With special techniques, they were able to camera-track right through space, stars, and planets to a closeup shot of the craft and actually show the astronauts moving around inside. Multiple exposure shots, employing the original negative, were used in place of the more modern techniques of "traveling mattes" or blue screens. The system of "roto-scoping," which involves taking a sequence frame by frame and handpainting various mattes, was also employed to simulate the complex orbiting and landing sequences. Budgetary constraints forced Allder and Johnson to abandon any plans to incorporate the motion control technology developed by John Dykstra for the movie STAR WARS (1977) into ALIEN.

Allder was also responsible for constructing several of the film's working props. His team had little trouble constructing such things as a flame-thrower and cattle prod, but the motion tracker and medical tools had to be both functional and futuristic. He was later asked to produce a dozen mess-room props, from plates and cups to cans of beer and food. By the close of the production, his special signature was in most every scene.

THE CAST

Nineteen Eighty-Four star John Hurt portrayed the first victim of the Alien, Kane (photo copyright ©1984 Atlantic Releasing Corporation) Ad-Slick (right) courtesy United Artists Theatres

While Gordon Carroll, David Giler and Ridley Scott worked on preproduction at Shepperton Studios, Casting Directors Mary Selway and Mary Goldberg began looking for the five actors and two actresses to fill the roles of ALIEN. Their initial choice for the role of Kane, however, proved problematic. Jon Finch was first signed to play the executive officer; but after several days of shooting the noted British thespian was hospitalized with a diabetic ailment and had to be replaced by John Hurt. Hurt, who was born in 1940, had already spent years on stage and in front of the camera, in productions as diverse as A MAN FOR ALL SEASONS (1966), FORBUSH AND THE

PENGUINS (1968), and TEN RILLINGTON PLACE (1970). He was the husband in SHOUT (1978) and the NAKED CIVIL SERVANT (1976). His portrayal of Max in MIDNIGHT EXPRESS (1978) won him critical acclaim, and brought him to the attention of Selway and Goldberg. For the role of Kane, Hurt projected an air of inner tension and vulnerability behind a reserved exterior. His strong characterization of the executive officer ultimately made the film come to life. John later spoofed his role in Mel Brooks' SPACEBALLS (1987).

Tom Skerritt (Captain Dallas) armed against a killer of a different kind in Stephen King's The Dead Zone (photo copyright ©1983 Dino De Laurentiis Corporation) Ad-Slick (right) courtesy United Artists Theatres

Tom Skerritt was cast against type as Dallas, the Nostromo's low-key captain. A native of Detroit, Skerritt was born in 1933, and made his motion picture debut twenty nine years later in THE WAR HUNT (1962). His other roles in M*A*S*H (1970), FUZZ (1972), THE TURNING POINT (1977) and ICE CASTLES (1979) helped him further refine his acting talents. For Dallas, he brought the same quiet, confident air that he had established in his previous work. Following ALIEN, he would be featured in THE DEAD ZONE (1983), TOP GUN (1986), SPACE CAMP (1986), POLTERGEIST III (1988), STEEL MAGNOLIAS (1989) and the television series PICKET FENCES (1992, CBS).

Ian Holm, who portrayed the murderous android Ash, as viewed in **Greystoke: The Legend of Tarzan, Lord of the Apes** *(photo copyright ©1988 Warner Bros.) Ad-Slick (right) courtesy* **United Artists Theatres**

The role of Ash, the ship's uptight science officer, was awarded to Ian Holm. A former student of the Royal College of Dramatic Arts and one of England's most rep-utable Shakespearean actors, Holm found the character of Ash very different from the kinds of role he had often played. Prior to ALIEN, the Britisher had appeared in THE FIXER (1968), NICHOLAS & ALEXANDRA (1971), THE MAN IN THE IRON MASK (1977) and the miniseries JESUS OF NAZARETH (1977). He continued in TIME BANDITS (1980), CHARIOTS OF FIRE (1981), WITHERBY (1985) and ANOTHER WOMAN (1988). He also recently appeared in two Shakespearean films, Kenneth Branagh's remake of HENRY V (1989) and Franco Zeffirelli's version of HAMLET (1990).

Yaphet Kotto (Parker) portrayed Dr. Kananga, villain to James Bond in **Live and Let Die** *(photo copyright ©1973 Danjaq, S.A.) Ad-Slick (right) courtesy* **United Artists Theatres**

Yaphet Kotto also brought an impressive body of stage and motion picture work to his characterization of Parker, the ship's sarcastic engineer. Roles in THE THOMAS CROWN AFFAIR (1968), FIVE CARD STUD (1968) and LIVE AND LET DIE (1973) had made him a highly-sought-after performer. His work following ALIEN was equally impressive, including important featured roles in BRUBAKER (1980), THE STAR CHAMBER (1983) and THE RUNNING MAN (1987).

The well-known character actor Harry Dean-Stanton was cast, partially for comic relief, in the role of Brett, the ship's laconic engineering technician who blind-ly follows Parker's instructions. Born in 1926, Harry first began working in motion pictures as "Dean Stanton" in THE PROUD REBEL (1958). His early work still reads like a list of classic motion pictures, from COOL HAND LUKE (1967) to PAT GARRETT AND BILLY THE KID (1973) and THE MISSOURI BREAKS (1976). Stanton's portrayal of Dustin Hoffman's partner in STRAIGHT TIME (1978) earned him much critical praise, and offers from many

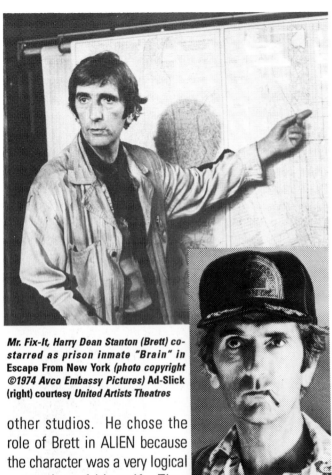

Mr. Fix-It, Harry Dean Stanton (Brett) co-starred as prison inmate "Brain" in Escape From New York (photo copyright ©1974 Avco Embassy Pictures) Ad-Slick (right) courtesy United Artists Theatres

Veronica Cartwright (Lambert) is constantly imperiled by aliens, as witnessed in this scene from the remake of Invasion of the Body Snatchers (photo copyright ©1978 United Artists Corporation) Ad-Slick (right) courtesy United Artists Theatres

other studios. He chose the role of Brett in ALIEN because the character was a very logical extension of himself. They shared at least one thing in common: both were chain-smokers. His work in ALIEN led to key roles in PRIVATE BENJAMIN (1980), UFORIA (1980), ESCAPE FROM NEW YORK (1981), CHRISTINE (1983), REPO MAN (1984), THE LAST TEMPTATION OF CHRIST (1988), WILD AT HEART (1990) and MAN TROUBLE (1992).

British-born Veronica Cartwright, who grew up in the United States with her equally-famous sister Angela, was the perfect choice for Lambert, the ship's high-strung navigator. Fresh from her encounter with the pod people in Philip Kaufman's remake of INVASION OF THE BODY SNATCHERS (1978), Veronica had been working in motion pictures and television since she was six. Born in 1949, she began performing in commercials at age six, and made her film debut IN LOVE AND WAR (1958). Her first important break came as Violet Rutherford, the Beaver's girlfriend, in LEAVE IT TO BEAVER. She won an Emmy at

age fourteen for her role in TELL ME NOT IN NUMBERS, in which she played a girl who "spoke" in numbers—substituting numbers for words. Subsequent roles in THE BIRDS (1963) and THE CHILDREN'S HOUR (1963) landed her a recurring role in television's DANIEL BOONE. She gained a certain notoriety for INSERTS (1976), baring herself literally for Richard Dreyfuss, and GOIN' SOUTH (1978), with Jack Nicholson. After completing her work on ALIEN, Cartwright continued making genre films, notably THE RIGHT STUFF (1983), NIGHTMARES (1983), FLIGHT OF THE NAVIGATOR (1986), and THE WITCHES OF EASTWICK (1987).

The pivotal role of Warrant Officer Ripley was given to a relative unknown, Sigourney Weaver. Initially, David Giler and Gordon Carroll had considered Meryl Streep for the part. Even though she had yet to make her mark as the tortured wife in THE DEER HUNTER (1978) and in other high profile roles, Streep was still well regarded by the industry. Her turn as "Inga" in the television miniseries HOLOCAUST (1978) had critics buzzing, so much in fact that Meryl passed on the role of Ripley because it was after all only a horror film. The part was then offered to Weaver, who voiced similar objections. "I didn't want to be in a science fiction picture," she reflected years later, "but I thought this was an interesting woman to play." Sigourney tentatively accepted Carroll's offer, and flew into London for a screen test. The test, taken from the cocoon scene later discarded, was all that Ridley Scott needed to assure him he had found his Ripley.

Born "Susan" Weaver in 1949 to Elizabeth Inglis, a British actress, and Sylvester "Pat" Weaver, a former NBC-TV executive and one of the true pioneers of television programming, she later changed her name to "Sigourney" from a reference in F. Scott Fitzgerald's THE

Sigourney Weaver (Ripley) seen with a simian friend in Gorillas in the Mist *(photo copyright ©1988 Warner Bros. Inc.)* **Ad-Slick (left) courtesy** *United Artists Theatres*

GREAT GATSBY. After being raised in Manhattan, Weaver studied at Stanford University and the Yale Drama School. Returning to New York, she found work in a variety of comic stage roles off-Broadway and did a handful of television shows, including the daytime drama SOMERSET and the prime time BEST OF FAMILIES. Her first screen appearance was a brief one as Woody Allen's date in ANNIE HALL (1977). She next appeared in the Israeli-produced MADMAN (1978). The role of Ripley in ALIEN was her professional debut in a big-budget motion picture, and the critical acclaim for her performance rocketed her to stardom. She soon became a popular leading actress with lead roles in EYEWITNESS (1981), THE YEAR OF LIVING DANGEROUSLY (1983), DEAL OF THE CENTURY (1983), and GHOSTBUSTERS (1984).

The actors decided that the characterizations were too thin, and they fleshed them out by adding lines and bringing much of themselves to the roles.

In addition to the seven actors, Selway and Goldberg were also responsible for hiring a cat to fill the role of "Jones." Jones was supplied by Animals Unlimited. Three small children, including Ridley Scott's two sons, were also hired to stand-in for the principal players as a further enhancement of scale in several key sequences. Of course, Bolaji Badejo had already been secured by H.R. Giger as the Alien.

PRODUCTION DETAILS

Principal photography on ALIEN was scheduled to begin on July 5, 1978, at Shepperton Studios, but was pushed back to July 25th to give the technicians enough time to finish the sets. Throughout the first four weeks, with the three phases of the Alien yet to be completed, Director Ridley Scott concentrated on the sequences leading to the discovery of the derelict on the planetoid Acheron. Since the Nostromo sets were still not complete, things got off to a slow start. A major sequence photographed during this period was the landing party's descent onto the planetoid surface. Subsequent scenes were filmed in some of the ship's completed sections. Because rehearsal time had been kept to a minimum, this was the first time most of the actors had worked with one another. The early scenes were tense and business-like, reflecting the distrust and tension the crew of the Nostromo was supposed to have towards each other.

The "chest-burster" scene, ALIEN's most talked about and most copied visual sequence, was filmed late in August 1978. Since the "chest-burster" was the first alien form to be completed by Roger Dicken and his crew, it was also the first creature to be filmed. The scene held a few shocking surprises for the cast, since none of them knew exactly what they were going to see. On the day before, all shots leading up to the alien's unexpected appearance were completed, consisting mostly of the crew eating dinner and Kane's initial convulsions. When filming wrapped for the night, the production crew went to work preparing for the next day's difficult shoot.

In the morning, no actors except John Hurt were allowed onto the set. The table in the mess had a large hole cut into it in which the actor was fitted with just his head, shoulders and arms above. A fiberglass chest piece was attached to Hurt's shoulders, and then fitted with a t-shirt, which gave the appearance he was still lying on the table. The artificial chest was then filled with several tubes to squirt fake blood, and a single hand puppet, operated by Roger Dicken and Nick Allder, was positioned below. The director and crew also dressed in white smocks and covered their equipment in plastic. After several hours, the scene was ready for the rest of the cast members. On cue, with three cameras rolling to capture effective reaction shots which were of genuine surprise, the "chest-burster" ripped through Hurt's artificial chest and sprayed blood all over the others, most especially Veronica Cartwright. The scene was then completed using wires to help the alien race across the table.

On September 6, the Alien appeared on the set for the first time for a scene which corresponded to the creature's first appearance in the film. While searching for the cat on "C" level, Brett wanders into the chamber which houses the landing gear, and passes to refresh himself under the stream of water flowing from above. The Alien suddenly appears, and carries him away. Ridley Scott filmed several variations of the scene with the monster descending from above onto Harry Dean Stanton, but none of them worked. In one set-up, Badejo was strapped to a see-saw which, when raised into the air more than twenty feet, made him very dizzy and nauseous. He declined a second take, and stunt man Eddie Powell took over. Eventually, after several more tries, Scott successfully filmed the stuntman being lowered head-first by wires.

The infamous cocoon scene, which was later discarded, was filmed on September 25, 1978. Ripley, alone in the Nostromo with the alien patiently stalking her, hears a sound coming from one of the ship's storage areas. She enters the compartment with a flame-thrower in hand only to discover Dallas, partially devoured yet still alive, caught in a cocoon. Near him, Brett is gradually being transformed into one of the alien spores. The Captain begs Ripley to kill him, and she accedes to his wishes by incinerating the whole compartment. The scene took several days to complete, and was printed for inclusion in the final cut. "That sequence was quite spooky, and it actually worked very well," Ridley Scott declared. "I like it because it was a brief way of explaining what had happened on the derelict and what was now happening on the Nostromo." (But Scott later relented, believing the scene slowed the pace of the film, and ended up cutting it from the final print.)

In December of 1978, with the final shots of Ripley in the hypersleep chamber having just been completed, principal photography on ALIEN wrapped. A few days later, all of the sets were completely gone, and the stages were ready for the next production.

*****

During post-production, Ridley Scott worked with editor Terry Rawlings to transform the thousands of feet of raw footage into a rough cut. They trimmed much of the footage in which the characters argued and openly insulted one another, and eliminated most of the overt sexual or violent actions. Scott also wisely chose to limit the number of appearances of the Alien. Citing the original JAWS (1975) by Steven Spielberg, the British director proved that the most convincing movie monsters were the ones that appear on screen the least.

Scott had some very definite ideas about the musical score as well, and discussed the possibility of hiring the Japanese composer Tomita with Gordon Carroll and David Giler, but they were reluctant to deal with someone who had never scored a motion picture. Jerry Goldsmith, the veteran of hundreds of film and television scores, was subsequently hired to produce the musical score for ALIEN. During the late seventies, Goldsmith was at the top of his form. Having just won an Academy Award for his haunting music in THE OMEN (1976), the veteran composer had already produced themes for a half dozen films, including ISLANDS IN THE STREAM (1977), CAPRICORN ONE (1978), DAMIEN- OMEN II (1978), THE BOYS FROM BRAZIL (1978), COMA (1978) and THE SWARM (1978) when he turned to ALIEN. His work was well received by Carroll and Giler, and dominates much of the final film. Unfortunately, Scott was dissatisfied with several key themes, including the climatic one, and had conductor Lionel Newman replace them with material from FREUD (1962) and Howard Hanson's Symphony #2.

With less than a few weeks remaining, the film was ready for its cinematic debut.

THE THEATRICAL RELEASE

Released on Friday, May 25, 1979, two years to the day after STAR WARS burst onto the scene, ALIEN quickly shot to the top of the box office in its first weekend. Although the motion picture faced stiff competition from other major releases, including ROCKY II, ESCAPE FROM ALCATRAZ, THE JERK, MOONRAKER, AIRPORT 1979, MEATBALLS and reissues of JAWS and STAR WARS, it continued selling tickets throughout the summer. Critical reaction to the film was generally mixed, with some reviewers crediting Ridley Scott with its breathtaking pace and nonstop action, while others proclaimed its derivative nature. David Denby wrote in the June 4th New Yorker: "ALIEN . . . works on your nerves and emotions with the practiced hand of a torturer extracting a confession. They movie is terrifying, but not in a way that is remotely enjoyable." Frederick Pohl, a noted science fiction author, wrote: "The story of ALIEN is a lot like the early work of A.E. Van Vogt....and not very complicated, though....the effects are superb." Most moviegoers, some who had spent hours in front of their local theatre lined up around the block, declared the film a success. The film grossed a whopping $40 million in domestic theatre rentals ($100 million worldwide), and

proved that science fiction and horror films were worthy summer blockbusters.

The film, however, was not without its controversy. Science fiction author A.E. Van Vogt, who had written The Voyage of the Space Beagle, found far too many parallels between his novel and the film. He requested payment from producers Gordon Carroll and David Giler for using his original story. But no one at Brandywine Productions took his claim seriously. Similar accusations were also made by United Artists and director Edward L Cahn over the various similarities between IT! THE TERROR FROM BEYOND SPACE (1958) and Twentieth Century-Fox's ALIEN, but nothing ever came of these accusations either.

In February of 1980, ALIEN was honored with two award nominations from the Academy of Motion Picture Arts and Sciences for the Best Achievement in Art Direction (for Michael Seymour, Les Dilley, Roger Christian and Ian Whittaker) and the Best Achievement in Visual Effects (H.R. Giger, Nick Allder and Brian Johnson). At the actual Academy Awards ceremony, ALIEN lost out in the category of Art Direction, but won against STAR TREK-THE MOTION PICTURE, Disney's THE BLACK HOLE and Steven Spielberg's 1941 in the category of visual effects. H.R. Giger's work on ALIEN was not only recognized by his peers for outstanding achievement but also his creation has become one of the legendary movie monsters. The film was also honored with a "Hugo" award from the World Science Fiction community.

Learning much from the promotional campaign for STAR WARS (1977), Twentieth Century-Fox had also licensed a number of companies to produce merchandise and promotional items for ALIEN. A novelization of the screenplay by Alan Dean Foster was arranged through Warner Books, and a movie novel by Avon Books provided 1000 frame blowups and dialogue from the motion picture. Heavy Metal issued a comic book adaptation by Archie Goodwin and Walt Simonson, a trade paperback design book by Paul Scanlon and Michael Gross, and a calendar. Giger's Alien, a coffee table art book with 140 photographs from his personal collection, was put out by Morpheus International. Both a souvenir program and two poster magazines were licensed, as well as posters, custom-designed masks and Halloween costumes, t-

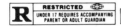
shirts, bubble-gum cards, mobiles, a model kit of the Alien, jigsaw puzzles, and children's pajamas. Kenner Products also made a board game and a twelve-inch posable doll of the Alien. Some of the products did very well, but most of them ended up being remaindered.

In the Spring of 1992, Halcyon, a Britain-based model company, released several original model kits inspired by the movie, including the "Space Jockey," the "Face Hugger," the Alien, and the Narcissus. Though somewhat pricey, these items continue to sell well in specialty stores and at science fiction conventions. Many unlicensed products from Japanese companies have also recently appeared, making the film's merchandising far more successful today than in its initial release.

THE LASERDISC RE-CONSTRUCTION

A Special Wide Screen Collector's Edition of ALIEN was released in 1992, featuring a new digital transfer of the film in the "letterbox" format—preserving the entire Panavision aspect ratio of 2.35:1 that was seen in the theatres. The mastering process, personally supervised by Ridley Scott, provided home video enthusiasts with a definitive version that preserves the integrity of the director's original vision. Utilizing the superior quality of Laser Disc presentation, the version enabled the home viewers to engage in a frame-by-frame analysis of the film or view material in a special section which documents the entire evolution and history of the film. Rare photographs, production art work, and exclusive footage took the viewer through every phase of the production and reveal how the various elements of the film were created. An exclusive interview with Ridley Scott also provided fans with an insight into the creative process. The section on Pre-production included original material, some never before released to the public, on the screenplay, the director, Giger, the Alien Production unit and casting. The Production section included the design of props and costumes, the Nostromo, planetoid and the alien, while the section on Post-Production featured interesting facts about the film's theatrical release, promotion and a gallery of art from ALIEN.

From the mysterious-looking egg in the theatrical trailers to the tag line on the poster: "In space no one can hear you scream," audience members knew they were in for an exhilerating experience, a rollercoaster ride of sheer terror and suspense. And Twentieth Century-Fox's production of ALIEN delivered all the chills and excitement that it promised, and so much more. Over the years, since its initial release in May 1979, the film has become accepted as a genuine screen classic, a startling tale of otherworldly terror and primal human fear that fuses classic elements of science fiction and horror. ALIEN's enduring popularity and success can be attributed to many key elements, from the archetypal nature of the story to the visual style of its director Ridley Scott to the contributions of the many artists and technicians, but its true essence lies in the screen magic these numerous storytelling and filmmaking techniques combined to cre-

ate. Even though so few surprises remain today, audiences still continue to be hypnotized by the overall visual experience of the film.

H.R. Giger's incredible imagination for things that are both strange and frightening is largely responsible for ALIEN's most important element, the innovative design of the creature itself The film doesn't simply present a roaring monster in a rubber suit (with a visible zipper) like so many motion pictures before it, but takes the time to introduce not one but three distinct stages in the creature's evolution. The two early, post-egg stages are both provocative and compelling, disquieting and repulsive. The final, humanoid form, with its gargoyle-like head and shark-like jaws, is the ultimate movie monster, and by keeping the alien hidden or half-glimpsed by the audience, director Ridley Scott magnifies it beyond our wildest imaginations. Even more intriguing is that the title creature doesn't possess any sort of biological flaw. By creating a monster that could only be destroyed by human resourcefulness, the producers have added an extra dimension of true horror.

ALIEN is also a triumph of production design, set decoration, special effects, costumes, and makeup. Credit for the distinctive look of the film belongs entirely to the very gifted H.R. Giger. Although many of his designs for the motion picture seem somewhat familiar today, they established a pattern that would be copied in other films throughout the decade. Ron Cobb, Jean "Moebius" Giraud and Chris Foss also deserve special recognition for their contributions to the film. Particularly effective is the extraordinary way in which Michael Seymour, John Mollo, Les Dilley and Roger Christian helped to bring most of their designs to life. The film, as a whole, has relatively few special effects, but Brian Johnson's model work and the optical genius of Nick Allder's visual effects stand head-and-shoulders above what was currently being offered in other films. [If you need further convincing, simply rent MOONRAKER, THE BLACK HOLE or 1941, and you'll see a distinct difference.] Jerry Goldsmith's haunting score, which was orchestrated by Lionel Newman, contributes to the overall atmosphere, and binds the other elements nicely together.

Ridley Scott is truly a brilliant visual stylist. He

has taken special pains to create a believable environment in which to unleash his monster. His documentary-like style with the camera helps to evoke a much more realistic portrait of the central characters. The members of the Nostromo are not stereotyped as space-going philosophers, but rather are portrayed as interstellar truck drivers. They are not the least glamorized by his camera work; in fact, quite the opposite is true—he photographs them with warts and all. Scott also manages to avoid the trap of depicting helpless females in jeopardy; by treating Ripley and Lambert as equals of their male counterparts, they function much like real people. ALIEN is without a doubt Scott's most accomplished work.

Sigourney Weaver is very striking as Warrant Officer Ripley. She begins as one of the anonymous members of the crew, and gradually reveals a considerable depth of character as the film builds toward its dramatic climax. John Hurt is particularly effective as the doomed astronaut Kane. Ian Holm also performs wonders as the robot Ash, while Tom Skerritt continues a low-key performance as the soft-spoken Captain Dallas. Yaphet Kotto, Harry Dean Stanton and Veronica Cartwright provide the perfect balance for the larger-than-life alien creature which does attempt to command every scene.

ALIEN, like STAR WARS, may have had its roots in the pulp science fiction adventures of the thirties and forties, but the story itself is somewhat universal in nature—seemingly drawn from the earliest cave etchings of primitive man. No matter how familiar it may be to modern audiences, its superb depiction of the classic conflict between man and the unknown forces of nature continues to affect all who experience it. ALIEN is currently available on videocassette from Twentieth Century-Fox video, and a special letter-boxed edition is also available on laserdisc from Fox.

The following four page appendix on **Alien** *appeared in the original press book. (Courtesy United Artists Theatres.)*

tainly her starring role in "ALIEN" is a giant step in that direction.

British-born Veronica Cartwright, who grew up in America, portrays Lambert, the space-tug's navigator, a high-strung woman, readily responsive to the mood of a situation. This is undeniably a quality shared by Veronica. During one memorably horrifying sequence in "ALIEN," she almost fainted in terror at what was going on around her. ("When I'm into a scene, I often can't help feeling that everything's for real — and that's good I suppose, because it helps my performance and gives it a certain amount of authenticity," says the one-time Hollywood child star who has been acting since she was six.)

The well-known character actor Harry Dean Stanton plays the "Nostromo's" engineering technician, Brett, and sees the character as an extension of himself. They share one thing in particular. Brett is a heavy smoker. And so, it happens, is Stanton.

British actor John Hurt projects an air of vulnerability and inner tension behind a reserved exterior that is very much in keeping with the character he portrays, that of Kane, the executive officer of the space-tug and the first of the astronauts to encounter the dreaded Alien.

There is one other Britisher in "ALIEN," Ian Holm, who plays the role of Ash, the science officer. Holm finds himself essentially different from the character, saying, "Ash tends to become uptight and lose his head in an emergency situation. I flatter myself that I will keep mine."

And finally there is Yaphet Kotto who feels a bond with the ebullient humor of Parker, the engineer whom he portrays, particularly since the script calls for Parker to be a pal of Brett's and, in real life Yaphet and Harry Dean Stanton are very good friends.

Seven intriguing personalities, brought together in one of the most unusual and suspenseful situations the screen has ever known. They will make many films in the future. But they will never forget their roles in "ALIEN." Nor will you.

* * *

Twentieth Century-Fox presents "ALIEN," a futuristic suspense-thriller which tells of seven astronauts — five men and two women — working on a battered commercial space-tug, far away in space and time, who encounter an awesome galactic horror and of their desperate attempts to combat it. "ALIEN," which stars Tom Skerritt, Sigourney Weaver, Veronica Cartwright, Harry Dean Stanton, John Hurt, Ian Holm and Yaphet Kotto as "Parker," is produced by Gordon Carroll, David Giler and Walter Hill, with Ronald Shusett as executive producer. Ridley Scott directs the screenplay by Dan O'Bannon, based on a story by O'Bannon and Shusett. Music by Jerry Goldsmith.

Announcement Story

The fascinations of deep space provide a cinematic challenge which director Ridley Scott meets with astonishing results in Twentieth Century-Fox's futuristic suspense-thriller "ALIEN," opening on _____ at _____ Theatre.

Produced with breathtaking imagination by Gordon Carroll, David Giler and Walter Hill and utilizing some of the most innovative and spectacular special effects ever filmed, "ALIEN" plunges the viewer into a maelstrom of terror and suspense.

The screenplay by Dan O'Bannon, based on a story by O'Bannon and executive producer Ronald Shusett, tells of seven astronauts — five men and two women — working on a battered commercial spacetug, far away in space and time — who encounter an awesome galactic horror. The surprising character revelations which occur during their desperate attempt to combat this mysterious force provides seven extraordinary performances from the film's seven stars — Tom Skerritt, Sigourney Weaver, Veronica Cartwright, Harry Dean Stanton, John Hurt, Ian Holm and Yaphet Kotto.

Director Scott worked closely with special effects director Brian Johnson and supervisor Nick Allder, as well as noted artists H.R. Giger and Ronald Cobb, to evolve a totally original concept of space, while Academy Award winner Jerry Goldsmith has contributed a brilliant and evocative score.

Differences and Similarities

Twentieth Century-Fox's "ALIEN" deals with the exploits of seven astronauts working on the "Nostromo," a battered commercial space-tug, far away in space and time. Unusual characters to be sure. But what of the five actors and two actresses chosen to fill these roles? Do they bear any resemblance in real life to the characters they portray on the screen?

Surprisingly, the answer is yes in many instances.

Tom Skerritt, who plays Dallas, the Captain of the "Nostromo," carries himself with the same quiet, confident air the role requires. Like Dallas, he tends to be laconic ("I don't think it's necessary to fill the air with meaningless conversation," he grins amiably). He prefers reading history or developing his interest in writing screenplays. Both Skerritt and Dallas are men who view their capabilities realistically. They know what they have to do and do it well, with a minimum of fuss and nothing extraneous.

Sigourney Weaver makes her screen debut in "ALIEN" in a remarkable performance as Ripley, the beautiful, cool young warrant officer of the "Nostromo." Like Ripley, Sigourney is highly intelligent, purposeful, determined and not easily deflected from whatever course she chooses to pursue. Given her talent, her stage background and her good looks, these qualities will undoubtedly propel her to super-stardom in rapid time. Cer-

Ridley Scott Directs "Alien"

After building up a formidable reputation in British television, being probably the foremost maker of TV commercials in the country (close to three thousand), director Ridley Scott yearned for the larger motion picture screen as his canvas.

"The Duellists," his first feature-length film, made in 1976, fulfilled that dream.

Now comes his second motion picture, the new Twentieth Century-Fox futuristic suspense-thriller "ALIEN," which tells of seven astronauts — five men and two women — working on a battered commercial space-tug far away in space and time, who encounter an awesome galactic horror and of their desperate attempts to combat it.

"The fact that the story happens to be set in space is really incidental," says Scott. "The space-tug could be an old cargo ship in the South Seas, with a crew of seven who happen to land on an island (a planet in the film) and encounter a horror of some kind. It's the story that matters — the actual setting could be practically anywhere at any time."

Ridley Scott's first film "The Duellists" was based on a Conrad short story. And both Scott and the producers Gordon Carroll, David Giler and Walter Hill are all admirers of Conrad's work. The fact the name of the spacecraft — "Nostromo" — is the title of a famed Conrad novel, constitutes a tip of their caps in that master storyteller's direction.

Ridley Scott was born in 1939, in South Shields, Tyne and Wear, England, later being brought up in London, Cumbria, Wales and Germany, before returning to the Northeast to live in Stockton-on-Tees, where he completed his education. As a child, he showed little aptitude for any school subject other than art, and his parents encouraged him to study at the West Hartlepool College of Art, then at the Royal College of Art in London.

He also joined the newly-formed Film School at the latter college and, with a single Bolex movie camera, made his first film, a 16mm short subject called "Boy on a Bicycle," about a schoolboy playing truant from school. His younger brother played the boy and his father a madman he meets. He shot it for one hundred pounds, then the British Film Institute saw it and gave him another grant to refine and expand it. For Ridley Scott it was a start...

On graduation from the R.C.A., Scott won a travelling design scholarship which took him to New York, where he worked with Bob Drew Associates, took photographs, and watched theatre and documentary film directors at work.

On his return to London he joined BBC-TV as a set designer, later becoming a TV director and working on various productions and popular series such as "Z-Cars" and "The Informer." He left BBC-TV after three years and began to direct commercials, becoming so successful that he formed his own company and, working in London and America, was responsible for around three thousand commercials in ten years, winning many awards and prizes. His most famous commercials include those for Hovis Bread, Strongbow Cider and Levi Jeans.

"The Duellists," his first feature film, originally began as a film for French Television, eventually developing into a major

motion picture, produced by David Puttnam and starring Keith Carradine and Harvey Keitel. Critically acclaimed, it won the Special Jury Prize at the 1977 Cannes Festival, and firmly established Ridley Scott as a new filmmaker of the first rank.

On "ALIEN," as on "The Duellists," Scott works as camera operator as well as director, literally directing from behind the lens as he goes along. When he is working on a picture he is totally dedicated to the job in hand, from early morning to late at night, having no time for distractions of any kind.

Ridley Scott is a perfectionist. and it shows.

* * *

Twentieth Century-Fox presents "ALIEN," a futuristic suspense-thriller which tells of seven astronauts — five men and two women — working on a battered commercial space-tug, far away in space

and time, who encounter an awesome galactic horror and of their desperate attempts to combat it. "ALIEN," which stars Tom Skerritt, Sigourney Weaver, Veronica Cartwright, Harry Dean Stanton, John Hurt, Ian Holm and Yaphet Kotto as "Parker," is produced by Gordon Carroll, David Giler and Walter Hill, with Ronald Shusett as executive producer. Ridley Scott directs the screenplay by Dan O'Bannon, based on a story by O'Bannon and Shusett. Music by Jerry Goldsmith.

"ALIEN" and Its Special Effects

Imagine a London taxicab towing a quarter of London's vast Heathrow Airport. Or a bicycle pulling along London's entire Mayfair district. Or a normal-sized movie shooting stage tugging an area a mile-and-a-half square.

Then you'll have a rough idea of the relative sizes of the unique "Nostromo" space-tug and the vast oil refinery it tows through galactic space in Twentieth Century-Fox's futuristic suspense-thriller, "ALIEN."

All the interior and planet surface sequences for "ALIEN" were filmed at Shepperton Studios. But the six months of special effects and model photography were based at Bray Studios, Windsor (once the home of Hammer horror films) about fifteen miles away.

There, special effects director Brian Johnson, and supervisor Nick Allder, were in charge of the highly-complex and technical magical work that goes into the breathtaking sequences that movie audiences will eventually see of spacecraft hurtling through galaxies of stars and planets and of many other such shots.

Their work is obviously top secret and it would spoil audiences' eventual enjoyment to reveal too many of the intricate "tricks of the trade" that go into the movie special effects field.

But this is special effects supervisor Nick Allder talking — and not, it is hoped, giving too many technical secrets away:

"Our main model of the commercial space-tug 'Nostromo' is eight feet long, which represents eight hundred feet in the story. With our special techniques we're able to camera-track right through space, stars, planets and so on, up to a closeup shot of the craft and actually show the astronauts moving about inside — and all in one continuous shot. But I won't tell you how we do that!

"Generally, we use multiple exposure techniques, employing the original negative, thereby obtaining far better quality than we might otherwise have. We're not using 'travelling matte,' or blue screen backings for this picture for various reasons. The whole picture is shot in rather low-key lighting, so we can't suddenly cut from the space-tug interior to outside space and terrific high contrast quality, because it wouldn't look consistent. Consequently, our lighting of the models has to be fairly low-key as well. Using 'travelling matte' wouldn't work in these circumstances.

"We use the system of 'rotascoping' quite a lot, which involves taking a sequence frame by frame, making line-drawings, then hand-painted mattes, then shooting that in high-contrast, to actually create our matte and eventual effect."

If all that sounds complicated, then it is. Except to the "sfx" technicians who know exactly what they're doing.

Nick Allder, thirty-six, knew that he wanted to be involved in the movie business in some way, at the age of nine. His father was a camera engineer and nine-year-old Nick could "lace up" a Mitchell movie camera like an expert. On leaving school he started with a small commercials company, becoming a rostrum cameraman and working on many TV and cinema commercials and cartoons. He joined Les Bowie's special effects company in the early 1960's and worked on several Hammer pictures. Since then he has worked on the special effects for such films as "Gordon Of Khartoum," "The Long Duel," "Twist of Sand," "The Battle of Britian," (for two years), "The Medusa Touch," "The Wild Geese" and "The Revenge of the Pink Panther." Also on many TV series, including "Space 1999" (for three years). After "ALIEN," he was due to join Brian Johnson on the sequel to "Stars Wars" titled "The Empire Strikes Back."

* * *

Twentieth Century-Fox presents "ALIEN," a futuristic suspense-thriller which tells of seven astronauts — five men and two women — working on a battered commercial space-tug, far away in space and time, who encounter an awesome galactic horror and of their desperate attempts to combat it. "ALIEN," which stars Tom Skerritt, Sigourney Weaver, Veronica Cartwright, Harry Dean Stanton, John Hurt, Ian Holm and Yaphet Kotto as "Parker," is produced by Gordon Carroll, David Giler and Walter Hill, with Ronald Shusett as executive producer. Ridley Scott directs the screenplay by Dan O'Bannon, based on a story by O'Bannon and Shusett. Music by Jerry Goldsmith.

"ALIEN" Experience

"'ALIEN.' ABSOLUTELY NO VISITORS WITHOUT WRITTEN PERMISSION FROM THE PRODUCTION MANAGER."

So read the large notice, printed in stark red-and-black lettering, that greeted would-be visitors to the set of Twentieth Century-Fox's futuristic suspense-thriller "ALIEN," while it was filming at Shepperton Studios, just outside London.

And the notice meant just what it said. There were no actual armed guards at the massive doors to the sound stages. But if a strange face suddenly appeared in the vicinity of the filming area, a polite but firm assistant director would at once inquire as to his business, and then, if the stranger produced no valid reason for being there, guide him, politely but firmly, off the set.

From its inception, "ALIEN" was the top secret motion picture of the year. The story which deals with seven intergalactic astronauts who encounter an awesome and terrible being in space — contains so many surprises and remarkable special effects, it was decided not to spoil forthcoming audiences' enjoyment of the unique production, by letting them know too much in advance.

The seven astronauts — actually more like workaday truckers who happen to do their jobs in space rather than on earthbound highways — are played by Tom Skerritt, Sigourney Weaver, Veronica Cartwright, Harry Dean Stanton, John Hurt, Ian Holm, and Yaphet Kotto.

Had you managed to establish unimpeachable credentials and been allowed on the set, one of the first things you would have noticed was the sight and scent of incense. Director Ridley Scott used it to help give his photography an indefinable but highly-effective "diffused" effect. The special incense he uses is known as "Sanctuary" and is made by Benedictine Monks at Prinknash Abbey in Gloucester. It gives the movie set an almost church-like atmosphere which is appropriately matched by Ridley Scott's devout fervor as he single-mindedly both

directs and operates the camera.

"I enjoy working with designers very much," says co-producer Gordon Carroll, "and with the look and feel of a movie generally. Ridley is marvelous to work with because he has such a fabulous visual sense. Apart from anything else I know the film looks stunning."

"The structure of 'ALIEN' has essential elements of several cinematic genres, including aspects of science fiction and suspense, but those genres overlap considerably," points out co-producer David Giler.

And co-producer Walter Hill adds, "What we're hoping to create is a pure and linear suspense tale combined with an elaborate design texture. And also a classic story of terror and fear of the unexpected and unknown."

Production designer Michael Seymour supervised the design aspects of the film and his team included two Oscar winners from "Star Wars," Les Dilley and Roger Christian (co-art directors) and concept artists and designers H.R. Giger and Ron Cobb. Another "Star Wars" Academy Award winner was costume designer John Mollo.

Once on the "ALIEN" set, one was additionally struck by the intricate technological detail and apparent authenticity of everything on the space-tug (upon which ninety percent of the action takes

place). On the space-tug's upper level, endless corridors linked one section to another, from operational bridge (ablink with myriad twinkling lights and working television screens and computer read-outs) to the commissary, from the infirmary to the hyper-sleep chamber. With three levels in all, it adds up to one of the most complex and fascinating sets ever built for a movie.

In addition one would have come away with snapshot-like memories of the cast between takes:

Quiet, reflective, bearded Tom Skerritt, deep in a book on English history; laughing, short-haired (she had it shorn especially for the picture) Veronica Cartwright, enjoying a joke with the makeup girl; serene, dark-haired Sigourney Weaver, pensively stroking a ginger cat which sits comfortably on her lap (it is featured in the film); silent, poker-faced Harry Dean

Stanton puffing on a constant cigarette; British Ian Holm (noted for his many fine Shakespearean portrayals in the theatre) deep in a serious discussion with the continuity girl; another Englishman, John Hurt, animatedly describing a recent experience with his usual hilarious asides, to a group of appreciative technicians; and last, but certainly not least, the massive, dominant figure of Yaphet Kotto, grinning wickedly, white teeth flashing, in the midst of a chat with an assistant director.

"Quiet everyone, settle down, please!" the first assistant would shout and then turning to the director say, "All right, Ridley, it's all yours..."

* * *

Twentieth Century-Fox presents "ALIEN," a futuristic suspense-thriller which tells of seven astronauts — five men and two women — working on a battered commercial space-tug, far away in space and time, who encounter an awesome galactic horror and of their desperate attempts to combat it. "ALIEN," which stars Tom Skerritt, Sigourney Weaver, Veronica Cartwright, Harry Dean Stanton, John Hurt, Ian Holm and Yaphet Kotto as "Parker," is produced by Gordon Carroll, David Giler and Walter Hill, with Ronald Shusett as executive producer. Ridley Scott directs the screenplay by Dan O'Bannon, based on a story by O'Bannon and Shusett. Music by Jerry Goldsmith.

The Space-Tug "Nostromo" — An Authentic Galactic Technological Wonder And A Movie Set To Remember

One of the most remarkable, complex and ingenious sets ever designed for a motion picture will be seen in Twentieth Century-Fox's futuristic suspense-thriller "ALIEN." It's that of the gigantic commercial space-tug "Nostromo," aboard which most of the action of the spine-chilling story takes place.

The script called for a well-used, slightly battered spacecraft which acted as a kind of massive tug which towed through space a series of three vast oil refineries — rather like a huge intergalactic articulated truck — the whole supposedly 1½ kilometres long and weighing around an awesome two hundred million tons.

"We started by building model sets, then an actual section of a space-tug corridor of part of the operational bridge," explains production designer Michael Seymour. "Then, after further discussions, we began building the sets in earnest."

The "Nostromo" has three levels or "decks" and the designers first toyed with the notion of building a huge three-story set, but it was decided that this would prove impractical for filming purposes. So the "A" (or top) level was constructed first, filling much of the giant "C" sound stage at Shepperton Studios.

The "A" level comprised the astronauts' living areas, mess room, computer annex, infirmary, many linking corridors and, most important and spectacular, the operational bridge. Here, amidst a veritable technological wonderland, the seven astronauts sat at their own individual and immense, leather seats to navigate and operate the space-tug, surrounded by forty television screens (variously sized 5", 9", 13", 15", and 22") showing different pictures of computer readouts, technological and navigational information, maps, and views of the space area outside. Masses of other technical equipment were there, plus hundreds of switches and literally thousands of flashing indicator lights. The many TV screens were fed pictures and films from a special intricate video-centre situated at the side of the sound stage, headed by video coordinator Dick Hewitt.

The numerous banks of circuits and electronic equipment on the walls were prepared by the props and construction departments and largely made up ingeniously from old aircraft, automobiles, and radio and TV sets.

"We must have spent thousands of pounds on scrap from old jet-aircraft engines particularly," said Les Dilley (co-art director with Roger Christian). "And it's all paid off handsomely because it all looks so authentic." Dilley and Christian, incidentally, both won Oscars for their work on "Star Wars" — Dilley as co-art director and Christian as set decorator. "ALIEN" costume designer John Mollo also won an Oscar for his contribution to "Star Wars."

The operational bridge on the "Nostromo" is probably the most technologically detailed and authentic scientific movie set ever constructed. And especially when you realize that everything works! Walk onto the bridge, push a button or throw a switch and something happens, whether it's a light flashing, a door closing, an alarm buzzer sounding or a TV picture zooming into closeup. As Michael Seymour said: "This spacecraft does practically everything but fly..."

Walk down a corridor from the bridge and you come to the mess room, where the crew eat and relax. To one side is a small kitchen area, with every mod-con you could wish for and various foods neatly capsuled into powder and tablet form and often easily indentified by tiny

models of the food available, e.g. a miniature banana, orange or apple. Unbreakable crockery is neatly arranged on shelves and there's a sink too — even astronauts have to do the washing up sometimes!.

Stroll down another padded and illuminated corridor and you come to the infirmary, equipped with everything a doctor or nurse might need, including medicines, drugs, an operating table which glides out of sight into the wall, and a fearsome overhead-suspended set of surgical instruments.

In another section of "A" level is the remarkable "hyper-sleep" area where, in flower-petal-like, perspex-enclosed beds, the crew can "freeze" themselves into hyper-sleep for up to two years at a time.

In an intersecting lobby you can find two large, perspex-fronted wardrobe cases, containing spare space suits for the crew, complete with helmets and other accoutrements.

The "Nostromo's" movements are guided by a remarkable computer called "Mother" by the seven astronauts, who also rely on it for all kinds of other information and facts. Why "Mother?" Because its official technological identification is "MU/TH/UR/6000..."

Later sequences for "ALIEN" were filmed on the two lower levels of the space-tug, built separately on other stages: "B" level, the general maintenance area, and "C" level, containing the vast engine rooms plus a seemingly-endless network of complex machinery-filled corridors, and the giant "claw room," into which the huge landing claws of the space-tug retract when not in use.

"One of the basic ideas of all these complicated interior sets is that you can actually walk from corridor to corridor, from bridge to mess, from mess to infirmary, and so on, thus giving both the actors and the audience the feeling of being inside a vast spacecraft — both huge and claustrophobic at one and the same time," says production designer Michael Seymour. "We want people to have the impression that it's a real place, that it's more science-fact than science fiction, and also that the whole place is well used, lived in and slightly battered after years of service. After all, the crew members of the "Nostromo" are really inter-stellar truckers, just doing their ordinary day-to-day work. They're really top-level truckdrivers who happen to operate a complex space-tug instead of a truck along the motorways on Earth.

"They're freebooters, in a way, who extract appropriate oils and minerals from planets, tow them back to Earth, and share in the proceeds.

"Then their whole lives change when they're awakened from their hyper-sleep by the mysterious distress bleeps — which may well have been sounding out for millions of years, who knows?"

The "Nostromo" is a set to remember, a technological miracle come to movie life. While it doesn't actually achieve "lift-off" it does practically everything else.

"ALIEN" stars seven actors and the Alien itself. The "Nostromo" is the ninth wonder of this very special galactic world.

***

Twentieth Century-Fox presents "ALIEN," a futuristic suspense-thriller which tells of seven astronauts — five men and two women — working on a battered commercial space-tug, far away in space and time, who encounter an awesome galactic horror and of their desperate attempts to combat it. "ALIEN," which stars Tom Skerritt, Sigourney Weaver, Veronica Cartwright, Harry Dean Stanton, John Hurt, Ian Holm and Yaphet Kotto as "Parker," is produced by Gordon Carroll, David Giler and Walter Hill, with Ronald Shusett as executive producer. Ridley Scott directs the screenplay by Dan O'Bannon, based on a story by O'Bannon and Shusett. Music by Jerry Goldsmith.

CHAPTER TWO
"ALIENS"
THE MARINES VERSUS THE NIGHTMONSTERS

1986 - ALIENS - 20th Century Fox, in association with Brandywine Productions, 137 min, Panavision (released in 70mm, Dolby Stereo). Director: James Cameron. Producer: Gale Anne Hurd. Executive Producers: Gordon Carroll, Walter Hill and David Giler. Screen Story by Cameron, Hill and Giler. Screenwriter: James Cameron. Based on characters by Dan O'Bannon and Ronald Shusett. Music Composer: James Horner. Director of Photography: Adrian Biddle. Film Editor: Ray Lovejoy. Special Effects Supervisors: Brian Johnson, Stan Winston, Robert Skotak, and Dennis Skotak. Certain Special Effects by L.A. Effects Group. Conceptual Artists: Ron Cobb and Syd Mead. Alien Creature Design by H.R. Giger. Production Designer: Peter Lamont. Starring: Sigourney Weaver, Michael Biehn, Lance Henriksen, Carrie Henn, Jenette Goldstein, Paul Reiser, William Hope, Bill Paxton, Colette Hiller, Al Matthews, Mark Rolston, Ricco Ross, Daniel Kash, Cynthia Scott, Tip Tipping, and Trevor Steadman. Released on July 22, 1986

Fifty-seven years have passed since the destruction of the commercial starship Nostromo, her cargo and crew. The alien juggernaut that decimated most of the seven-man crew has likewise been destroyed. Only Warrant Officer Ripley survived the terrible events, and now sealed within a hypersleep chamber, cast adrift in the starship's shuttle craft Narcissus, she floats aimlessly through the countless star systems. Little does she know (or even care) that the planetoid Acheron, where her crew first encountered the alien creature in the cargo-hold of a derelict ship, has been colonized by terra-formers. When all communications from the colony suddenly cease, Ripley is the only one who knows the terrible secret . . .

Those first, tantalizing hints that Twentieth Century-Fox was mounting a sequel to ALIEN were revealed by Terry Erdmann during a slide show and presentation of upcoming films at the 1985 North American Science Fiction Convention held in Austin, Texas. Most fans greeted the news with wild enthusiasm, while some others grumbled with trepidation. At first glance, the notion of a sequel must have seemed like such a forgone conclusion. Next to STAR WARS (1977) and CLOSE ENCOUNTERS OF THE THIRD KIND (1977), Ridley Scott's stylish thriller had been one of the most popular films of the decade. But in the six years since its release, the

motion picture had also spawned a rash of forgettable clones. And in a period filled with sequels to almost every successful and popular Hollywood movie that rarely succeeded on their own merit as original entertainment, the new production appeared to be more of a tremendous gamble than a sure thing. Besides the challenge to bring something familiar and new under budget and on time to the screen, the project also had to deal with its share of preconceptions.

The most obvious problem writer and director James Cameron faced in developing a sequel to ALIEN, he said, was, "How do you beat a classic? You really have to dig deep into the bag of tricks and come up with some good ideas. And you have to do a proper homage to the original without being a mindless fan, something which is a piece of entertainment and a story in its own right."

DISCUSSIONS OF A SEQUEL

In the wake of ALIEN's success, many similar films soon began appearing at the local multi-plex. Just as ALIEN had been influenced by low budget science fiction films of the Fifties and Sixties, like IT! THE TERROR FROM BEYOND SPACE (1958), PLANET OF THE VAMPIRES (1965) and QUEEN OF BLOOD (1966), the critically-acclaimed motion picture inspired its own collection of imitators, including INSEMINOID (1980), THE CREATURE WASN'T NICE (1981), GALAXINA (1981), GALAXY OF TERROR (1981), THE THING (1982), CREATURE (1983) and many others. Most of those productions failed to generate any popular enthusiasm, and quickly died at the box office. Ridley Scott's stylish thriller and audience favorite, considered by many as a classic of the science fiction genre, had seemingly captured magic in a bottle. Executives at Twentieth Century-Fox were doubtful that task could again be accomplished, in light of the failure of numerous rip-offs and spoofs, and dismissed a sequel as an unrealistic option.

The partners at Brandywine Productions disagreed, and had faith that a sequel would eventually be made under their production banner. Three years after the release of ALIEN, writer-director Walter Hill, producer Gordon Carroll and writer David Giler held a conference at their offices on the lot at Twentieth Century-Fox to dis-

ALIENS

THE OFFICIAL MOVIE MAGAZINE

K48260 $3.95

Sigourney Weaver battles facehuggers and chestbursters!

Inside the ALIENS nest with James Cameron, director of TERMINATOR!

The film's spectacular story!

Nightmare war on a planet of ALIENS

Michael Biehn in savage combat with the ALIEN army!

*James Cameron took over the directorial reins of the **Alien** franchise from Ridley Scott. Here he's seen directing Arnold Schwarzenegger in* **Terminator 2: Judgment Day** *(photo copyright ©1993 Tri-Star Pictures)*

cuss the possibilities of a sequel. They all agreed that a fresh approach was clearly necessary if audiences were going to accept a follow-up, but none of them could agree what approach to take with the new film. After all, there were so many questions still left unanswered from the first film. Questions, like "Would Ripley safely make it back to Earth?" "Would her story be believed by her superiors?" "Would they then launch an investigation?" "And what about all those Alien eggs waiting to hatch their parasites in the cargo hold of the derelict ship?," continued to bother each of them. They reasoned that a continuation of the story would have to answer many of those questions, while at the same time being completely different in order to avoid simply rehashing the events of the first film. Carroll, who had been studying the success of the evolving home video market for several years, also reminded his partners how much money could be made from the sale of ALIEN on videocassette if the film's

integrity remained in tact. Finally, Hill and Giler concluded that it was better to have no sequel than one which compromised the internal logic of ALIEN, and turned to other projects, including a futuristic remake of SPARTA-CUS. Late in the fall of 1983, Brandywine Productions began considering applicants for writer and director of its next major project. Their decision to rework SPARTACUS with a science fiction setting, though hardly original, was the kind of high concept that Twentieth Century-Fox was willing to invest huge production dollars. The only drawback the partners faced was finding the right individual to pull the project together. Walter Hill briefly considered directing the film himself, but later withdrew his nomination for the less conventional STREETS OF FIRE (1984). Both he and David Giler had been impressed with the script for THE TERMINATOR (1984), and while that particular project had already been optioned by Hemdale (in association with Orion Pictures and HBO Entertainment), they felt its author possessed the kind of raw talent needed for their new film. They consequently met with James Cameron to discuss his participation. Even though he declined, freely expressing his major concerns about their idea, the producers were impressed enough to present the young filmmaker with a unique proposition, the idea of doing a sequel to ALIEN. (As Cameron was about to leave their meeting, Giler actually said, in a half-joking manner, "There's always ALIEN II.") Jim, a great admirer of the first film, readily accepted the difficult task of mounting a sequel.

"All they said was, 'Ripley and soldiers,'" James Cameron fondly remembered his first meeting with executive producers Walter Hill and David Giler. "They didn't really give me anything specific—just this idea of getting her together with some military types and having them all go back to the planet."

JAMES CAMERON

Born in 1955, James Cameron began learning cinematic storytelling techniques at the age of twelve when he first started drawing comic books. By designing each comic book literally frame for frame, with closeups, medium and wide shots, he taught himself the basics of visual narrative. Even though Jim always dreamed of becoming a professional comic-book artist, he eventually set all that aside to work as a graphic designer for Roger Corman's New World Pictures. (Cameron readily credits his development as a filmmaker to Corman, the legendary entrepreneur who produced hundreds of successful low-budget films in the late fifties and sixties from his basement.) While working for New World Pictures, Jim not only learned the pragmatic side of filmmaking, including the importance of efficiency and budgetary control, but also developed skills in art direction, special effects, and photography. His early credits as an art director include PLANET OF HORRORS (an ALIEN rip-off released in 1981 as GALAXY OF TERROR), ESCAPE FROM NEW YORK (1981), and FORBIDDEN WORLD (1982). He worked for the first time with future collaborator Gale Ann Hurd on BATTLE BEYOND THE STARS (1980), designing and shooting the special effects unit while she served as the production manager. When Corman offered him the director-

ial reigns of a PIRANHA sequel, Cameron delivered an effective low-budget thriller.

During post production on his first film, PIRANHA II: THE SPAWNING (a JAWS rip-off), James Cameron (then 27 years old) wrote a simple screen treatment for THE TERMINATOR. The treatment, which contained no dialogue or breakdown on special effects sequences, told the story of a battle-weary soldier from the future who must prevent an unstoppable robot (also from the future) from assassinating a distant relative of the resistance leader's family. While the story itself was hardly new, Cameron's sense of character delineation in a technological setting was what first clinched a development deal for his film at Hemdale. He was still regarded, in many circles, as merely a graphic artist and journeyman screenwriter, and not a talented filmmaker. In fact, at the time of his first meeting with Hill and Giler, Cameron was still waiting for the green light to begin production on THE TERMINATOR. To pay the bills, he accepted the commission to write a screenplay for RAMBO: FIRST BLOOD PART II (1985).

"I was writing RAMBO at the time, and I was getting into the whole Vietnam thing, and it occurred to me that 'grunts in space' was a wonderful concept," Jim

Cameron's writing of the first draft of Rambo: First Blood Part II *is what inspired his "grunts in space" approach to* Aliens *(photo copyright ©1985 Tri-Star Pictures)*

explained his reaction to the original concept for ALIEN II. "There's a whole list of science fiction going back to the twenties that explores the idea of military in space, but it hadn't really been done in film. So I took that idea and all the elements from the first film that I like and thought would be worth retaining, and from there the story crystallized very quickly—in about two days as a matter of fact. I just sort of sat down and drank a lot of coffee and wrote a treatment."

Before he could complete a finished script for Hill and Giler, however, Cameron received word from executives at Hemdale Entertainment that his production of THE TERMINATOR had been given the green light. Jim and co-writer/producer Gale Anne Hurd (then only 28) immediately went to work on the low-budgeted action film which would ultimately become the surprise box office hit of 1984. Based on pages of notes, character sketches and a very rough outline, the partners at Brandywine agreed to wait until Cameron was finished shooting THE TERMINATOR to continue work on their sequel. "I think it's probably safe to say that if THE TERMINATOR had come out and I had then been approached with the idea of doing ALIEN II, I probably would have shied away from it," said the writer/director. "But I did get emotionally involved, and I liked what I'd created. Once the imagery is in your head, you can't get rid of it. The only catharsis is to make the movie. Then you never have to deal with it again."

THE ORIGINAL STORY TREATMENT

James Cameron's original story—a forty-five page treatment, with notes on characters and effects, entitled ALIEN II—was submitted to the partners at Brandywine Productions on September 21, 1983. Although similar to the final film, several concepts in the original were altered or dropped from the latter drafts of the script. The most discernible difference was in the extensive background of the characters. Early in his development of the story, Cameron concluded that the first and most essential element was the central character of Ripley. If the sequel was to succeed, she would have to remain as the emotional core of the piece. He was determined to bring Sigourney Weaver back to

reprise her role, and knew that the actress would agree only if Ripley's character had been expanded beyond the anonymity of the first film. He spent a great deal of time detailing the Warrant Officer, by creating a past history and defining her motivations. According to his original notes, Ripley is a divorced mother with a young daughter who lives with the child's father. She promised to be with "Amanda" on her twelfth birthday; but Ripley learns, upon her fifty-seven year return to earth, that Amy is now a bitter old woman who accuses her mother of abandoning her. That element of guilt, coupled with her recurring nightmares about the alien, provides Ripley with the reason for going back.

Perhaps most crucial in Cameron's early draft was the introduction of Anne and Russ Jorden (who are the parents of Rebecca, "Newt"). Under orders from the Weyland-Yutani corporation, these two colonists investigate coordinates on the planetoid of Acheron (later changed to LV-426) that Ripley has provided for the derelict spaceship. Their discovery of the egg chamber re-introduces the threat from the first film. First, Russ Jorden is infected with the alien parasite, then a handful of rescuers, and finally the whole colony. Unfortunately, their pivotal roles were later reduced in subsequent drafts and completely eliminated from the final film. [During the painstakingly complex reconstruction of the film on laserdisc, the Jorden Family scenes were restored.] Cameron also applied the knowledge he had gained through his research on RAMBO and his interest in the Vietnam War to create a collection of hardened yet believable soldiers. His Colonial Marines, including Hicks, Hudson, Vasquez, Frost, Apone, Drake, Dietrich and the others, remain largely unchanged from the original treatment to the final script. Jim's rough notes, however, featured Lieutenant Gorman as the nominal villain. Carter Burke was not even introduced, and most of his early scenes were assigned to Dr. O'Neil (who does not join Ripley on the journey), with Gorman (in a state of panic) committing the acts of betrayal in the later scenes. The android Bishop was modeled on the character of Ash (from the first film) but changed in subsequent drafts. Because Bishop is merely a machine (and can't act with self-determination), his basic programming threatens the safety of the mission. At one point in the treatment, he is given a direct order from Ripley and Hicks to pilot the second "drop" ship to the surface in order to rescue them. But the ship's computer has issued a "quarantine command" for the entire planetoid, and he is unable to land. (Ripley is then forced to locate the colonists' shuttle, and pilot the craft to safety herself.) Other changes in the story offer interesting variations on the plot. Master Sergeant Apone is not killed during the attack at the processing center, but rather stung and paralyzed by an alien stinger. The others are forced to carry his body back to the infirmary, where Ripley (not Bishop) deduces the alien community is constructed like an insect hive with warriors, workers and a queen. Late in the story, after Bishop has disobeyed the direct order to land the rescue ship, Ripley and the marines begin looking for the evacuation shuttle. Newt is separated from the group during a pitched battle, and both Ripley and Hicks are captured and cocooned. Ripley manages to get free but has only enough time to save the little girl or the injured corporal. She opts for the little girl, and reluctantly leaves Hicks behind.

Cameron's original story treatment for ALIEN II, though impressive to Carroll, Hill and Giler, was little more than a reworking of Robert A. Heinlein's STARSHIP TROOPERS (1959), with elements of Joe Haldeman's FOREVER WAR (1974) added for good measure. One of science-fiction literature's most widely read classics, Heinlein's story follows the exploits of an elite group of soldiers in their battle with a race of large insect-like aliens (which they dub "Bugs"). Their combat is called a "bug-hunt" because the troopers are often forced to hunt down the loathsome creatures, which number in the hundreds, in a complex series of mazes and underground tunnels. At the lowest level, the soldiers discover "the queens....obscene monsters larger than a horse and utterly immobile." Heinlein equips his troopers with "powered battle suits" so that they can match the awesome strength of the aliens. His narrator describes the battle armor: "Two thousand pounds of it, maybe, in full kit....you look like a big steel gorilla, armed with gorilla-sized weapons. The suit has feedback which causes it to match any motion you make, exactly—but with great

force." The soldiers must also endure the "drop," a harrowing free-fall in tiny capsules from the infantry mothership to the planet below. Similar elements from Haldeman's story, not the least of which is the notion of time dilation during hypersleep travel, also seemed to find their way into the treatment.

THE FIRST DRAFT SCREENPLAY

The basic story for ALIENS, as originally conceived by James Cameron prior to his work on THE TERMINATOR, only later evolved, after numerous revisions and rewrites, into the blueprint for the highly successful film. While the similarities to Starship Troopers and The Forever War remained, other concepts needed reworking. But Hill and Giler had been impressed enough by his forty-five page treatment to give Cameron approval to continue. After completing work on THE TERMINATOR, the young filmmaker spent weeks, sorting through his stacks of notes and the partially conceived treatment. Finally, after nearly a month, Jim got right down to business and wrote his script. Almost two years after the completion of the treatment, he turned the first draft screenplay into Brandywine Productions on February 28, 1985. David Giler and Gordon Carroll reviewed the draft, and suggested that certain elements be changed. Cameron submitted a revised screenplay several weeks later. Within a month, Twentieth Century-Fox had approved his script and preproduction began on the expensive sequel.

Surprisingly similar to the final version, the first draft screenplay added a couple of new sequences and deleted a few others. The most dramatic inclusion was the introduction of Carter Burke, the company man who first befriends then later betrays Ripley. His presence in the script filled the void left by Ash (in the first film) and added an important subplot that would function as a catalyst for conflict when the aliens were off-screen. Most of the scenes featuring Dr. O'Neil at Earth Satellite Station Beta (changed to Gateway Station in the final film) were simply rewritten for him; other scenes portraying Lieutenant Gorman as the nominal villain were also revised for Burke. A major sequence, towards the end of the story, was also written (but never filmed) which

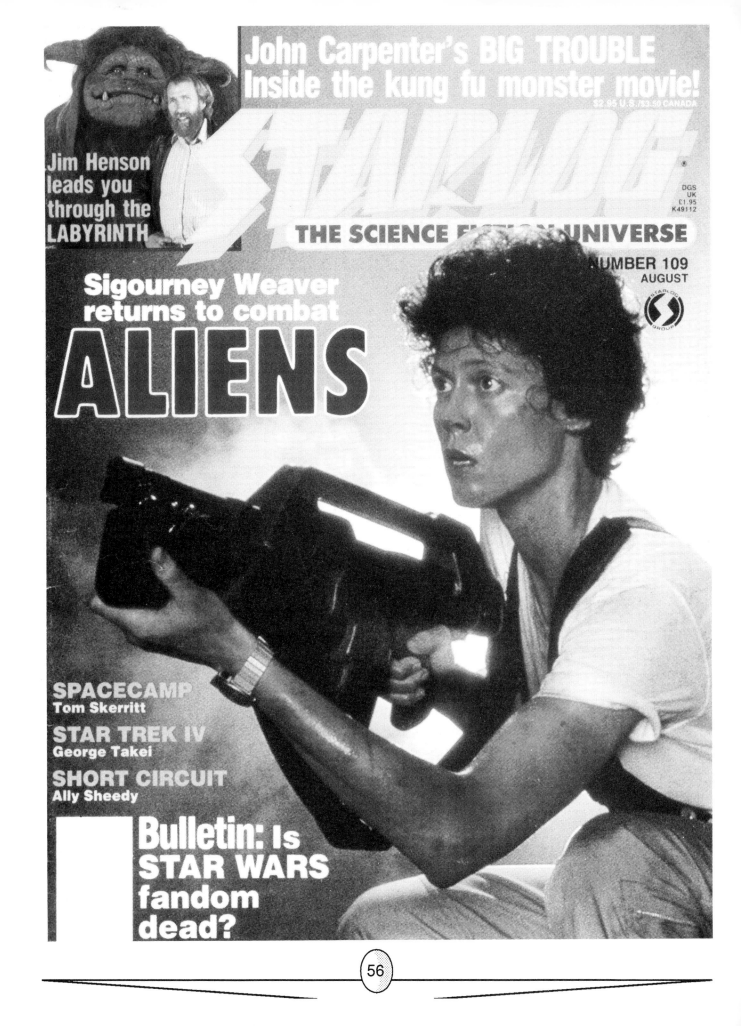

John Carpenter's BIG TROUBLE
Inside the kung fu monster movie!

$2.95 U.S /$3.50 CANADA

STARLOG

THE SCIENCE FICTION UNIVERSE

DGS
UK
£1.95
K49112

NUMBER 109
AUGUST

Jim Henson
leads you
through the
LABYRINTH

Sigourney Weaver
returns to combat
ALIENS

SPACECAMP
Tom Skerritt

STAR TREK IV
George Takei

SHORT CIRCUIT
Ally Sheedy

Bulletin: Is
STAR WARS
fandom
dead?

drop-ship toward the planetoid below. The small craft rocks and buckles as it plummets through the atmosphere, then penetrates the cloud cover on its way toward the distant landing beacons of the colony. Stumbling as the ship pitches back and forth, Ripley makes her way to Gorman's command center to get a better look. The colony looks completely deserted. The drop-ship sets down on the wet, wind-swept tarmac, deposits the armored personnel carrier, and lifts off in a swirling cloud of smoke. The APC, driven by Bishop and carrying Ripley, Burke and the Colonial Marines, screeches into the small colony of Hadley's Hope. Suddenly, the main compartment door flies open, and the troops hit the ground running. Inside the complex, they find huge blast holes, broken barricades, and fire-gutted offices but no bodies. Apparently, there was some incredible battle, but they are weeks, or even months, too late. Gorman orders his men to "stand down," then he and Ripley, accompanied by Private Wierzbowski (Trevor Steadman), Burke and Bishop, enter the seemingly deserted complex. Down in the devastated medical wing, Ripley and the others discover six face-huggers—two alive and the other four dead—preserved in transparent cylinders. Burke seems surprised to see the alien creatures, and asks Ripley if they are like the one her crew found. She nods, her whole body frozen with paralysis. This is the first real evidence to support her allegations, but before they can investigate further, a loud beep on Hicks' motion tracker alerts them to a possible intruder. The tension continues to mount as Ripley and the others follow the signal to a most unusual source. Cowering in the darkness is a dirty, frightened little girl named Newt (Carrie Henn).

Ripley gathers the little girl lovingly into her arms, and cradles her like the lost daughter she left on earth so long ago. Newt, like the former Warrant Officer, is a survivor; she has been hiding in the air ducts since her parents were killed by the aliens.

Meanwhile, Burke and Hudson have managed to locate the missing colonists through their homing transmitters. They seem to be gathered "for a town meeting" at the Atmosphere Processing Station. (Little do they know the colonists have actually been entombed alive there in a labyrinthine cocoon, awaiting the incubation of

baby aliens.) The soldiers mount a rescue mission, boldily rushing into the alien's lair, despite Ripley's warnings. Then all hell breaks loose, as the "bugs" emerge from the walls of the chamber. Using pulse-rifles, flame-throwers, smart-guns, and other weaponry, the Marines battle their fearsome alien opponents, but they are simply outmatched.

"*Get them out of there!*" Ripley screams, moments before grabbing the wheel of the APC from Gorman. The armored personnel carrier races into the labyrinth, and smashes through the alien barricades. But she is too late! The aliens have already killed or captured most of the squad. Hicks, Hudson and Vasquez are the only ones left, and they must struggle to get free. Once safely aboard the APC, the survivors race toward freedom. (Lt. Gorman is knocked unconscious during their escape.) They manage to get half a kilometer away from the Atmosphere Processing Station before the gears of the vehicle grind to a halt. Ripley has not only stripped the gears in her desperate attempt to save the others but also blown the trans-axle. The APC is finished.

Ripley has had enough of battling these monsters and suggests they "take off and nuke the entire site from orbit." Burke disagrees, reminding her of the cost of the installation. But he is quickly overruled by the ranking officer, Corporal Hicks, who signals the "drop-ship" to pick them up. Their plan may, however, be a trifle premature. Before Corporal Ferro (Colette Hiller) and Private Spunkmeyer can reach their location, an alien hidden inside the craft attacks. The drop-ship veers wildly, strikes a rock formation with its landing gear, and crashes to the surface. Ripley, Newt and the others are completely stranded.

Later, in the colony operations center, Ripley takes charge of the squad. The earliest they can expect to be rescued is in seventeen days, so they must devise defensive strategy strong enough to hold the aliens until then. She orders Hudson and Vasquez to weld several barricades in place, while Hicks begins assembling all of the weapons they've managed to salvage. She then tucks Newt safely in bed, and confronts the android. Bishop seems enthralled with the "face-hugger" creature, declaring its anatomy to be very unique. He also reasons, through a complex series of tests, that there must be a queen who is responsible for laying the eggs. Ripley doesn't really care about his speculation, and orders him to destroy the specimens "as soon as possible." Bishop can't. Burke has ordered him to preserve them for further study back in laboratories on earth. Enraged, the former Warrant Officer hunts Burke down, and warns him about the laws against shipping dangerous organisms. But he doesn't see the problem, claiming "Those specimens are worth millions to the bio-weapons division. Now, if you're smart we can both come out of this heroes, set up for life." Ripley adamantly disagrees, and threatens to expose his negligence with information linking him to the deaths of 157 colonists. (She has checked the colony radio log. Apparently, Burke was the person responsible for sending colonists out to investigate the derelict craft without warning them what they might find.) He shrugs it off as "a bad call...."

Just when it seems that things couldn't get much worse, the android interrupts with even more bad news. The Atmosphere Processing Station, damaged during the crash of the drop-ship, is building towards overload. They have less than four hours until it blows, and the blast radius will be more than thirty kilometers, about equal to a forty megaton nuclear explosion. Their only chance is to get the other drop-ship from the Sulaco, and bring it down by remote control. With their transmitter destroyed in the APC wreckage, the only hope is the colony up-link tower (if it's still in tact). Someone has to go out there and manually work the controls. Bishop volunteers, minding them that it will be close.

Ripley knows the aliens will eventually get into the complex, and convinces Hicks to teach her how to use a pulse-rifle equipped with grenade launcher. She intends to fight, right to the end. Then, exhausted and stressed beyond human capacity, Ripley retires to the infirmary for a few hours rest with Newt. Little does she know or even suspect that Burke intends to impregnate both her and Newt with the alien parasites.

About an hour later, Ripley wakes up with a start, as if yanked out of another nightmare. She looks around the room, and everything seems quiet....perhaps, too quiet for her sensibilities. She suddenly notices the two

empty jars, which once held face huggers, and realizes to her own horror that they are in trouble. In a frenzied scramble, she grabs Newt, rolls under the cot and flips it over, trapping the first creature. Child in arms, she races to the door, and finds it sealed. The second face hugger strikes. Ripley struggles to keep the other creature at bay, while calling for help. At first, Hicks is distracted in the communications center by Burke, and fails to notice her screams on the surveillance monitors. Then, several desperate moments later, her room erupts with gunfire as the Marines come to the rescue. Within heartbeats, the two creatures are dead.

Hicks and Vasquez catch Burke and drag him back to the operations center. But before they can execute him for his treachery, the lights suddenly go out. The aliens have penetrated the barricades, and are clawing their way through the crawlspace into the center. Hudson opens fire, just as Ripley scoops Newt into her arms and Burke bolts for the only escape. The other Marines stagger back, firing blindly as the aliens appear from above the ceiling and below the floor. They are once again vastly outnumbered by the "bug"-like creatures.

Gorman orders them to retreat, but their escape hatch has been locked by Burke. They blast through with welding torches, but lose Hudson in the struggle. (Burke continues closing off exits, until he stumbles upon an alien warrior himself. He has no time to scream.) Unable to breakthrough the last hatch, the Marines soon realize they are trapped. Newt tugs Ripley across the room to an air vent, and the others follow closely behind. The duct leads to a larger shaft, which runs the length of the complex, and may ultimately deposit them on the landing strip. If Bishop was successful, the second drop-ship should be waiting or them on the wet, wind-swept tarmac.... Vasquez is suddenly cut off from the others. Gorman hears her screams, and crawls back to help. But he is also cut off, as the aliens appear from every conceivable direction. Unwilling to submit, the Lieutenant primes a grenade. He then pulls Vasquez close to him, and the two die in a blaze of glory.

Ironically, the shock wave from the exploding grenade rocks the air shaft, causing Newt to loose her footing and tumble down a long, narrow chute into the murky darkness of the complex. Ripley leaps to grab her hand, but she is inches too late. Before she and Hicks can get down to her, an alien warrior carries the little girl away. Ripley is so devastated by the loss that she is literally paralyzed from the neck down. Hicks drags her toward an elevator t the far end of the tunnel and pushes her inside, while at the same time blasting away at another alien. The acid-blood splashes through the doors onto the corporal's armor, and the skin below. Ripley finally comes to her senses, and takes the injured man into her arms. She really has no time to mourn Newt; her first duty is to carry Hicks to safety of the drop-ship, then may be she'll have time to think about her little girl.

Bishop is waiting at the drop-ship; they have less than twenty-six minutes before the area "turns into a cloud of vapor the size of Nebraska." But Ripley can't just leave, if there's a chance to save Newt.

After strapping on a flame-thrower and a pulse-rifle, Ripley descends into the alien hive, ten stories below the Atmosphere Processing Station. Several explosions rock the complex like earthquakes, as a computer voice counts down the seconds to destruction. Ripley searches the catacombs, and finds Newt entombed inside a cluster of eggs. The little girl screams, soon to be the victim of a face-hugger; but Ripley is there, in the nick of time, with her formidable weapons. The former Warrant Officer blasts away at the creature, then tears Newt free from her cocoon. The worst is not over, however. As Ripley whirls around to leave, with the little girl tucked safely in her arms, she glimpses the most terrifying thing she has ever seen— the alien queen. Ripley tries backing away from the queen, which towers above her by several feet, but soon realizes that the queen has other plans for them. Pissed off, Ripley unleashes an awesome display of firepower, blasting the queen's swollen abdomen and igniting the field of eggs. She and Newt then race for the safety of the drop-ship with the angry queen in hot pursuit.

Anxious to leave the planetoid far behind, Ripley orders Bishop to take off for the Sulaco, unaware that the drop-ship now harbors the alien queen in its landing gear. The spacecraft surges through the clouds into the black-

ness of space, moments before the surface erupts with a nuclear blast. Shortly after touch-down, while she and Bishop are looking for a stretcher to carry Hicks, the alien queen slowly emerges from the craft and tears the android in half like a rag doll. The creature then turns on the little girl. Thinking fast, Ripley climbs into a "power-loader" suit, and confronts the alien queen, shouting, "Get away from her, you bitch!" The alien lashes out with unbelievable fury, but Ripley blocks her attack with a blow from the powerful steel forks of the loader. They battle, one-on-one, demolishing everything in their path. Ripley finally manages to close the forks, crushing several of the alien queen's ribs, then carries the obscene creature to the airlock. The alien fights back, and intertwined, they crash fifty feet to the bottom of the shaft. The former Warrant Officer claws her way out of the "powerloader." She then fumbles with air lock mechanism, and blasts the queen into the depths of space. With all her remaining strength, Ripley fights the hurricane of decompression, clawing her way to the top of the emergency airlock. She hits the "close" button, and collapses to the deck.

Later, in the Sulaco's hibernation center, Ripley secures both Hicks and Bishop in their own stainless steel chambers, then tucks Newt securely away for the long journey home. She retires into hypersleep herself, knowing that the nightmare is finally over.

*****

James Cameron's final shooting script was viewed by Walter Hill and David Giler as a worthy successor to the honored original. Even though he had moved the action from the claustrophobic interiors of a space ship to the wide open battlefield of the colony base, Cameron had still maintained the relentless death-struggle between a small group of rugged individuals and a cosmic creature. He had also centered the action around the nominal "hero" of the first film. But Hill and Giler knew that his screenplay was more than simply a logical extension of ALIEN. By expanding the role of Ripley and delving deeper into her background, Cameron had created a believable character who would engage a potential audience's sympathy and goodwill. Only reluctantly does Ripley first decide to confront her demons by

Movie Classics

Class II
Power Loader
with Ripley
1/12th scale

ALIENS

going on the expedition then later choose to take command of the squad. As portrayed by Jim Cameron, she is clearly not a female Rambo but merely a victim of extraordinary circumstances. Her "masculine" strength and assertiveness are soon tempered by a maternal devotion to Newt, who like herself is a survivor. In comforting and protecting the little girl, Ripley also overcomes the guilt she feels having abandoned her daughter. The partners at Brandywine Productions knew these elements combined to make their new project a winner. Sigourney Weaver was equally impressed with the story, and agreed to play Ripley a second time. With her involvement in the project secure, Twentieth Century-Fox gave Brandywine its final approval and preproduction began.

THE PRODUCTION STAFF

Once the script had been approved, and the title of the film had changed from ALIEN II to ALIENS, James Cameron knew his selection of the right production team was crucial to the success of the film. Walter Hill, David Giler and Gordon Carroll had decided to act as executive producers rather than producers (as in the first film), and that left Cameron free to bring in his own producer. Even though he had worked with a handful of very successful producers over the years, his collaborative experience on THE TERMINATOR (1984) revealed that there was only one person for the position—Gale Anne Hurd, a woman he had worked with during the early Corman years. Hurd, a graduate of the Stanford University with a combined degree in communications and economics, had begun her career as a publicist for SAINTJACK (1979), LOVE ON THE RUN (1979) and THE BROOD (1979). She eventually moved from publicity to producing feature films at Roger Corman's New World Pictures. Her first credits came as an assistant production manager on BATTLE BEYOND THE STARS (1980), in which she worked with Cameron, and GEORGIA PEACHES (1980). Not long after, she became a co-producer (with Corman) on 1981's SMOKEY BITES THE DUST. She later co-wrote and produced THE TERMINATOR, turning a modest little thriller into one of the year's ten best motion pictures. She married James Cameron during the production of ALIENS, and helped him launch his next major project, THE ABYSS (1989), before embarking upon a successful producing career of her own.

In producing ALIENS, Hurd was extended a tremendous amount of autonomy and creative input by Cameron. He knew that she was the only person in the industry who could take their modest budget of $18 million, and see that every dollar went right onto the screen by hiring the best cast and crew. She made no attempt to achieve a continuity of personnel between the new film and its highly praised predecessor. "We didn't want to put ourselves in the position of trying to reassemble the Ridley Scott crew because then you get into a position of unconstructive second-guessing," she explained. "We went out to find people who could bring Jim's vision to the screen. It just so happened that there were a few people who had worked on ALIEN who came to work for us."

Among the people returning from the first film were several very familiar faces. Adrian Biddle, who had worked as a focus puller on ALIEN, had become a first rate cinematographer in the intervening seven years. The former clapper-loader for Ridley Scott Associates had earned quite a reputation as a director of photography in England, and he was Jim Cameron's first choice. Crispian Sallis, who had been a trainee of Les Dilley, Roger Christian and Ian Whittaker in the art department on ALIEN, had gone on to become a seasoned set decorator. His impressive skills were called upon to decorate both the Gateway Station's medical lab and the huge colony complex. And finally Ron Cobb, who had produced literally hundreds of sketches for the first film, seemed like the ideal choice to produce a number of important designs. The former political cartoonist had become one of the most sought after art designers since his work on ALIEN. He had contributed sketches to RAIDERS OF THE LOST ARK (1981), and later headed the art departments for CONAN THE BARBARIAN (1982) and THE LAST STARFIGHTER (1984). He was initially hired by Gale Anne Hurd to help Cameron (during the early stages) brainstorm many of the film's key sequences, then kept on as one of the two principal designers.

Like the first film, ALIENS required a skilled art department to bring the otherworldly nightmare to life. "Part of the attraction of doing the film was that it was a design fest," said Cameron, "an opportunity to do all sorts of wonderful hardware. I knew that the only way we could get the job done was to bring on two top designers and divide up the workload—with me taking on certain parts of it myself to fill in the gaps." With Cobb already aboard sketching everything from the vehicles to the weapons to the patches on uniforms, the young writer/director hired Syd Mead as his other designer. Mead, a major figure in industrial design, had contributed futuristic designs for Paramount's first STAR TREK film (1979) and Ridley Scott's BLADERUNNER (1982). Disney had called upon him to realize the inner world of the computer in TRON (1982), and his designs for Peter Hyams' 2010: THE YEAR WE MAKE CONTACT (1984) won him enormous critical praise.

Since Ron Cobb had already been familiar with the world of ALIEN, he was assigned the task of designing the colony of LV-426. Those conceptual designs included the Atmosphere Processing Station, the colony complex (both interior and exterior), and the colonists' vehicles. His sketches all looked fully-functional and very realistic. Syd Mead was given the assignment of envisioning most of the military designs, including the troop carrier Sulaco. Cameron, an accomplished art designer in his own right, produced dozens of sketches as inspiration for the two artists, including one which would eventually become the drop-ship. ALIENS, like its predecessor, had one of the strongest art departments of any motion picture currently in production.

Peter Lamont, a highly-celebrated production designer, was hired to translate the imaginative graphics of Ron Cobb and Syd Mead into functional sets. Lamont had studied art at the High Wycombe School of Art and started working in film as a print boy in a huge art department. He later graduated to set decorator, and won an Academy Award for his work on FIDDLER ON THE ROOF (1971). Albert R. Broccoli recognized his budding talent, and put him to work with legendary production designer Ken Adam on the 10th James Bond film THE SPY WHO LOVED ME (1977). He soon took over as the chief production designer on the 007 adventures FOR YOUR EYES ONLY (1981), OCTOPUSSY (1983) and A VIEW TO A KILL (1985). He also designed the first Bond film to star Pierce Brosnan, GOLDENEYE (1995), which is number 17 in the series. In addition to bringing many of the designs to "life," Lamont also worked closely with Crispian Sallis creating many of the Gateway sets from his own designs. He was later called upon to transform a deserted electrical generating plant into the interior for the Atmosphere Processing Station.

The actual job of supervising the extensive floor effects, as well as overseeing the special effects, was awarded to John Richardson. Richardson had been involved early-on with the original ALIEN—when Walter Hill was still planning to direct—but was forced to withdraw from the project during its numerous delays. A veteran of THE OMEN (1976) and SUPERMAN (1978), he had gone on to distinguish himself by directing the visual effects for RAISE THE TITANIC (1980), LADYHAWKE (1985), and three James Bond Films. He would have the most difficult task of not only supervising the floor effects but also bringing the special effects, being completed by various groups around the world, into a unified whole. He was also singularly responsible for the creation of the power-loader.

*****

For reasons of economy, Cameron and Hurd decided to shoot their ambitious sequel at Pinewood Studios, just outside London. Their budget of $18.5 million would go much further in the United Kingdom, where the dollar was much stronger than the pound. Carroll and Giler also negotiated with Twentieth Century-Fox for an 18-week shooting schedule with four months for post-production. Fox had originally planned to release the motion picture on July 1, 1986, during the highly lucrative Fourth of July holiday; but they soon realized that, even with a tight production schedule, the film would never be ready. They eventually conceded to a July 15th release date, which was later changed to July 22nd to avoid other scheduling conflicts. With time of the essence, Cameron took the script and drew storyboards for every key sequence in the film based on the designs from Cobb and Mead. Jim knew that he could deliver the film on time if he simply followed his storyboards. He would also have to oversee the set construction and the special effects.

One of the most remarkable and ingenious miniature sets ever designed for a motion picture—that of the colony complex and its gigantic Atmosphere Processing Station—was built one sixth-scale over an entire soundstage. Since the script called for a well-used, slightly battered collection of buildings to represent the colony complex, the idea of modular sections, converted from space ship containers, was conceived. "We're not talking technical prophecy here," said Ron Cobb of his original designs. "It was understood from the very beginning that what we wanted was not a serious consideration of a believable future, but rather something more stylized. If we were being serious about all this, it isn't likely that the colonists would even try to build on the planet surface. They'd probably go underground. But if we'd done that we'd have missed out on dusty streets and people huddled against the wind—the real frontier western look."

Originally, Cameron and his designers toyed with the notion of building several modular sections which could be moved around, but it was decided that this would prove impractical for budgetary reasons. So, Jim and Gale Anne Hurd selected the L.A. Effects Group (under the direction of Larry Benson and Alan Markowitz), a fledging optical house that had recently finished work on CREATURE (1985), to construct an elaborate miniature of the colony complex. Cameron avoided going to Boss Film or Industrial Light and Magic because he didn't really know anyone there personally who would remain directly involved. The young filmmaker did know two members of the L.A. Effects Group, Robert and Dennis Skotak. He had worked with both of them on GALAXY OF TERROR (1981) and THE TERMINATOR (1984), and entrusted them with the miniature work.   Together with technical adviser Pat McClung, Robert and Dennis collected an assortment of precious junk, which had been left over from the previous Bond movie, and assembled a massive complex. Because of its overall length, the colony was laid out diagonally over a eighty by ninety-foot stage. Several paintings flanked the makeshift boomtown to provide a forced perspective. A second, smaller version of the colony, roughly eight-foot square, was also built for the drop-ship fly-over sequences.

THE SPECIAL EFFECTS

While most of the interior and planet surface sets for ALIENS were being built at Pinewood Studios by L.A. Effects Group, some of the special effects and model photography were sub-contracted to Arkadon Motion Control, an 11,000 square-foot facility beside the River Thames near the Buckinghamshire-Berkshire border. Most of the visual effects were completed under the direction of Brian Johnson, who had worked with Nick Allder on the original film. His company contributed most of the motion control shots in the sequel, particularly those involving the Narcissus and the deep-space salvage ship, the Sulaco, and the various shots of the dropship in space and on the planet's surface.

Brian Johnson had long been a fan of science fiction. Johnson became involved in the motion picture industry in 1958, and with the hopes of one day making his own film, he joined the camera department of Shepperton Studios to learn all that he could about cinematography. Later, he began to study special effects under the tutelage of Les Bowie, one of the true pioneers who would later receive an Academy Award for the first SUPERMAN (1978). Brian was given his first chance supervising special effects for Val Guest on THE DAY THE EARTH CAUGHT FIRE (1962). In the late sixties and early seventies, he emerged as the predominant special effects wizard in England, and was soon hired to produce extensive work for the television series SPACE 1999 and numerous other projects. Most of the special effects and model work centered around the troop carrier Sulaco and its two drop-ships. Although the warship was supposed to be hundreds of feet in length, the model of the Sulaco was actually about six feet long. The ship was assembled in rough form by outside contractor Peter Astin, then detailed and painted at the studio by Pat McClung. With special techniques, Johnson and his crew made the Sulaco appear much larger, and more deadlier, than the model. Similar miracles, making use of bluescreen and computer-controlled camera-tracking, were employed to simulate the complex orbiting and landing sequences. Peerless Camera Company in London was also called upon by Johnson to provide several motion control shots for the film.

Certain visual effects were also supplied by the Los Angeles Effects Group. Larry Benson, Steven Benson, Susan Benson, and Alan Markowitz had not only contracted to supply most of the models for the projects but also to complete several key effects. Chief among these effects were the reconstruction of the derelict alien craft, the creation of a volcanic environment for it, and work on a base model for Gateway Station. Most of the work was done at LAE's North Follywood facility under the supervision of Steve Benson and Jay Roth. Their work, along with dozens of highly-skilled technicians, comprised all but the last stage of the special effects process. The designs for the "aliens" still remained.

STAN WINSTON AND THE "ALIENS" DESIGNS

During the very early stages of pre-production, James Cameron tried to involve H.R. Giger in his ambitious project; but the Swiss surrealist was far too busy creating otherworldly monsters for POLTERGEIST II (1986) to consider his offer. Cameron then acquired Giger's original drawings for the egg, the face-hugger, the chest-burster, and the alien warriors from Brandywine, and began making sketches of his own. The life cycle of the Alien had already been clearly established in the first film: the creature begins as a pod containing a face-hugger, then springs out and attaches itself to a host; by way of a tube inserted in the victim's throat, the face-hugger deposits an embryo which grows into a parasite; the parasite emerges by bursting from the victim's chest, and grows quickly into an adult alien; the adult then cocoons its victims, depositing an alien larva, which consumes the host alive and grows into a pod. That last stage in the alien's life cycle had been unceremoniously removed by Ridley Scott during the final editing of ALIEN, and left room for Cameron to re-imagine the origins of the eggs.

"The version of cocooning that was shot for the first film involved the concept of the host's body slowly forming into the egg itself from which the face-hugger would ultimately emerge. Had that existed in the first film, my story wouldn't have worked," Cameron revealed. "In my story, the eggs came from somewhere else. I focused on the idea of a hierarchical hive structure where the central figure is a giant queen whose role it is to fur-

This model showcases the look of the Alien Queen.

ther the species." Carrying the alien life cycle to its logical conclusion, Jim made dozens of sketches that rendered his gigantic queen in loving detail. But with Hans Giger unavailable, the young filmmaker needed a first rate creature effects designer. He did not have to look far to find Stan Winston.

Winston, who had previously worked with Cameron and producer Gale Anne Hurd designing the robot version of THE TERMINATOR, seemed the ideal choice. "I was aware of ALIENS from the outset when Jim was actually doing his first draft screenplay," Winston explained. "I remember talking to Jim, and him saying, 'What do you think, Stan, should I do a sequel to ALIEN?' And I said, 'Absolutely, Jim—I need the job."

One of the world's premiere special make-up effects designers, Stan Winston actually came to Hollywood to become an actor. He had always loved motion pictures, particularly horror movies, and as a child dreamed of fighting monsters alongside Peter Cushing and Vincent Price. Winston eventually used his talents as an artist, painter and sculptor to find odd jobs within the industry to keep him employed. While waiting for some studio to discover him as an actor, he worked developing his skills in make-up on several highly-prestigious television projects. He soon received two Emmy Awards for his work on GARGOYLES (1972) and THE AUTOBIOGRAPHY OF MISS JANE PITTMAN (1974). Stan made the transition to film with little difficulty, and was nominated for the first Academy Award given in the field for make-up for HEARTBEEPS (1981). He received a Saturn Award for his robot effects in THE TERMINATOR from the Academy of Science Fiction, Fantasy and Horror in June of 1985. (Winston also served as the film's second unit director.) When the elaborate, multi-jointed creature failed to work in the ALIEN-inspired PREDATOR (1987), he stepped in and created the now-famous alien-predator. He would later make his directorial debut with PUMPKINHEAD (1988) before earning a second Academy Award for his work on TERMINATOR TWO: JUDGMENT DAY (1991). His more recent accomplishments include JURRASIC PARK (1993) and INTERVIEW WITH THE VAMPIRE (1994).

Once in production, a major part of Winston's job on ALIENS was the construction of the new alien character, the Queen. Working from sketches provided by Cameron, he first constructed a miniature prototype with the help of his team of sculptors, including John Rosengrant, Alec Gillis, Willie Whitten, Greg Figiel, Brian Penikas, Shawn McEnroe, and Shane Mahan. The four-limbed, fifteen-foot creature was built around two men on stilts, using fiberglass and aluminum plating, and its heavy bulk was supported by a crane. The head and neck movements were controlled by hydraulics and cables, while the legs and tail were puppeted externally. Stan spent a major amount of his time and budget working out the rough details of how the creature would move realistically without revealing the stuntman in the rubber suit. Later, as he became more involved in the project, he realized that a smaller version would also be necessary for certain shots. (Doug Beswick was hired to produce a quarter-scale one that was cable-controlled.) Winston also made several full-scale mock-ups of certain body features, such as the head and tail, for those inevitable close-up shots.

With the exception of the queen, the other creatures remained largely unchanged from the first film. "I had access to just about everything except the original chest-burster," Winston said. "But there had been a number of photographs and books on the first ALIEN, so anything we didn't have actual access to, we had pictures of. We tried to be as true to the original film as we could, without disallowing ourselves a little bit of artistic freedom to do things that we considered—if not an improvement—something to keep your head above water so you're not just doing what was done before."

The biggest difference affected the design of the alien warrior but only in a very subtle way. "On the original alien," Cameron continued, "there was a translucent cowl covering the whole top of the head that looked kind of like a porpoise back. We planned to do the same thing with ours, and to that end Stan had Tom Woodruff sculpt a ribbed, bone-like understructure that would fit underneath and be slightly visible through the cowl. When it was finished, they gave it a real nice paint job and I took a look at it and said, 'Hey this looks much more interesting the way it is.' So we just pitched the cowl and decided it was just another generation of aliens."

ALIENS

Alien Warrior Boxed Set
Six 25mm Lead Miniatures and a Figure Storage Case

Sculpted by Bob Ridolfi   Painted by Tim Olsen

LEADING EDGE
GAMES

Warning: This product contains lead, and should not be used by children under 12 years of age.

Other alterations in the way the creature moved also made the alien warrior more insect-like and less like a man in a rubber suit. To this end, Winston not only created fifteen suits out of a spandex material but also almost a dozen puppets. The suits were made to fit stuntmen, actors and dancers, depending on what movements were required for the scene. The puppets were designed —in some case even larger than the suits— to make it easier to accomplish fantastic movements a man in a rubber suit could not possibly achieve. Only the most discerning eye would notice any change between the two; but when that element of animation or puppetry was added, the special effect offered audiences something they had not seen before. "I get a great deal of pleasure knowing that the things I put on film will scare people in a healthy way. There are films out there that are based on scaring people with the realities of life, with the horror of real life. I would rather not do that," Winston concluded. "I prefer to scare people for fun. Scare them with things that are the boogey man and things that we can really look at and say, 'That's not real.' That's just make-believe and it's a big monster on the screen and get a lot of fun out of being scared, then being able to walk away and sleep at night knowing that's not something that walks around your own neighborhood."

THE CAST

While James Cameron and Gale Anne Hurd worked with Stan Winston and others on the various phases of preproduction at Pinewood Studios in England, casting directors Mike Fenton, Jane Feinberg and Judy Taylor (in Los Angeles) and Mary Selway (in England) began looking for the actors and actresses who would fill the roles in ALIENS. They hoped to re-create the casting magic of the first film, and looked for performers who would bring much of themselves to the roles. Of course, the lead role of Warrant Officer Ripley had already been predetermined by the first film, and what better actress could they ask for than Sigourney Weaver?

Following the success of ALIEN (1979), Sigourney Weaver developed a string of winning performances in EYEWITNESS (1981), THE YEAR OF LIVING DANGEROUSLY (1983), and DEAL OF THE CENTURY (1983). She reluc-

tantly accepted the role of Dana Barrett in GHOST-BUSTERS (1984), but demonstrated she could handle comedy as well as serious drama. Shortly after the phenomenal success of GHOSTBUSTERS, she returned to the New York stage, and earned a Tony nomination for her performance in the Broadway production of HURLYBURLY. At first, Weaver was somewhat hesitant about reprising the character of Ripley in ALIENS. She had just landed the starring role of a high-priced call girl in HALF MOON STREET (1986), and was working her way towards the "A" list of leading actresses. Sigourney did not really need to do the motion picture, but she was intrigued by James Cameron's new take on her character.

Sigourney Weaver, looking more glamorous in this shot from Ghostbusters II *than she usually does as Ripley (photo copyright ©1989 Columbia Pictures)*

"Ellen Ripley's emotional content is so much greater in ALIENS, and that really appealed to me," the actress confessed. "I tried to imagine and comprehend something like her situation, coming back to a whole different world, and yet haunted by the other one. And

Ripley's personal situation is so bleak. I know I'm playing the same character, but I feel that she has changed, so utterly, by what happens to her early in ALIENS—she's not the earnest young warrant officer she was when she went into space the first time. She's had to become very strong in order to deal with what she's seen and felt."

In addition to Ripley, Cameron created several other strong female characters for pivotal roles. Private First Class Vasquez was written as the toughest of the squad of Marines, and finding the right person for the role produced some anxiety for the casting directors. Eventually, they settled for an unknown stage actress who had received much critical notice, Jenette Goldstein. She was born in Los Angeles and studied drama at the University of Southern California at Santa Barbara, and in

New York at the Circle in the Square Theater, where she appeared in numerous plays. Besides jazz, modern and folk dancing, and singing (soprano), her interests include body-building, gymnastics, acrobatics, soccer, and baseball. Even though ALIENS was Jenette Goldstein's film debut, she later went onto appear in key roles in NEAR DARK (1987), MIRACLE MILE (1989), and LETHAL WEAPON II (1989). She worked again for Cameron on TERMINATOR TWO: JUDGMENT DAY (1991).

Nine year-old Carrie Henn, who had never before worked in front of a camera, was cast in the pivotal role of Newt, the lone survivor of the colony who develops a very special relationship with Ripley. (Louise Head and Kiran Shah were also hired to double for Newt during the more complex and dangerous action scenes.) Newcomer

An Aliens reunion of sorts on the set of Near Dark, with Lance Henriksen (Bishop), Jenette Goldstein (Vasquez) and Bill Paxton (Hudson) (photo copyright ©1987 De Laurentiis Entertainment Group)

Cynthia Scott was hired to play Corporal Dietrich, the squad's medical officer, and Colette Hiller was brought aboard as Corporal Ferro, the drop-ship pilot. While neither of their parts were particularly substantial, they were important members of the ensemble cast. Cameron was most insistent that these five women be viewed as the bravest and most resourceful characters in the story.

Michael Biehn, seen here in the original Terminator, *picked up the action as Hicks in* Aliens *(photo copyright ©1984 Orion Pictures)*

The young writer/director insisted his male soldiers were equally vital, and challenged Fenton, Feinberg, Taylor and Selway to find vital actors to round out his ensemble cast. Their initial choice for the role of Hicks, however, proved problematic. James Remar was first signed to play the young corporal; but after several days of shooting Cameron was not pleased with his performance, and replaced him with a much more familiar face, Michael Biehn. Biehn had just completed a rather intensive shoot with Jim on THE TERMINATOR (1984), so he was very familiar with the writer/director's ardent desire for perfection. Born in 1957, Biehn had studied drama at the University of Arizona before beginning his profession-

al acting career. His first screen role in the television pilot for the LOGAN'S RUN series gave him less than two lines, but he did leave an indelible impression. He later appeared in episodes of OPERATION RUNAWAY, JAMES AT 15, POLICE STORY, and FAMILY, and co-starred in television movies FIRE IN THE SKY (1978) and ZUMA BEACH (1978). Finding opportunities limited in television, Michael began perfecting his own collection of psychotics, racists, weirdos, and other nasty characters, in films as diverse as THE FAN (1981), THE LORDS OF DISCIPLINE (1983), and DEADLY INTENTIONS (1983). He was cast against type as the heroic Kyle Reese in THE TERMINATOR, and proved that he could hold his own against heavy-weight Arnold Schwarzenegger. He would later return to bad guy roles in Cameron's THE ABYSS (1989), turning in an Oscar-worthy performance as the crazed Navy seal. Other more recent performances have included NAVY SEALS (1990), a cameo as Kyle Reese in TERMINATOR TWO: JUDGMENT DAY (1991), and K2 (1992).

Paul Reiser, a lovable schnook in TV's Mad About You, *was considerably slimier as Burke in* Aliens *(photo copyright ©1990 Paramount Pictures)*

Paul Reiser was also cast against type as Carter Burke, the sleazy company executive who endangers the lives of Ripley and the others. A native of New York, Reiser was a rising star in the late seventies on the New York comedy circuit at clubs like "Catch a Rising Star," "The Comic" and "The Improv." The stand-up comedian made an easy transition from nightclubs to motion pictures with an impressive debut in Barry Levinson's DINER (1982). That celebrated performance was followed by a hilarious turn, opposite Eddie Murphy, in BEVERLY HILLS COP (1984). His role in ALIENS was a major departure from his previous work. Following ALIENS, he reprised his 1984 role in BEVERLY HILLS COP II (1987), and went on to headline the popular television series MY TWO DADS and MAD ABOUT YOU.

The role of Bishop, the squad's mysterious android, was awarded to Lance Henriksen, a veteran of several Cameron movies. Regarded by many in the industry as a "chameleon," because of his incredible ability to create new characters, Henriksen was born in New York City and had lived all over the world by the time he was thirteen. He made his motion picture debut as Murphy, an impressive turn as a hired killer, in DOG DAY AFTER-NOON (1975), and followed that with small roles in NET-WORK (1975), CLOSE ENCOUNTERS OF THE THIRD KIND (1977) and THE VISITOR (1979). In DAMIEN: OMEN II (1978), he turned in another incredible performance as the evil Sergeant Neff. Other noteworthy performances followed in THE PRINCE OF THE CITY (1980), NIGHT-MARES (1983), THE RIGHT STUFF (1983), and THE JAGGED EDGE (1985). Lance first worked with James Cameron on PIRANHA II: THE SPAWNING (1982); Cameron was so impressed with his work that he wrote the evil robot in THE TERMINATOR with the talented actor in mind. When it finally came time for casting the role, Henriksen kicked his way through a production meeting door, dressed in a leather coat, with foil teeth and slicked-back hair. The film's distributor was suitably terrified and impressed, but ultimately the role went to Schwarzenegger. (Henriksen appeared in the film as a police detective.) He tried a similar stunt to land the role of Bishop, by purchasing special contact lenses which gave the illusion he had two pupils. This time, the stunt worked, and even though Cameron chose not to make use of the lenses during filming, he was certain he had the right

actor as Bishop.

The well-know character actor Bill Paxton was cast, partially for comic relief, in the role of Private Hudson, whose constant joking and nervous complaining causes tension for the rest of the squad. Born in Fort Worth, Texas, Paxton first began working in motion pictures as a set decorator for Roger Corman on BIG BAD MAMA (1974) and DARKTOWN STRUTTERS (1975). He was working behind the scenes when Jonathan Demme offered him a bit part in CRAZY MAMA (1975). Other roles in a handful of forgettable motion pictures followed. Cameron remembered his face from several of those films, and cast him as a street punk in THE TERMINATOR, which earned him much critical praise. Paxton would later star opposite Henriksen in NEAR DARK (1987) and Biehn in NAVY SEALS (1990) before tackling PREDATOR II (1990) and THE DARK BACKWARD (1991).

Al Matthews also brought an impressive body of stage and motion picture work to his characterization of Master Sergeant Apone, the unit leader. Canadian-born William Hope was the perfect choice for Lieutenant Gorman, the squad's by-the-books commanding officer. The other key roles of Privates Spunkmeyer, Drake, Wierzbowski, Crowe and Frost were filled with seasoned performers Daniel Kash, Mark Ralston, Trevor Steadman, Tip Tipping and Ricco Ross. Even though most of them were given very little screen time, they helped mold Cameron's potentially anonymous group of soldiers into a real unit.

PRODUCTION DETAILS

Principal photography on ALIENS was scheduled to begin in September of 1985 at Pinewood Studios with the shooting of the opening sequence aboard the Narcissus, in which the deep salvage team first discover Ripley. But when word reached the production office that HALF MOON STREET—currently shooting across town at EMI Elstree Studios with Sigourney Weaver—was running seriously behind schedule, panic began to spread. Weaver could not make the film's fall start date, and would now be unavailable for the first three weeks of principal photography. Cameron's carefully worked-out shooting schedule was suddenly obsolete. Gale Anne

Hurd reminded Jim that, in order to be ready for a Summer '86 release, they needed to begin shooting no later than October of 1985. Since so much of the project revolved around Weaver's participation, the young writer/director was left in a real quandary.

"Rehearsal time was something that we didn't have on this film," Cameron later admitted. "Sigourney not being available was a severe handicap; but as I rehearsed the troopers, the military characters, who were part of a close-knit squad with a close camaraderie, as a separate unit from the rest of the cast, I think her absence helped actually contribute to the tension and distance between her and the others." Jim drilled his Colonial Marines with military precision, forcing them to do calisthenics, close order drill around the backlot, weapons prep, and target practice. Most of the cast stayed in character off the set, and when they were interacting, they would treat each other as their characters treated each other. But the writer/director could only work them so much. He still had a motion picture to film, and according to his producer, he was already behind schedule.

One of the few sequences that did not directly involve Weaver was the assault team's foray into the Atmosphere Processing Station which had been taken over by aliens. Rather than build an elaborate set on the Pinewood lot or a complex miniature (that required special processing shots), Peter Lamont and his location crew had converted a decommissioned electrical generating station in the London suburb of Acton (about fourteen miles away) into the eerie bio-mechanical nest of the creatures. During the first couple of weeks, Cameron concentrated on the sequences leading to the discovery of the alien hideout, the one and only chest-burster scene, and the first of two major battles with the army of alien warriors. Since Lamont and his crew had been forced to remove dangerous asbestos from the station, much of the retrofitting (over the existing machinery) was still not complete, and things got off to a slow start. (Principal photography at Acton had been scheduled much later in the shoot.)

A major sequence photographed during this period was the troopers' descent into the station. Inside the

alien structure, they find the first physical evidence that confirms Ripley's story. They also discover a colonist who is still alive but trapped in a cocoon. Only moments later, she begins screaming as a chest-burster erupts from her body. Stan Winston and his crew were responsible for creating this illusion. They started by attaching a fiberglass chest piece to Barbara Coles' shoulders, and surrounding her head and neck with a resinous substance, which gave the appearance she was trapped in the wall. The artificial chest was then filled with several tubes to squirt fake blood, and a single hand puppet, operated by Tom Woodruff, was positioned inside. Much like the setup in the first film, the chest-buster hand-puppet was designed to burst through the foam rubber appliance and t-shirt. But Winston soon learned, what the technicians on ALIEN had already discovered, that it was not easy to tear through cotton shirts. He was forced to distress several t-shirts with battery acid, as in the first film; but the early frustration caused more than a few tense moments for cast and crew. Subsequent scenes were filmed at some of the station's completed sections, including one that involved a complicated hanging miniature built by Steve Begg and Chrissy Overs. Many of the sequences were also duplicated with a hand-held video camera, so that Jim could later interpolate these shots with those captured on film to lend an air of credibility.

After about two weeks of intensive shooting, Cameron decided to replace actor James Remar—originally cast in the key role of Hicks—with Michael Biehn. This change meant that several scenes which featured Hicks had to be restaged with Biehn. He was falling even further behind his shooting schedule.

By the time the cast and crew returned from Acton, Sigourney Weaver had joined them on the sets at Pinewood Studios. Her first scenes on the schedule included several key sequences that followed sequentially the troopers' demoralizing rout at the power station. Ironically, most of the cast and crew felt demoralized by the less than perfect shoot. The realistic performances in the next few scenes attest to their own feelings of distress. But that was soon to change. Weaver's enthusiasm for the project was apparent to everyone right from the beginning, and was very contagious. When filming wrapped for the fourth week, the production crew and cast were in very high spirits, having rebounded nicely from the earlier disappointments on the shoot.

Principal photography, involving the first and second units, continued for the next several weeks without any major problems or difficulty. Peter Lamont and his crew were scrambling to keep ahead of the first unit, as Cameron moved quickly from scenes in the Sulaco's cargo hold to Gateway Station to the colony complex itself. About mid-way through the shoot, problems developed between the production company and the L.A. Effects Group. Many of the miniatures, which Jim had hoped to combine with live action sequences for in-camera effects, were not yet ready, and other special effects sequences were running far behind schedule. "Originally," Brian Johnson explained, "L.A. Effects said that they could handle the work, so Jim and Gale hired them. But as time went on, it became obvious that they weren't equipped to handle all of it, so they came to me and asked if Akadon Motion Control could help them out."

Later, when Cameron realized they would never be done in time, he himself hired Johnson to complete other aspects of their assignment. That decision not only caused some hurt feelings and discontent between the production company and the L.A. Effects Group, but also led to a legal dispute regarding credit.

Towards the end of the year, with many scenes still remaining to be shot and the eighteen-week schedule drawing to a close, the first and second units began working overtime. Sequences featuring Ripley's rescue of Newt in the alien nest, the drop-ship's last minute arrival, and the struggle with the alien queen aboard the Sulaco were set up very quickly and filmed. Cameron felt comfortable with the fast pace, but his cast and crew were again showing signs of fatigue. Several variations of the scene with the monster descending from the drop-ship and tearing Bishop to pieces were shot under the supervision of Stan Winston and his crew. But none of them seemed to capture the true essence of the scene. Eventually, after several more tries, Jim successfully filmed the sequence which would become legendary.

In late January of 1986, with the final shots of Ripley in the hypersleep chamber of the Narcissus having just been completed, principal photography on ALIENS wrapped. A few days later, Peter Lamont and his crew began disassembling the remaining sets, so that the soundstages could be readied for the next production.

*****

During post-production, James Cameron shut down the production for a week so that he could work with editor Ray Lovejoy on a rough cut of the film. Cameron knew that he had to cut thousands of feet of raw footage down into a workable, two-hour time frame, or Twentieth Century-Fox would hire its own editor to do the job. He and Lovejoy reluctantly trimmed much of the footage involving the colonists' discovery of the derelict craft, and eliminated several references to Ripley's daughter. Executives at Fox still weren't satisfied, and cut two additional minutes of footage considered crucial to Ripley's relationship with the space orphan Newt. Jim was later upset with himself that he let that happen. (Many of these compelling sequences were later restored to the televised and laserdisc versions of the film.)

Cameron and Gale Anne Hurd also hired James Horner to produce the musical score for ALIENS. The writer/director had met Horner during his tenure at New World Pictures, and respected his tremendous talent as a composer. The veteran of half a dozen motion pictures, Horner began his career in the early eighties, producing scores for Roger Corman in projects as diverse as BATTLE BEYOND THE STARS (1980) and HUMANOIDS FROM THE DEEP (1980). His first real break in the industry came in 1982 when Harve Bennett approached him to score STAR TREK II: THE WRATH OF KHAN. That prestigious assignment led to STAR TREK III: THE SEARCH FOR SPOCK (1984), COCOON (1985), and other high-profile films. Following his work on ALIENS, Horner went on to compose the music for BATTERIES NOT INCLUDED (1987), COCOON-THE RETURN(1988), AN AMERICAN TAIL (1989), and others. Cameron did not care much for Goldsmith's original theme for ALIEN, and instructed Horner to produce a rousing score which placed an emphasis on action over suspense. The composer worked on the main themes for several weeks, and literally overwhelmed Cameron with his work

With less than a few weeks remaining, the film

was ready for its cinematic debut. With the tag-line "This time—it's war," the studio promoted the picture as a straight action-adventure, highlighting guns and the battle with the aliens and de-emphasizing the character development of Ripley.

THE THEATRICAL RELEASE

When it was released on Friday, July 22, 1986, ALIENS faced incredibly stiff competition from John Carpenter's BIG TROUBLE IN LITTLE CHINA, Ridley Scott's LEGEND, David Cronenberg's remake of THE FLY, Sylvester Stallone's COBRA and Arnold Schwarzenegger's RAW DEAL. But its real nemesis at the box office was the hugely popular TOP GUN, directed by Ridley's younger brother, Tony Scott. ALIENS debuted in over a thousand theatres, and sent its competition running for cover. In its first week of release the movie easily knocked TOP GUN off the top of the charts and later, while grossing an incredible $40 million in its initial three weeks, committed serious damage to its other foes. Both theatre audiences and critics alike praised the film's nonstop action and impressive special effects, but some reviewers did find fault with its violence. Regardless of the criticism, ALIENS continued to perform well at the box office all throughout the summer and fall, and netted more than $170 million in receipts (worldwide), emerging as the third highest grossing film of the year.

In February of 1987, ALIENS was honored with three award nominations from the Academy of Motion Picture Arts and Sciences. Sigourney Weaver's nomination as Best Actress in a Leading Role was an unexpected surprise for the tall, statuesque actress. Because the studio had cut so much of her character in order to focus more on the action and adventure, she realized that her chances of capturing the coveted award were slim. But the honor of being recognized by her peers with a nomination was really reward enough to her. Nominations were also given to James Horner for Best Musical Score and Stan Winston, Brian Johnson, Robert and Dennis Skotak for the Best Achievement in Visual Effects. At the actual Academy Awards ceremony, ALIEN lost out in two of its three categories, but won in the category of visual effects. Later in the year, the film was also honored with a "Hugo"

award from the World Science Fiction community.

Early in its promotional campaign for ALIENS, Twentieth Century-Fox made the decision to limit the number of licensed products, refusing to flood the market like it had with the first film. A novelization of the screenplay was again arranged through Warner Books, but there were no trade paperback design books, no comic adaptations, no calendars, and no coffee table art books authorized by the studio. Only a souvenir program and movie magazine with posters were licensed to Starlog publications. In the Spring of 1992, Halcyon, a Britain-based model company, released several original model kits inspired by the movie, including the "Power Loader," the "Drop-Ship," and the "Armored Personnel Carrier." Though somewhat expensive, these items still continue to sell well in specialty stores and at science fiction conventions. Dark Horse Publishing also began releasing comic books inspired by ALIENS, and in the Winter of 1993, Kenner Products began issuing action figures based on the characters in the movie and original designs for its aliens.

THE LASERDISC RE-CONSTRUCTION

A Special Wide Screen Collector's Edition of ALIENS was released in 1991, featuring a new digital transfer of the film in the "letterbox" format — preserving the aspect ratio of 1.85:1 that was seen in the theatres. The mastering process, painstakingly supervised by James Cameron, provided home video enthusiasts with a definitive version that preserves the integrity of the director's original vision.

Utilizing the superior quality of Laser Disc presentation, the version enabled the home viewers to engage in a frame-by-frame analysis of the film or view material in a special section which documents the entire evolution and history of the film. Rare photographs, production art work, and exclusive footage took the viewer through every phase of the production and revealed how the various elements of the film were created. An exclusive interview with Cameron also provided fans with an insight into the creative process. The section on Pre-production included material about the development of the screenplay, the ALIENS production unit and casting. The

Production section included an extensive look at the design of props and costumes, the Sulaco, Gateway Station, and the alien queen, while the section on Post-Production featured interesting facts about the film's theatrical release and promotion. In addition to sections dealing with production, the disc restored many of the film's edited sequences, including the introduction of the Jordens and mention of Ripley's daughter.

CRITICAL COMMENTARY

ALIENS is not only a worthy successor to the honored original but also surpasses Ridley Scott's thriller, in many respects, by delivering all the chills and excitement of a rollercoaster ride out-of-control. Meticulously crafted and beautifully filmed, James Cameron's spectacle offers more other worldly terror and suspense, more rousing action and more in-depth feeling than any three films of its kind. The film's enduring popularity and success can be attributed to many of the same elements that made ALIEN popular and successful, including the archetypal nature of the story, the extraordinary visual style and the many contributions of the artists and technicians who labored for nearly a year on the project. But its true essence lies in the screen magic of writer/director James Cameron. Even after repeating viewings of the work, audiences continue to be mesmerized by the overall visual experience of the film.

The film owes so much of its strength and magic to Cameron. Prior to ALIENS, he was a struggling filmmaker who had an eye for art direction and special effects. Like veterans Stanley Kubrick and Ridley Scott, he sought to prove that motion pictures could provide a narrative approach through its visual medium. His film generates a high premium excitement from the opening frame, dispensing with the need for traditional storytelling in favor of explosive action and nerve-jangling adventure. Cameron's involvement in the project, from writing and directing to supervising the special effects, is apparent in nearly every facet of the production, and his genius is apparent throughout the film. Part tech noir, part heavy metal, and all action, the director brilliantly leads audiences on a reconnoiter into the heart of darkness and back again. But Cameron is equally effective in the smaller, more personal scenes. He evokes a truly compelling performance from Sigourney Weaver as the troubled survivor of the Nostromo, who must go back and face her worst nightmares. Her scenes with Newt provide the emotional core of the film, for we realize that Ripley is not only fighting for herself but also for motherhood and humanity itself. Cameron forces his central character to take responsibility for her own fate as well as the fate of the universe, and that represents high drama for the director. Juggling all of these elements at once, Cameron combines plot, characterization, hard-hitting action, and special effects to create a truly unique film experience.

Of course, at the emotional center of the film, is Sigourney Weaver in what may be her best performance as Warrant Officer Ripley. Even though she began the first movie as one of the anonymous members of the crew, her character is firmly established here by Cameron with several key scenes. Awakened from her unusually long hypersleep, she begins experiencing the first signs of post-traumatic stress disorder. She hallucinates the presence of an alien parasite in her body. Then, burdened with the knowledge that her daughter has died of old age despising her, Ripley continues her descent into a personal hell, and begins to fall to pieces. She finally decides to fight the continuous nightmares by returning to the LV-426, and by facing the creature, once and for all. Ripley is then thrust into the role of protector, and surrogate mother, when the soldiers discover Newt, the colony's sole survivor. Each of these sequences allows Weaver to express a different facet of Ripley: first, as a survivor, then, a victim (of her nightmares), next, a warrior, and finally, a mother (the role she once abandoned). Her multi-leveled performance was clearly worthy of the Academy Award for Best Actress of 1986.

Supporting Weaver throughout the film, Cameron has assembled a wonderful collection of actors and actresses to turn his potentially anonymous cast of soldiers into a group of very realistic characters. The members of his squad are not stereotyped as macho, Rambo-like warriors, but rather are portrayed as enlisted men and women who gripe, joke and risk their lives for each other. By focusing on their basic humanity and their determination for survival, Jim Cameron transforms his "grunts" into individuals the audience can relate to. Played mostly by fresh screen faces, each of the actors is given a moment in the spotlight. First among Cameron's collection of characters is Michael Biehn as Corporal Hicks. Boyishly handsome but with cat-like reflexes and cold, dead eyes, he provides a powerhouse of pure adrenaline with his performance. In fact, when Hicks first pulls out his TERMINATOR shotgun, the audience always reacts with raucus approval. Jenette Goldstein, with her Hispanic accent and Ms. Olympia physique, is equally compelling in the role of Vasquez. She is not only the toughest of the marines but also a counterpoint to Weaver's very assertive Ripley. Bill Paxton is very good as Hudson, the private who first laughs in the face of danger then falls apart. His comic pacing provides the film with some of its funnier movements. Lance Henriksen and Paul Reiser also contribute memorable performances to the film.

Like its predecessor, ALIENS is also a triumph of production design, set decoration and special effects. Credit for the distinctive look of the film is shared equally by Ron Cobb, Syd Mead and Cameron. Stan Winston and his team of specialists also deserve praise for not only bringing the alien creatures to life but also making them appear much more than men-in-rubber-suits. Brian Johnson, Robert and Dennis Skotak also provide some stunning visual effects, worthy of the Academy Award. Horner's rousing score, which was clearly better orchestrated than Goldsmith's score from the first movie, contributes to the overall atmosphere, and underscores the non-stop action.

Over the years, since its initial release in the summer of 1986, ALIENS has become accepted as a genuine screen classic. In fact, the two films are often mentioned in many ten-best lists of science fiction. While its roots may be traced back to Robert Heinlein's STARSHIP TROOPERS, Joe Haldeman's FOREVER WAR or other pulp fantasy adventures of the thirties and forties, the film does manage to transcend those simple stories in order to reach exceptional heights of its own.

ALIENS is currently available on videocassettes and laser discs from Twentieth Century-Fox video. A spe-

cial wide-screen version, which includes informative background material, is also available on laserdisc from Fox.

THE OFFICIAL MOVIE BOOK

ALIENS

The year's most spectacular science-fiction adventure!

Sigourney Weaver in a duel to the death with the ultimate horror! The making of this chilling sequel. From the director of TERMINATOR—James Cameron! Includes eight explosive posters.

CHAPTER THREE
THE LOST WORLDS OF "ALIEN THREE"

1992 - ALIEN THREE - 20th Century Fox, in association with Brandywine Productions, 115 min, Panavision (released in 70mm, Dolby Stereo). Director: David Fincher. Producers: Gordon Carroll, Walter Hill and David Giler. Associate Producer: Sigourney Weaver. Screen Story by Vincent Ward. Screenwriters: Hill, Giler and Larry Ferguson. Based on characters by Dan O'Bannon and Ronald Shusett. Music Composer: Elliot Goldenthal. Director of Photography: Alex Thompson. Film Editor: Terry Rawlings. Special Effects Supervisor: Richard Edlund. Alien Creature Design by H.R. Giger. Alien Effects by Alec Gillis and Tom Woodruff Jr. Production Designer: Norman Reynolds. Starring: Sigourney Weaver, Lance Henriksen, Charles S. Dutton, Charles Dance, Paul McGann, Brian Glover, Pete Postlethwaite, and Ralph Brown. Released on May 22, 1992

Returning from her death struggle on Acheron, LV-426, Ellen Ripley relaxes comfortably in her hypersleep chamber aboard the military carrier Sulaco as it traverses the cold darkness of space. The former Warrant Officer is suddenly roused from her dreamless slumber to again face her worst nightmare....aliens....in a retrofitted New York City of the future....in an abandoned shopping mall in space....on a man-made planetoid inhabited by hillbilly farmers....aboard a wooden fourteenth century spaceship from earth, crewed by monks....or in a run-down penal colony.

Eleven years after the original ALIEN, and less than four years since its rousing sequel ALIENS, the Twentieth Century-Fox franchise had finally reached a creative impasse. Not only had the many plotlines under consideration for the new sequel finally revealed just how clearly derivative of other genres the series had become, but also how dramatically limited the whole concept was from the very start. Nevertheless, Fox was determined to release a third (and possibly fourth) film, aware that the first two installments in the series had combined grosses over $200 million. Planned for an Easter 1990 release, the troubled sequel eventually went through three directors, eight screenwriters, innumerable script drafts and rewrites, a Writers Guild strike, the Gulf War, criticism about massive cost overruns, a change in studio leadership, a problematic production, expensive reshoots and a power struggle over creative control

before debuting to negative reviews and lukewarm box office receipts. The project seemed doomed to failure from the start.

"Money men now seem to be in control of the studios rather than filmmakers," said a disgruntled crew member who chose to remain anonymous. "They know if they release ALIEN 3 people are going to see it out of pure curiosity. They're going to make millions of dollars, so they don't care what the picture's like."

Much like the mythical, malevolent "Company" of the series, some evidence does seem to suggest that Twentieth Century-Fox was motivated more by profit margins than creative integrity . But perhaps that opinion is far too simplistic or naive. Perhaps the blame for ALIEN 3's failure belongs clearly with the creative brain-trust who have nurtured the series from the beginning. Others seem to find fault with the unsatisfactory screenplay. Though carefully engineered to plunge audiences into a maelstrom of terror and suspense, the relentless death-struggle between Ripley and the cosmic creature may have simply become too familiar. Still others choose to blame the novice director whose work, though stylish, lacked the proper focus. The answers lie somewhere between that first story idea and the motion picture that finally debuted in movie theatres.

The final motion picture of ALIEN 3 evolved from dozens of scripts, treatments and story conferences involving many successful writers and directors. While few in the industry will publicly acknowledge it, the film suffered through a process known as "development hell" on its way to the big screen. In their quest to make a movie which packs a huge box office wallop, the executives at Fox and the producers at Brandywine went through a dizzying array of Hollywood's talented visionaries, often at the expense of true genius and genuine vision. That process first began in 1987 with the first discussions of a sequel.

DISCUSSIONS OF A SEQUEL

The overwhelming and unexpected success of ALIENS prompted Roger Birnbaum, president of world-wide production at Twentieth Century-Fox, and other key executives to begin referring to the ALIEN series as "the

CINEFANTASTIQUE®

June 1992

$5.50
CAN $6.50
UK £3.50

ALIEN³

IT CAME FROM DEVELOPMENT HELL

COOL WORLD
Ralph Bakshi makes whoopee in cartoonland

HELLRAISER III
The horror continues, but without Clive Barker

Volume 22 Number 6

Walter Hill, seen here directing Nick Nolte and Eddie Murphy in *Another 48 Hrs.*, is a producer of the *Alien* film series *(photo copyright ©1990 Paramount Pictures)*

franchise." Both Ridley Scott's stylish thriller and James Cameron's rousing action-adventure had not only proven to be money-spinning crowd-pleasers but also that the concept was potent enough to survive sequel after sequel. Science fiction and horror films were continually demonstrating their versatility at the box office and on home video, raking in over $800 million annually in profits. Like George Lucas' epic STAR WARS space saga and Paramount's perennial STAR TREK franchise, their series had seemingly managed to capture that same magic in a bottle. Executives at Fox were convinced that they could continue to profit from ALIEN, and approached the partners at Brandywine Productions with the notion of one, possibly two, films.

Accordingly, producers David Giler, Walter Hill and Gordon Carroll began exploring the possibilities of a sequel. They all agreed that a different approach was clearly necessary to distinguish from the horrific aspects of the first movie or the all-out warfare of the second if audiences were going to embrace the franchise, but none of them could agree what approach to take with the new film. They considered such story ideas as having the aliens come to New York and fuse into a giant, Godzilla-like monster that threatens the city, and another in which Ripley and the orphan are trapped in a BLADE RUNNEResque metropolis with the creature. They ultimately acknowledged that bringing the alien creature to earth was probably not a good idea. Giler explained it best, by saying, "Drop the alien in Death Valley and you drop a nuke on him — end of story." The partners knew that the storyline worked best in a dark, claustrophobic setting. They also reasoned that a continuation of the story would have to feature the character of Ripley in some capacity, while at the same time being completely different from her previous encounters with the creature in order to avoid simply rehashing past events. They soon found themselves turning to Sigourney Weaver for input. Over the years, she had become friendly with both Gordon Carroll and David Giler, and that friendship eventually led to a key role in the decision process.

"There wasn't any given time where the masterminds just said, 'Oh, let's just do another one,'" Sigourney Weaver explained her new role as co-producer. "It was a very slow process and a long struggle. The impetus for the third film was primarily due to the huge success of ALIENS. Clearly audiences wanted more. But we approached it with a lot of trepidation because the first two movies were so successful and so well done — well, in my opinion — that everyone was worried a third wouldn't measure up to the standards set by Scott and Cameron. It took a long time figuring out what story we should tell and what elements we would try and duplicate. We decided early on Cameron had done guns so brilliantly that it would be best not to reprise that aspect. Only when we could come up with an original idea and a wonderful director to match, did we all agree to go ahead with work on the sequel."

Hill and Giler each labored on several highly original concepts before settling upon a complex, two-part story in which the "Company" must confront a separate, space-faring earth culture (of a socialist or communist bent) that was developing the alien as a weapon of war. The first film (ALIEN 3) would merely feature a cameo appearance of Ripley with Hicks in the lead role, and the second (ALIEN 4) would re-establish her character as she battled the creatures in an earth-like setting. Weaver particularly liked the political allegory, and consented to the diminishment in her role. "I felt Ripley was going to become a burden to the story," she concluded. "There are only so many aspects to that character you can do."

Although somewhat skeptical about their plans to demote Ripley to cameo status, Twentieth Century-Fox agreed to front some development money for the new film — with one or two provisions. The first provision was that the partners at Brandywine approach Ridley Scott to direct ALIEN 3, and the second was that both films be produced concurrently to keep down mounting production costs. "We talked to Ridley briefly," said Weaver. "There was an idea at one time to film ALIEN 3 and 4 back-to-back. Ridley was going to direct one of those but he could never get it together." Scott had just completed SOMEONE TO WATCH OVER ME (1987), and was preparing BLACK RAIN (1989), with Michael Douglas and Andy Garcia. He was also scheduled to shoot THELMA AND LOUISE (1991), the controversial picture for which he received an Academy Award nomination, and later 1492 (1992). Ridley was simply too busy with other projects to commit to the unscripted sequel.

After their attempt to enlist Scott had failed, Gordon Carroll and Walter Hill made a list of suitable directors who were, at the same time, available. Their list included Vincent Ward and David Fincher, among others. But Fox was pushing a young Finnish director, named Renny Harlin, based on the box office success of A NIGHTMARE ON ELM STREET 4: THE DREAM MASTER (1988). David Giler arranged a screening of the film, and the partners all agreed that his work was exceptional. Harlin was subsequently contacted by the partners at Brandywine, and following an enthusiastic first meeting, he was signed to helm the new sequel. Less than two years later, Harlin would drop out of the project to make DIE HARD 2 (1989) and THE ADVENTURES OF FORD FAIRLANE (1989) for Fox.

WILLIAM GIBSON AND THE FIRST SCREENPLAY

Late in September 1987, while they were still searching for a suitable replacement for Ridley Scott, David Giler recommended acclaimed science fiction novelist William Gibson to Hill as a possible screenwriter for ALIEN 3. Giler had read Gibson's Nebula and Hugo award-winning novel NEUROMANCER (1985) while relaxing on a beach in the south of Thailand soon after the release of ALIENS, and felt that his grasp of cyberpunk sensibilities was just the kind of touch that was needed. The central assumption of Gibson's writing (including COUNT ZERO, MONA LISA OVERDRIVE and the short story collection BURNING CHROME) was that mankind, though trapped in some vaguely post-apocalyptic ruin, could be radically reprogrammed or redesigned through artificial evolution to become more useful as an instrument of technology and less a product of humanity. Hill agreed to meet with the Vancouver-based author, and the three forged a meaningful alliance, particularly after Gibson revealed that ALIEN had had such a strong influence on his writing NEUROMANCER.

"I found a lot of things in the original that were interesting even when it first came out," said William Gibson, singling out its "lived-in future" look as something that immediately appealed to him. "I though there were germs of stories implicit in the art direction. I always wanted to know more about these guys. Why they were wearing dirty sneakers in this funky spaceship? I think it influenced my prose SF writing because it was the first funked up, dirty kitchen-sink spaceship and it made a big impression on me. When I started writing science fiction I went for that."

One of the brightest and most widely-celebrated stars of the science fiction genre, Gibson had some very strong ideas about the sequel. Even though he had very little in the way of actual screenwriting experience, the author still knew how to master a well-textured story. He was given the scripts for the first two films and a twelve-page story treatment. Gibson read the story producers Walter Hill and David Giler had devised for ALIEN 3 first, and was delighted to find that it combined aspects of two separate scenarios he had come up with himself. "I was glad to have something to hang onto storywise," the novice screenwriter explained. "Being given free rein really means an infinite budget. The impression I had, though, was that budget parameters argued against introducing the aliens into something that was the equivalent of the BLADE RUNNER set, which I admit would have been my natural impulse." William Gibson began work on the script almost immediately. Aware that a Writers Guild strike was imminent, he knew that he was under pressure to deliver a completed manuscript before December.

*****

Gibson's script for ALIEN 3 begins in deep space with the Sulaco. Due to a failure in the on-board navigational circuitry, the former troop carrier accidentally strays into a sector of space claimed by the Union of Progressive Peoples. The ship is intercepted by a small shuttlecraft, and searched by three U.P.P. commandos. They find Ripley, Newt, and Hicks slumbering in deep-sleep hibernation; but upon closer examination of Bishop, an alien face-hugger launches out of the android's synthetic entrails, and attaches to one of the soldiers. The others blast him into space, fearing what the parasite might do to them, and take Bishop for further study. Returned back to its original course by one of the men, the Sulaco eventually reaches its destination, Anchorpoint — a space station and shopping mall that's

nearing completion.

Several days pass, while the quarantined ship undergoes a thorough examination by "Company" representatives of the Bio-weapons Division and military personnel. (Apparently, upon arrival at the station, the Sulaco was boarded by a deck squad of Marines who were subsequently attacked by alien predators. During the one-sided skirmish, Ripley's hypersleep chamber was consumed by fire, and the former Warrant Officer was severely injured. Hicks and Newt were able to escape, unharmed.) Corporal Hicks awakes in the medlab quarantine, and learns from Spence (a female tissue culture tech) that the ship is now completely off limits to all but authorized personnel. When both he and Newt are reunited, they learn together than Ripley has suffered a stroke, and that she is comatose. They also discover that Bishop has been taken by U.P.P. members.

On Rodina, the Union of Progressive Peoples' space station, Colonel-Doctor Suslov and other scientists learn from their study of Bishop's basic programming about the alien menace on LV-426. The strange globules that he carries in his chest cavity — the result of an alien parasite — can not only be cloned but also used as killing machines to eliminate their enemies. Because the Weyland-Yutani corporation has a similar interest in bio-weapons research, Suslov fears that further deliberation and study will only result in a technology gap. They decide to begin work immediately making their own alien.

Meanwhile, Colonel Rosetti warns Kevin Fox and Susan Welles, "Company" representatives from the Bio-weapons Division, that Anchorpoint is not a military station but a civilian operation under the control of the Colonial Administration Authority. He cannot simply close down the shopping concourse and impose martial law simply because they want information about the alien kept to a minimum. They attempt to frighten him with news that the U.P.P. is developing a xenomorph based on top secret information carelessly leaked from the station, but he still doesn't budge. Their meeting is rudely interrupted by Corporal Hicks, who demands to know what they've done with Bishop. Fox and Welles explain that the android was taken right out from under

ALIENS™

DARK HORSE COMICS

1 (of 4)
$2.25 U.S.
$2.80 Canada

their noses by the other side.

In the "mall," a high-tech cross between a Hyatt atrium and an airport shopping center, Charles Tully, a worker in the tissue culture lab, fears the military industrial complex may be collecting alien samples to use in weapons research. Even though he has been forced to sign an oath not to reveal what he knows, Tully can't help telling his girlfriend Spence. Later, in the tissue culture lab, the two specialists compare notes, and come to the conclusion that the Weyland-Yutani corporation (in conjunction with the military) have isolated an alien microorganism from which they plan to construct the ultimate killing machine, an alien warrior. That research would violate all the existing treaties with the U.P.P.

Hicks has a tearful send-off with Newt. She's returning to earth aboard the Sulaco to be with her grandparents in Oregon. (Little do either of them suspect that tissue samples of the alien are also being dispatched to Gateway Station aboard the cleared ship.) Hicks promises the little girl to tell Ripley where she's gone, and even takes a hand-drawn map for the former Warrant Officer when she awakens from her coma. At about the same time, in a nearby docking bay, a mysterious shuttle arrives with the android Bishop on board. He has been repaired and returned in the interest of galactic peace by scientists of the Union of Progressive Peoples. Of course, Bishop has been totally stripped of the alien globules.

Professor Trent, the leading authority in bio-weaponsresearch, arrives from earth to supervise the whole operation. Under the pretext of cancer research (to fool the local administrator, Rosetti), Trent proposes to fuse human DNA with the alien tissue samples in order to create the ultimate weapon. He doesn't really care how many people have to die in order to perfect this thing, noting that the entire station is expendable.

Reporting to his first duty assignment in months, the young corporal soon learns from his talkative co-worker, Tully, that the "Company" is planning to clone an entire army of the alien warriors. Hicks becomes instantly enraged, recalling what those monsters did to his squad of Colonial Marines. Tully calms him down, and convinces him to meet with his girlfriend, Spence. They might have a plan to shut the research down before it reaches a critical phase. Later that night, the three concur that the alien was probably the results of some ancient arms race between two long-dead civilizations. Spence thinks she can sneak Hicks into one of the main labs, if Tully agrees to provide a worthy distraction....but on the way to the labs, they are intercepted by Bishop.

The android fears that he may have been reprogrammed by either the U.P.P. or the "Company," and that he may no longer be trustworthy. Hicks simply doesn't have time to find out, convincing Bishop that their only priority should be the destruction of the alien. Suddenly, alarms and klaxons begin sounding....the seal in decontamination has been "accidentally" broken by Tully, in clear view of Welles. They have both been exposed and possibly contaminated by the alien tissue samples. Corporal Hicks uses the mass panic to slip into the main lab, and destroy all the remaining samples. Unfortunately, both he and Bishop are captured, and placed in restraints. Hicks fears he will be tried and court-martialed, and the android will be forever disassembled.

On Rodina, the Union of Progressive Peoples' space station, they have had their own accident but far, far worse. Suslov and his fellow scientists have fallen victims to the alien parasite, and chest-bursters are now appearing all over the station. Frantically, their special forces commandos fight a losing battle.

Trent calls a meeting with Welles and Fox to discuss plans for dealing with Corporal Hicks' treachery. The "Company" knows it was no simple accident, and has already taken steps to preserve the alien creature by sending samples to earth aboard the Sulaco. Perhaps they should use the young corporal as a subject in one of their cloning tests. Hicks curses them all for endangering Newt and the rest of the planet. But before his words can register in the small meeting room, Welles suddenly doubles over at the waist and begins convulsing. She then grasps at her chest and an alien emerges. Hicks, who has seen the same thing happen before on LV-426, acts swiftly to destroy Welles and the alien creature. Tully must also be infected, along with any others who were exposed to the samples. Their only safe course of action is to abandon and then destroy the station.

Corporal Hicks goes to the radio center to dispatch a rescue signal to the closest starship, the Kansas City, but Bishop warns him that they all must die in order to be absolutely certain the alien parasite never gets off the station. His haunting words remind Hicks that there are alien samples already headed to earth aboard the military carrier Sulaco. That ship must also be stopped, but before he can send a message to the android pilot of the ship, a "may-day" comes in from Rodina. A lone female commando — the same one that first boarded the Sulaco and kidnapped Bishop — warns that her entire station has been infected. She requests permission to activate self-destruct codes in order to prevent the alien contagion from spreading to other stations. Her message is rudely interrupted by the captain of the U.P.P. cruiser Nikolai Stoiko. He has been given orders to nuke the site in the interest of galactic peace. Hicks listens as they destroy their own station, and realizes Bishop may be

right. Perhaps, they can still save the 138 people who were not infected because of their isolation in the shopping center.

Gathering together a detachment of young recruits to help him save the others, Hicks finds Ripley still comatose in the infirmary. He presses Newt's map into her lifeless hands, and launches Ripley into space aboard a one-man lifeboat. He figures that he owes her that much, knowing that she's safe and unaffected by the alien virus. He then calls to Bishop (on his comlink) to activate the self-destruct mechanism. Rosetti, the station administrator, cowardly prevents the android from carrying out the directive.

Outraged, Hicks dons a spacesuit, and follows Bishop and Spence into space in order to detonate the station from an emergency access panel. They are pursued by the alien horde, which continues to increase in number. At the last moment, the sole survivor from the Rodina (who apparently ejected from the station prior to its destruction) arrives in a heavily-armed shuttle. She begins blasting away at the aliens, while Hicks and the others struggle to activate the self-destruct mechanism. Mere heartbeats later, they are aboard the shuttle, watching Anchorpoint's destruction at a safe distance. Bishop notes that the earth humans are now united against a common enemy. They must now track the aliens back to their source, and destroy them once and for all. "This is a Darwinian universe, Hicks," the android explains. "Will the alien be the ultimate survivor, or will man....?"

*****

William Gibson delivered his completed manuscript, which he comically describes today in terms of a TV GUIDE synopsis as "space commies hijack alien eggs — big trouble in Mallworld," in December of 1987, shortly before the Writers Guild strike. He had successfully crafted a suspense-filled story based upon Giler and Hill's ideas, while at the same time remaining faithful to the original source material. Ironically, fast-breaking events in the Soviet Union and other communist countries would quickly date the conceptual metaphor of a political face-off between superpowers.

"We got the opposite of what we expected," said

Giler. "We figured we'd get a script that was all over the place, but which would have many good ideas we could mine. It turned out to be a competently written screenplay but not as inventive as we wanted it to be. That was probably our fault, though, because it was our story. We had hoped he'd open up the story and don't know why it didn't happen." The producers were pleased with the subtext which viewed the aliens as some type of cancer or HIV virus, and with the cliffhanger-like ending which nicely set up the story for ALIEN 4. But the underlying cyberpunk aesthetic, which had first attracted David Giler to Gibson's work, was clearly missing from his story.

For the duration of the Writers Guild strike, Gibson waited patiently for word from the producers on the outcome of his script. Eventually, he learned that his first draft had been rejected. Walter Hill and David Giler soon after introduced the young novelist to their director, Renny Harlin. The four spoke at length about their expectations for ALIEN 3 over a power lunch, then suggested that Gibson undertake a rewrite with Harlin. William Gibson declined, citing other commitments, which were far more meaningful to him personally. He had been asked to write scripts based upon his own stories (BURNING CHROME and JOHNNY PNEUMATIC) for Carolco.

ERIC RED AND THE SECOND SCREENPLAY

Following Gibson's departure, Renny Harlin recommended Eric Red, a screenwriter he had met at a film festival some months before. Hill and Giler had resigned themselves to hire a big name screenwriter, and Red seemed a likely candidate for the position. By age twenty-eight, the young writer had already distinguished himself in the Hollywood community by turning marginal material, like THE HITCHER (1986), NEAR DARK (1987) and BLUE STEEL (1988), into popular box office hits. He was hard at work on the screen story for COHEN & TATE (1989), and preparing for his directorial debut on BODY PARTS (1991), when the partners at Brandywine approached him with ALIEN 3.

"The basic problem when I was involved, for five weeks, was they didn't know what they really wanted," Red recalled some time later. "They went through a real waste of talent because of that. Another major problem was they didn't want Sigourney [Weaver] back, so I had to go through a whole series of new characters."

*****

Eric Red's screenplay begins, much like Gibson's, in deep space with the Sulaco. Due to a malfunction in the on-board navigational circuitry, the former troop carrier has drifted aimlessly in space for many years. The ship is intercepted by a small shuttlecraft, and searched by five Special Forces Green Berets and their captain, Sam Smith. They find the hypersleep chambers, which once held Ripley, Newt, Hicks and Bishop, have been smashed open, and alien eggs now reside in each. Upon closer examination, they find a sticky-like substance and cocoons hanging from the ceiling to the floor. Suddenly, an alien warrior drops down upon the soldiers. They blast away at the creature with their superior weapons, but the Green Berets are ill-matched, and are nearly all wiped out. Mysteriously returned back to its original course, the Sulaco reaches its destination, North Star — a space station and farming outpost populated mostly by redneck farmers.

Several weeks pass, while Sam Smith, the only survivor of the massacre, recuperates at his parents' farmhouse on the surface of the orbiting station. (Not only does Sam learn that all his men are dead but he also discovers, much to his dismay, that one arm and leg have been replaced with mechanical parts.) Tired of resting, he decides to accompany his father, General John Smith, to the base. Along the way, several farmers question John about the huge military build-up in personnel and armored vehicles, and Sam notices that the families of his men have mysteriously vanished. Fifty stories below the golden wheat fields and the pastoral farm-like settings, the "Company," in conjunction with the military, has constructed a massive complex. Bio-medical laboratories, conference rooms, troop training centers, docking bays for spaceships, fifty-story tall air and water tanks, all enclosed within huge glass windows, make up the mile in diameter complex. When Sam asks his father about the Sulaco, he is told that the ship (now stored in one of the docking bays) is completely off limits to all but authorized personnel.

General Smith and his son are greeted by

Sergeant Chong, the station's security chief, who informs them that Sam is wanted by "Company" officials. In the debriefing room, Dr. Alice Rand, Colonel Harold Sinclair, and three representatives from the Bio-weapons Division question him about his skirmish aboard the Sulaco. Sam doesn't remember much about it, having suffered a temporary memory loss, other than losing his men. Rand seems pleased that he has no memory of the alien creatures. Less than an hour later, Sam and his father are confronted by some of the redneck farmers. Briggs and Agar remind them that North Star is not a military station but a civilian operation under the control of the Colonial Administration Authority. The military cannot simply impose martial law to take their livestock. Willie Ray, another terra-farmer, accuses them of secret radiation experiments. John feigns ignorance but promises to look into their complaints. Later that night on their drive home, the two Smiths notice several armed squads of soldiers loading pigs, chickens and cattle onto trucks under the cover of darkness.

Far too bothered by what he has seen to sleep, Sam wakes his father in the middle of the night, and confronts him about what has happened. He "remembers" parts of his battle with an alien, but he cannot seem to grasp the whole. John first dismisses his son's memories of his struggle aboard the Sulaco as a nightmare, then tells him the truth. The "Company" might have ordered the young man lobotomized if he remembered too much of what had happened aboard the ship. They plan to develop the alien as a weapon. Sam has to see for himself, and penetrates the security of Section "C," where the former troop transport is housed, to discover a scene from hell. They have used the farmers' livestock to create pig-aliens, cattle-aliens, chicken-aliens, dog-aliens, etc. Apparently, the alien parasite gestates inside a living organism, and then takes on the physical attributes or characteristics of that organism when it finally emerges. Sam is sickened by what he has seen, and scrambles down an airduct to avoid becoming the alien's next victim.

Sam crawls past the Science Division, and overhears a lecture, which confirms most of his suspicions. Dr. Rand, the leading authority in bio-weapons research,

tells a group composed of earth scientists, technicians, "Company" officials, and military leaders (including General Smith) that the alien is "the soldier of the future." She has managed to isolate the alien's DNA cells, and learned that those cells "attack and assimilate the cells of whatever it encounters." "Imagine," she intones, "a living, organic jet fighter or alien tank." Rand then instructs members of her research team to bring in an alien warrior whose arms and legs are pinned in a hydraulic clamp. "Ladies and gentleman," the doctor continues, "a living war machine, utterly violent and utterly effective. I wouldn't want to be you if you were Russians and we released an army of these things by airdrop on Moscow." Alice Rand releases the creature from its clamps, claiming to have mastered its control. But when her back is turned, the alien warrior attacks, and tears her apart. It then begins ripping human after human limb-from-limb.

Reporting immediately to the duty officer on deck, the young captain takes command of a small squad of Special Forces Green Berets, and charges into the room to rescue his father. On his way to save the other survivors, though, his men are attacked by the army of alien warriors developed and perfected by the "Company." (These monsters include the pig-aliens, chicken-aliens and cattle-aliens Sam discovered earlier.) His specially-trained soldiers fight nobly against the horde of aliens, but they are simply ill-matched. Smith manages to slip away during the battle to help his father and some other key figures to safety, then realizes there's nothing he can do to stop the slaughterfest. Sam becomes instantly enraged, recalling what those monsters did to his men aboard the Sulaco, and curses them all (including General Smith) for allowing such madness to happen in the first place.

Above, on the surface of North Star, the terra-farmers have felt the first tremors of an earthquake. Briggs and the others know that the military has been up to something no good, and begin arming themselves with pitchforks, hoes, shovels, and shotguns. They plan to finally get even just as soon as day-break arrives.

With their path to the surface cut off, Sam and his father, accompanied by thirty Green Berets, climb into spacesuits, and head through the emergency escape-hatch into space. (They plan to climb around the dome, and enter North Star from above.) They are followed into space by a horde of alien warriors. Meanwhile, the aliens have penetrated the surface, and are striking innocent farmers in their wheat fields, at the local 7-11 store, and at the golden arches of McDonalds. By the time Sam Smith and his father arrive with reinforcements, the redneck farmers are already embroiled in a massive battle at the town's meeting hall. Against the backdrop of small-town Americana of Woolworths and hardware stores, hundreds of alien warriors attack. Scuttling, staggering, crawling down the street, the creatures appear totally invincible. But the terrified townsfolk mount a defensive line which temporarily drives the aliens back.

During the lull in battle, Sam rescues his mother and siblings from their farmhouse, and tries to place them safely aboard a space shuttle with the other women and children. But they refuse. The terra-farmers subsequently launch the shuttle, without them, hoping that the ship's distress beacon will summon a rescue ship for the rest of them. The remaining soldiers and redneck farmers then barricade themselves in the town's meeting hall, and await the next wave. John Smith suddenly starts to act funny, confessing to his wife and children that he volunteered to test a new alien strain. But before Sam can get to him, the General suddenly doubles over at the waist and begins convulsing. He then grasps at his chest and an alien creature, more deadly than before, emerges. Sam, who has never seen this happen before, panics, destroying the barricade instead of his father. Other hybrid aliens, notably a rooster-alien and a mosquito-alien, swarm through the opening, and attack without mercy.

Sam and his family race to the safety of a second space shuttle (which suddenly appears in the script without prior mention), and blast off right through the dome. The explosive decompression causes the space station to dissolve, and reform as a tremendous alien thing — a living bio-mechanoid space blob, ten miles across, with octopus-like tentacles formed from the beams and girders of the station. Captain Smith tries to pilot their shuttle away from the creature, but it simply reaches out and grabs the tiny craft. Fearing a hull-breach, the Smith family climb into spacesuits. Sam then remembers the ship carries nuclear weapons, and sets the payload to explode once they have gotten away.

Seconds later, Sam and the others watch North Star's destruction at a safe distance. The alien menace has hopefully, once and for all, been destroyed! They continue to float in deep space, and are eventually rescued by the other shuttle.

*****

Eric Red's "five-week job," first intended to coax more development money out of Twentieth Century-Fox, turned into a two-month ordeal. When he finally delivered his completed manuscript on February 7, 1989, no one seemed to like the script, despite the author's introduction of a new kind of alien. "In the third film, you needed a new alien, so I suggested doing genetic experiments with one of them," Red defended his screenplay. "[Hill and Giler] had no story or treatment or any real plan for the picture. They were very disorganized and irresponsible." Renny Harlin would have been the first to agree with Red, but after reading Red's uninspired script, the Finnish director simply asked to be released from his contract. Fox offered him THE ADVENTURES OF FORD FAIRLANE and DIE-HARD 2 instead. Sigourney Weaver also read the script, and concurred with David Giler's appraisal that "it was a real disaster, absolutely dreadful." Hill seemed to like the gene-splicing idea but little else. Eric Red was paid for his efforts, then dismissed from the project. The partners at Brandywine were no closer to making ALIEN 3 than before, and now they were short a director.

DAVID TWOHY AND THE THIRD SCREENPLAY

At this point, Hill and Giler abandoned all plans to develop two ALIEN sequels concurrently, and turned back to basics. The Gibson script, while clearly pedestrian in scope, contained many of the elements that audiences had come to expect from "the franchise." They hired David Twohy on the basis of his script for CRITTERS 2, a low budget ALIEN rip-off, and instructed him to not only punch up the dialogue but also to add a dimension to Gibson's story that would give the classic B-movie plot a sense of purpose and theme.

When Twentieth Century-Fox finally agreed to finance a rewrite of the first screenplay, late in March 1989, the decision was based entirely upon David Giler and Walter Hill's assertion that the story would be very contemporary. "By then it was a Soviet Union ship versus Gateway [the space station Ripley finds herself on at the start of ALIENS]," Giler explained their high concept. Completed over a six-month period, Twohy's rewrite maintained much of William Gibson's original material, including the commando raid on the Sulaco, the development of the alien virus, and the infestation of the station. Descriptions of action and dialogue were either shortened or tightened, and some scenes were completely rewritten from scratch. Even certain character names were changed to give the story a more contemporary feel.

Midway through Twohy's rewrite, however, several key incidents had occurred throughout the world that would eventually date or invalidate many of his central premises. Political changes within the Soviet Union and other Eastern-bloc countries signaled the end of the cold war. Genetic splicing had become a chilling reality, much more interesting than fiction. And Metro-Goldwyn-Mayer had just released its own watery version of ALIEN, called LEVIATHAN (1989), in which some bio-mechanical creature in a sunken Russian ship is inadvertently taken aboard an underwater drilling platform and unleashed to destroy its crew. The screenplay that David Twohy was developing for Brandywine would simply never work. He quickly changed the setting of his story to a penal colony in space, and eliminated all references to the Russians. But there was still one major problem. Since Hill and Giler had originally planned to leave Ripley out of the third film and bring her back for the fourth, Twohy had specifically written a story without her as the central figure. And no one had bothered to tell the novice screenwriter differently.

Joe Roth, then Twentieth Century-Fox's new president, reviewed Twohy's screenplay and rejected it swiftly and irrevocably, voicing his displeasure in very simple terms: "This is a great script, but I won't make this film without Sigourney. She is the centerpiece of the series. She's really the only female warrior we have in our movie mythology. In successful sequels you have a fine line between old and new ingredients. But we feel it would be cataclysmic to proceed without her."

Twohy's first collaborative efforts on ALIEN 3 with producers Walter Hill and David Giler had been a disaster, but he agreed to rewrite the story for a third time with Ripley as the central figure. "The Ripley character can be written as a man or a woman," Giler summarily dismissed the additional work. "In fact, it was originally written as a man. To change it for Sigourney isn't all that tough — she brings a lot of it herself." Since Fox had been upset over the omission of Ripley's character from his story, David Twohy concentrated on adding or altering sequences in the script in order to build the action around the former Warrant Officer. Sigourney Weaver also helped with the creative process by suggesting certain plot and dialogue changes. Not surprisingly,

most of Twohy's material is close to the final shooting script for ALIEN 3, with one or two exceptions. The single, most important difference between his version and the one audiences eventually saw in theatres centered around Newt. She survives the crash landing on the penal colony, and ultimately goes to live with her grandparents on earth.

While Twohy was busily working on his third rewrite, Hill and Giler were still searching for a director to replace Harlin. Back in New York City for other, unrelated business, Hill accompanied friends to an art-house showing of THE NAVIGATOR: AN ODYSSEY ACROSS TIME (1988) by an obscure New Zealand director named Vincent Ward. The engrossing yet esoteric tale of a young psychic boy who leads his plague-threatened, medieval English village on a tunneling expedition to a modern city struck a particular chord with Walter Hill. He

contacted Joe Roth at Fox, and got him excited enough to call Ward in London, where he was engaged in preproduction on his pet project, MAP OF THE HUMAN HEART (released in 1993).

The telephone call from the president of Twentieth Century-Fox came as somewhat of a surprise to Vincent Ward, but he did agree to consider Roth's proposal once he had read Twohy's script. Ward didn't like the story much, and began formulating his own. "During my flight [from London to Los Angeles]," Ward revealed, "I had an idea that was totally different: Sigourney would land in a community of monks in outer space and not be accepted by them." His neo-Luddite former religious heretics would live on a wooden planet that looked like something Hieronymus Bosch might imagine, with glass-blowing furnaces and windmills but no weapons.

The New Zealand director pitched his idea first to Hill and Giler, then to Roth, and they were all astounded. Even though Ward did not look upon himself a screenwriter, he had brought a vision to the production that had been lacking in the other stories. "It was a little far out," said Giler, "but that's what we wanted, to push this thing a little bit." Ward was immediately signed to direct, and Fox hired screenwriter John Fasano, who was known as a fast writer, to craft his ideas into a workable story. "We were supposedly writing ALIEN 4," Fasano recalled, "but if ours came in first, it would be ALIEN 3."

Meanwhile, across town, David Twohy was putting the finishing touches on his script when he learned from a Los Angeles Times reporter that Hill and Giler had brought in another writer. At first, the rumor of competing drafts went against everything Twohy had been told by the partners at Brandywine, and he readily dismissed the rumors as unfounded. But later, after he had been given the runaround with the production office, he realized the idea of filming two ALIEN sequels back-to-back was merely a smokescreen. "At that point," he said bitterly, "I just slapped my script together and went off to make my own film. And that was the last I ever heard from them. The old adage is true: Hollywood pays its writers well but treats them like shit to make up for it." Twohy left to write the very popular WARLOCK (1991).

THE FOURTH SCREENPLAY

Vincent Ward insisted on writing the script with John Fasano, in spite of the New Zealander's lack of experience as a screenwriter, and the two argued for months about plot and structure. Ward seemed very taken with his monks and wooden spaceship, and less interested in telling a story about aliens. On the other hand, Fasano, who had worked with Walter Hill before, felt he knew what was expected by both Fox and Brandywine, and rewrote much of their script after hours. Their first draft, delivered early in 1990, received a less than spectacular review by Hill and Giler. "Vincent's wood idea didn't work at all," Giler commented. "We couldn't figure out why it should be made of wood. We could never get a simple answer from them. Why would they fly all that wood out there, and why was it crummy wood, at that? The picture would have had a great look, but it didn't really make sense."

Although the studio continued to support Ward's unique vision, the partners at Brandywine were determined to get a workable screenplay. They hired Greg Pruss to replace Fasano, who had given up in disgust. (John Fasano would later write ANOTHER 48 HRS (1990) for Walter Hill, and complete yet another rewrite on the Ward story.) Pruss wrote "five arduous drafts" before journeying with Vincent Ward to London, where Twentieth Century-Fox was going to shoot the film with the hopes of saving money. The veteran screenwriter eventually came up with the idea of killing Ripley off, but he could never produce a script that Ward approved. "The movie's called ALIEN because it's about the alien," Pruss said, but his very valid complaints fell on deaf ears. "I couldn't get that across to Vincent. He and the studio were at odds, clear and simple, and I was caught in the middle."

At the same time, Vincent Ward complicated matters by offending members of the crew with his abrasive personality during the key stages of preproduction. The crew was already at work designing and building sets based on Ward's storyboards; but as the script changed with his each new idea and whim, sets were taken down and rebuilt. The New Zealander also dismissed special effect supervisor John Richardson, who was still completing work on HIGHLANDER 2: THE QUICKENING (1991), and Stan Winston. He replaced them with George Gibb, the effects designer for the INDIANA JONES films, and Winston protégés Alec Gillis and Tom Woodruff. He also attempted unsuccessfully to involve H.R Giger. Ward never bothered to consult with anyone at the studio over his seemingly compulsive choices, and soon found himself in conflict with both Fox and Brandywine. Citing "artistic differences," Ward was paid off, and released from his contract.

Twentieth Century-Fox had invested nearly $13 million in scripts, sets and pay-or-play commitments, and the studio was no closer to a completed film than before. Roth was very disappointed with Brandywine Productions. Hill and Giler offered to make amends by revising the script themselves, and embarked upon the complicated task of pulling all the ideas into a unified whole. Their first attempt to streamline Ward's vision produced an interesting if totally unfilmable story.

*****

The fourth screenplay, which was revised by Walter Hill and David Giler on March 29, 1990, opens cryptically with a quote from Hesse: "But how will you die when your time comes, Narcissus, since you have no mother?" At a Medieval monastery on the wooden planetoid of Arceon, a five-mile-in-diameter penal colony constructed by the "Company" to hold 350 political heretics, Brother John tends to the wounds of a fellow monk who has been injured in their glassworks factory. Gregorian chant reverberates through the complex, combining with the creaky wooden floorboards to produce a most unusual sound. That sound echoes down through the many layers of the station, which are patterned after the medieval concept of the universe. Heaven is visible above, through the planetoid's thin atmosphere, and Hell is below, in the dungeons of the planetoid. The area in the middle contains the monastery, a great library, some farms and wheat fields, the glassworks factory, and windmill air pumps.

John and other members of his monastic order have been banished to Arceon for having spoken against technology. Ostensibly sequestered from the rest of humanity to preserve mankind's legacy in books, the monks are, in fact, facing a death sentence. (Their wooden planetoid is gradually growing colder, and to keep from freezing to death in the coldness of space, they are burning the wooden interiors of their "home." But each layer of wood they remove for heat only makes the planetoid grow colder.) The Abbot knows that Arceon was built for planned obsolescence, but he keeps assuring them that their mission to preserve the combined knowledge of mankind is vitally essential. According to him, earth civilization has succumbed to another great plague (a computer virus), which has wiped out all technology, and fallen into a New Dark Age. John and his close friend Brother Kyle have no reason to doubt the Abbot, and they simply accept his word as truth just like the others.

Then, one cold winter's night, a comet, or rather what appears to be a comet, appears in the sky. Brother John is the first one to see it, but later he is joined by hundreds of others on the surface. The comet gradually draws closer, then crashes into their man-made sea. John rows a small boat over to the "comet," and discovers, much to his surprise and the anguish of the Abbot, that it is really the Sulaco's escape vehicle #4. (It has been decades since John has seen any kind of technology.) Carefully boarding the spacecraft, the monk finds a single survivor — Lt. Ellen Ripley — and evidence of a bloody conflict. The ship's flight recorder keeps replaying the details of its infestation by a xenomorph and the subsequent deaths of Hicks, Bishop and Newt; but John, with all his apparent sophistication, simply doesn't understand what any of it means. He carries the unconscious woman ashore.

Later in the abbey, Ripley wakes to hear the sawing and hammering of wood, whispered prayers, and lilting songs to God. She struggles to consciousness, and peers from her window at a pastoral scene of monks tending sheep next to a golden field of wheat. At first, Ripley thinks that she is still dreaming, but then she catches site of the escape vehicle being sealed in a primitive wood structure. She seeks out the governing Abbot, and quickly learns that his rigidity prevents him from not only accepting her story about the alien but also that she is from earth. Earth was, after all, on the brink of a New Dark Age when they left for Arceon. He refuses

to listens to her "ravings" about an indestructible, death-dealing xenomorph, and warns Ripley to keep quiet.

When a hysterical monk arrives with an incredible story about a demon exploding from his sheep's stomach, the Abbot accuses Ripley of bringing Satan with her to Arceon aboard her spaceship. He convinces a court of inquiry, and they find the "Comet Woman" guilty of witchcraft and conspiring with the devil. She tries to tell them what they're facing, but no one will believe her.

Thrown into the dungeons for insisting that an alien menace is loose on the planetoid, Ripley befriends a white-haired monk named Anthony who is, in reality, an android spy. He was sent by the "Company" to eavesdrop on their activities, and send regular reports. But when Anthony started experiencing demonic visions of fish-head sprites and birdmen, he was ordered to undergo treatments by Father Anselm, Brother John's predecessor as physician. Anselm soon discovered that he was an android, and cast him into the bowels of the planetoid. He has been in solitary there for nearly thirty years.

Several other mysterious deaths among the livestock lead Brother John to the inescapable conclusion that Ripley was telling the truth. Studying an old text in the library, he also discovers some striking similarities between these deaths and others that occurred in 1348 (during the time of the Black Death). One engraving in the book shows a creature similar to Ripley's description tattooed on the devil's posterior. He tries to confront the Abbot with his newly found answers, but the older monk simply dismisses his findings as coincidental. He is also warned by the Abbot to keep the deaths a secret.

John disobeys his superior, and climbs down a five-mile ladder to free Ripley from her captivity. She insists they take Anthony with them, and the unlikely trio head toward the "technology room" to search for weapons. Meanwhile, in the wheat fields above, a fierce battle between a "platoon" of monks, armed with scythes, pitchforks and hoes, and a horde of alien-hybrids is taking place. The holy men are simply out-matched by the death-dealing monsters, which can now blend into their environment, and are eventually killed or cocooned. Only the Abbot escapes, relentlessly pursued by the alien menace to the "technology room" where Ripley and the others have gathered. The "technology" turns out to be a collection of wooden windmills that channel air and water to the various levels.

The planetoid's planned obsolescence is now very clear to Ripley; as she collapses to the floor in surrender, she explains to the others how the "Company" must have built the station purposely to fail, so that the resources would eventually run out and everyone of them would have frozen to death. Ripley suddenly starts to feel dizzy, confessing to the others that the strange sensation may be an alien parasite growing inside her. But before John can get to her, the former Warrant Officer suddenly doubles over at the waist and begins convulsing. She then grasps at her chest and forces the pain back down. The Abbot, who has never seen anything like this happen before, panics, declaring that she is possessed by the devil. The words are barely out of his mouth when his head explodes with an alien head-burster.

John and Anthony chase the little creature into the hall, and are surprised by an alien which has adapted itself to look like wood. The android valiantly sacrifices his life for the others, allowing Ripley and John to escape to the surface. Along the way, John rescues his dog Mattias from the clutches of several face-huggers, and helps Ripley destroy all but one of the creatures in a great bonfire, which destroys the library. Finally, trapping the last one in the glassworks factory, they drown the alien menace in molten glass. When it rises out of the vat as a molten-glass creature, Ripley quickly dumps cold water from a huge tank, and shatters the alien in a million glass pieces.

The two struggle through the fire, which is now raging out of control, and reach the Sulaco escape vehicle. Once inside the craft, the monk performs a make-shift exorcism, using a strange potion concocted from his study of the Black Death. Ripley vomits the chest-burster up, but the reptilian-like creature slithers instantly out of reach and into John's mouth. The monk accepts the demonic creature like a true exorcist, and abandons ship moments before it blasts into deep space....

*****

Hill and Giler's rewrite, which was remarkably close to Vincent Ward's original vision for ALIEN 3, still left many questions unanswered. Chief among these questions, in the producers' minds, was how could they make Ward's wooden space station believable to contemporary audiences. Since neither one of them was interested in completing another rewrite, they coaxed an additional $500,000 from Roth to hire yet another writer — Larry Ferguson.

For several years, Larry Ferguson had been making his name well-known around Hollywood. He had scripted the hit sequel BEVERLY HILLS COP II (1987), the highly-underrated HIGHLANDER (1986) and THE PRESIDIO (1988). Ferguson began his career as an actor in San Francisco before moving to writing. He eventually did make his film acting debut in THE HUNT FOR RED OCTOBER, playing the Captain of the Deep Submergence Rescue Vehicle attached to the U.S.S. Dallas, but by that time Larry was far better known for writing the screenplay to the best-selling novel by Tom Clancy. He knew that he was expected to bring some fresh ideas to the franchise, but he was also experienced enough to know what the studio didn't want to see. "Sequels are like Big Macs," he once joked. "If you went into McDonalds and ordered a Big Mac, and it came out different, you wouldn't order it every time."

Ferguson worked on the screenplay with the new director for about four weeks, and brought a number of important ideas to the story. Towards the end of the year, however, Walter Hill and David Giler became embroiled with Gordon Carroll, Sigourney Weaver, James Cameron and Gale Ann Hurd in a legal battle with Fox over an alleged non-payment of profit shares from ALIENS. The lawsuit was quickly settled to everyone's mutual satisfaction, but left Hill and Giler feeling very proprietary about their franchise. They reviewed Larry's work in progress and deemed that it was not suitable. (According to Weaver, he had written Ripley so that she sounded like "a very pissed-off gym instructor" and she was really not interested in playing the character like that.) Larry Ferguson was paid for his efforts, then dismissed from the project.

THE FINAL SHOOTING SCRIPT

With the start of production just weeks away, Twentieth Century-Fox agreed to pay Hill and Giler another $600,000 for an emergency rewrite. Working in Hill's office in Los Angeles, the producers quickly scrapped the monastery setting, and returned to Twohy's prison planet locale. At least a penal colony, stationed on some faraway planet, made much more sense than a wooden asteroid. They changed the prison inmates from monks to, what Giler describes as, "your basic militant Christian fundamentalist millenarian apocalyptic" types, primarily to appease Weaver and the new director. The producers also reduced the number of alien creatures to one, and significantly altered the ending. In just three weeks, they had produced a draft that most of the principals involved could agree upon.

*****

Like many of the previous drafts, the final shooting script begins in deep space with the Sulaco. Due to a fire in the ship's circuitry and the subsequent malfunction of the on-board life-support systems, the still-hibernating bodies of Ripley and the others are ejected in an emergency escape pod. Apparently, and it is never fully explained how they got aboard the ship, several alien eggs have hatched (at least) one face-hugger which is responsible for the fire. Ripley's evacuation capsule crashes on Fiorina 161, a lice-infected planet in a distant solar system. Nicknamed "Fury 1" by its inhabitants, the planet is home to a small community of violent criminals who discovered religion and chose to stay behind when the prison facility was closed.

As a woman, Ripley (Sigourney Weaver) is the ultimate outcast. Her arrival on the planet causes a major conflict between Warden Andrews (Brian Glover) and his all-male population of inmates, by endangering the uneasy balance of power. Her presence among them also reminds many of the reformed members of the monastic community that they were once killers and rapists. But she is not the only threat to their little world. A single face-hugger, which has stowed-away aboard the capsule, is far more dangerous for it not only threatens the inhabitants of the planet but also the entire galaxy. Unfortunately, both she and her capsule are carried safely to shore.

Later, in the infirmary, Ripley rouses from a terrible nightmare that concludes with the deaths of her beloved Newt and Corporal Hicks. As she struggles to consciousness, Clemens (Charles Dance) informs her that the other members of her party are, in fact, dead, and that she was the sole survivor. At first, Ripley believes that she still must be dreaming; but when she finally sees their bodies in the morgue, the former Warrant Officer accepts the horrible truth. She then persuades Clemens, who is the chief medical officer, to conduct an autopsy, under the ruse that both may have died of cholera. The former inmate consents but only if Ripley will be honest with him. She tries to tell him about the monster she first faced aboard the Nostromo, then on LV-426. Her words about the "xenomorph" choke up unpleasant memories, and cause her to falter. Warden Andrews abruptly appears, interrupting their private conversation. He is most displeased with Ripley's appearance, and demands that she remain in isolation until her rescue ship arrives.

Meanwhile, the stowaway face-hugger has impregnated its first victim — an inmate's pet dog — in the lower bowels of the correctional facility. Within a matter of hours, the poor animal is whining and convulsing in extreme pain, as the alien parasite struggles to get free. The little demon that explodes from his dog's stomach shares characteristics with its host. It moves very fast, has a strong upper body, rabidnous teeth, and can scamper along the floor or ceiling. The alien is described by Golic (Paul McGann), the only prisoner to get a good look at it, as a "dragon," but his account of the creature is hastily dismissed as the ravings of a lunatic.

Dillon (Charles Dutton), the inmates' spiritual leader, arranges to have the bodies cremated in the molten lead of their mineral ore refinery, and prays to God for His mercy in their deliverance. Ripley is very moved by their simple ceremony, and after shaving her head (to eliminate a potential lice problem), she joins them in the mess hall for dinner. Even though they have all sworn an oath of celibacy, the inmates are still bothered by her presence. She helps to remind them that they were once murders, thieves and rapists. Ripley tries to thank Dillon for his kind words about Newt, but he wants nothing to do with her; she makes him "nervous."

After several mysterious deaths occur — first the dog, then the dog's owner, and finally a second man — Clemens arrives at the inescapable conclusion that Ripley was telling the truth. He follows her to the smashed hull of her ship, and eavesdrops while she interfaces with the damaged android. Bishop (Lance Henriksen) reveals that there was an alien aboard the Sulaco. Following the fire, the alien creature must have stowed-away on the escape pod, and could now be stalking them. Bishop also tells her that the "Company" has sent a top priority message to capture Ripley and the alien alive at all costs. Still conscious but in great pain, the android begs her to kill him, and she obliges by pulling the plug.

Alone, and near the point of collapse, Ripley returns to the infirmary. She feels very nauseous, and confesses to Clemens that she is experiencing morning sickness and a bad sore throat. She is also having frequent nose-bleeds. He dismisses her symptoms as simple fatigue, precipitated by an unusually long period in hypersleep, but Ripley knows better. After sharing a brief but intimate moment with Clemens, the chief medical officer is attacked and killed by the alien. The familiar creature, though somehow different in its appearance, closes to within inches of Ripley but doesn't kill her. It senses, what the former Warrant Officer already suspects, that she is carrying an alien embryo inside. (Ripley later confirms her suspicions by running a full bio-scan diagnostic in her spacecraft, and discovers she carries an alien queen.)

Ripley attempts to warn Andrews, and quickly learns that his rigidity prevents him from not only accepting her story about the alien but also that the deaths were caused by anything other than a crazed inmate. No sooner have the words crossed his lips then the alien strikes, carrying the Warden through an airduct. Once things finally settle down, she again tries to reason with them. Aaron (Ralph Brown), the dim-witted simpleton (nicknamed "85" for his I.Q.) who's next in charge, agrees to listen to her "ravings" about the indestructible, death-dealing xenomorph, and then chooses to do nothing except wait for the rescue team. Ripley warns him that the "Company" will probably kill all of them for having simply seen it, but he remains determined to wait.

Faced with extinction, the prisoners band together under Ripley's leadership, and despite a lack of advanced technology and modern weapons, they battle the creature in the ten miles of airducts, basements and dark corridors of the complex. The inmates first try to drive the alien into a toxic waste containment unit with walls several feet thick, but a prisoner smoking a cigar ignites the flammable fluid, incinerating several of his cellmates. Later, when they have the creature trapped in the sewer system, Golic (who has begun to worship the alien as a god) kills several more inmates in order to set it free. During their various encounters with the creature, Ripley discovers that it will not harm her, and insists Dillon kill her before the alien queen emerges. But the prisoner's spiritual leader wisely uses her to lure the alien into the furnace where they plan to drown it in molten lead.

Above, in the freezing, sub-zero temperatures of the surface, a "Company" rescue ship arrives. Aaron rushes to greet them with open arms, but quickly learns that Ripley was right. The elite group of Colonial Marines, in special protective gear, commanded by Bishop II (Henriksen) and accompanied by a Weyland-Yutani representative (Hi Chang), mean business. They dispense with pleasantries, and demand to be taken to Ripley.

Moments later, Ripley and the others manage to trap the alien creature in the lead works. Morse (Danny Webb) releases the molten lead, while Dillon, in a supreme act of sacrifice, holds the monster in place. Unfortunately, the alien is only stunned by the hot lead. Thinking quickly, Ripley douses the creature with cold water from a huge overhead tank, and shatters it in a million pieces. Even before she's able to catch her breath, Bishop and the soldiers are upon her. The "Company" offers to remove the alien parasite surgically from her body, but Ripley doesn't trust their intentions. They have wanted the alien for the Bio-weapons Division since the Nostromo first set down on Archeron, and they would do anything — would say anything—simply to get their hands on it.

Ripley decides to end her life, and thus save mankind from what may be the ultimate doomsday weapon. Both Aaron and Morse attempt to help her, but they are brutally shot dead by the soldiers. Ultimately, Ripley does plunge from atop the lead works' scaffolding, her arms spread out Christ-like as she falls in the fiery pit. The alien chest-burster tries to wrangle free, but she clutches it to her body moments before dying in the molten lead. Bishop and his soldiers collect Golic, the sole survivor, and seal the prison forever. In the escape capsule, the flight recorder replays Ripley's last words after the destruction of the Nostromo: "This is Ripley, last survivor of the Nostromo, signing off...."

*****

The final shooting script, which had combined elements from Vincent Ward's vision with ideas drawn from David Towhy's prison planet, met with Joe Roth's tentative approval. Hill and Giler's basic story still had a

number of problems, not the least of which was an explanation of where the eggs aboard the Sulaco came from in the first place; but since everyone was so eager to start production on the film, those problems were left unresolved. The Fox executive would later hire Rex Pickett, behind the backs of his producers, to run fixes on the second half of the script, notably those scenes involving Golic, the worthless psychotic who becomes the nominal "hero" survivor of the piece. But once Hill and Giler found out, Pickett was dismissed after less than a month of rewrites. Additional changes continued throughout production in London, and no one copy of the script, including a late draft submitted by the producers in April 1991, could possibly contain a complete list of the revisions.

Because the final shooting script had undergone so many significant changes from the first screenplay by William Gibson, through the others by Red, Ward and Fasano, Twohy, Pruss, Hill and Giler, Ferguson, and Pickett, Twentieth Century-Fox recommended the Writers Guild of America determine credit for the script and story. The Guild began that arduous task by sending stacks of scripts and story treatments to each of the writers for their review. They were asked to identify which elements they had created for the film. Arbitrators then reviewed all scripts and their subsequent rewrites, and ultimately found that substantial amounts of new material had been added by Larry Ferguson, Walter Hill and David Giler. They were awarded credit for the screenplay. Even though these three people were largely responsible for the final shooting script, the WGA awarded sole story credit to Vincent Ward. The Guild felt that his vision, while significantly altered, dominated the overall stylistic premise of the film.

THE DIRECTOR—DAVID FINCHER

Once the producers had finally settled on the story for the third film, they turned to an avid fan of the first two movies, David Fincher, to direct. The departures of Renny Harlin and Vincent Ward and the unavailability of Ridley Scott had caused innumerable difficulties for the project, and they hoped that Fincher would help pull ALIEN 3 back together. Little did Hill and Giler know that he would eventually fight with them, and the studio, over the script, the budget, the sets, the shooting schedule, and the final cut of the film.

David Fincher, who was twenty-seven at the time of the shoot, was born in 1963, the son of a Life magazine reporter. As a child, he showed little aptitude for any school subject other than art, and was producing a local news show while still in high school. He joined George Lucas's Industrial Light & Magic at age nineteen, and not only worked as a matte painter but also shot some of RETURN OF THE JEDI (1983). His first commercial for the American Cancer Society, featuring a smoking fetus, won him enormous critical praise. David directed his first music video at age twenty-one, and helped found the ultra-chic Propaganda Pictures, which several years later was annually grossing $50 million. He also directed three Madonna videos (including "Vogue," "Express Yourself" and "Oh, Father"). He was recognized for his visual panache with several prestigious MTV awards for his Paula Abdul and REO Speedwagon rock videos.

"Although ALIEN 3 was his feature debut, he'd shot miles of rock video film," Sigourney Weaver recalled. "We looked at his whole body of work. David being unknown was the least of our problems. Remember, Ridley Scott had only directed THE DUELLISTS before ALIEN and James Cameron really had only done PIRANHA 2 and TERMINATOR before ALIENS. Are those any better qualifications for making an ALIEN movie?"

Fincher had some very definite ideas in mind as to what the third film should be, and expressed those ideas during his first meeting with Fox world-wide production president Roger Birnbaum, the producers and Weaver. He took one look at Sigourney, and said, "How do you feel about....bald?" From that instant, it became apparent to everyone Fincher was not afraid to take chances, and that was exactly what the beleaguered project needed. In addition to Ripley's appearance, the novice director was also concerned with the final look of the creature

THE DESIGN OF THE NEW ALIEN

David Fincher knew that the central element in each of the three films was ultimately the alien creature

itself, and that devising a new creature, which was both familiar and different, required the fertile imagination of Hans Rudi Giger. Unfortunately, for the production company, Giger had gone into seclusion, vowing never to get suckered into another Hollywood deal. Even though he had won an Academy Award for his goundbreaking designs for Ridley Scott's ALIEN (1979), the artist had seen his hard work exploited in one failed project after another. His unusual designs for FUTUREKILL (1985), POLTERGEIST II (1986), and the low low-budget MIRROR (1988) were never adequately translated onto film. Fincher first approached the Swiss surrealist to redesign the titular creature, but the artist flatly refused. (Vincent Ward had already tried coaxing him out of his self-imposed retirement to work on his version of the movie.) Later, Gordon Carroll and David Giler spoke with him at his home in Zurich, and he reluctantly agreed to render a few sketches.

Giger worked meticulously for about a month, rethinking his now-famous creation. "This time around it had to be more animal-like, more elegant," he explained their demands. "You shouldn't get the feeling that it was a man wearing a suit. Basically, the head had to remain unaltered but the body had to change." Fincher gave him total freedom over the design. His only directive was that the creature should be like "a freight train with teeth." During the four-week period, Giger produced dozens of drawings, which each revealed a hidden language of its own, and finally settled on one or two recurring themes. Totally dissimilar from those aliens which had come before, his dominant themes sought to combine the features of a predatory cat (like a panther) with an insect to create the new four-legged alien. His final design for the creature was clearly more unique than its predecessors, but was never used by the production staff.

"I came up with some nice improvements even though I wasn't given too much time," Giger explained. "For instance, the skin of the creature was designed to produce tones; it had valves on it, like a saxophone. Maybe they just ran out of money . . ."

Inexplicably, Fincher discarded Giger's designs and turned to Alec Gillis and Tom Woodruff Jr., the creature effects artists who had originally been hired by

ALIEN CREATURE

Vincent Ward. He asked them to design several new forms of the maturing alien, and the creature itself. The two artists, both thirty-three at the time of the production, readily accepted the assignment, and began constructing a virtual army of beasts to portray the monster as it changed form throughout the film.

Creating believable movie monsters was precisely the reason why Alec Gillis and Tom Woodruff Jr. became interested in motion pictures in the first place. Alec and Tom grew up during the sixties, watching classic films like THE CREATURE FROM THE BLACK LAGOON (1954) on the late show and drawing their own horrible monsters. In art school they both learned the finer points of anatomy and physiology, and began developing creatures that were even more lifelike. Both had worked extensively on ALIENS as part of Stan Winston's team. Among the many tasks they were called upon to complete, Alec Gillis rendered several new face-huggers for Winston and worked on parts of the alien queen, while Woodruff supervised suit construction, built several new chest-bursters, and helped sculpt the alien's ribbed,

bone-like head. Following ALIENS, Gillis and Woodruff formed their own company, Amalgamated Dynamics, Inc. (ADI), and honed their techniques on several projects, including TREMORS (1990) and the cult television series ALIEN NATION.

For ALIEN 3, they reworked the chest-burster so that it would appear as two distinct stages in the creature's maturing process. The first stage was essentially a hand puppet thrust through the chest of a mechanical rottweiler, not unlike the creature seen in both the first and second films. The second stage, nicknamed the "Bambi-burster" by the ADI crew because it featured a newborn alien clambering unsteadily to its feet, was executed through a large, cable-controlled puppet (with a slimy substance called methylcellulose slathered onto its skin). Gillis and Woodruff also designed an adolescent stage, built again as a cable-controlled puppet, to show the creature at a phase never before seen on film.

The Alien itself, the film's most important design and greatest technical achievement, was imagined as a cross between a dog and some carnivorous insect. Not unlike the designs submitted by Giger, the final creature appears part insectoid, part serpentine and part predatory animal in appearance. The alien was executed by Gillis and Woodruff in two forms: one, an elaborate, cable-controlled puppet, and the other, a man (actually Tom Woodruff himself) in a rubber suit.

THE SPECIAL EFFECTS

Because Twentieth Century-Fox had agreed to pay for only twenty-five special effects shots, less than half the number of effects ALIENS had, David Fincher and his producers concluded that they would need to hire a crack team of professionals to produce the effects cheaply and within a specified period of time. Hill and Giler first approached Brian Johnson, but he was already working on several others projects. They then turned back to the States, and selected one of the most prestigious companies in the business. Once Fincher had filmed all the live action sequences for ALIEN 3 (with Alec Gillis and Tom Woodruff) at Pinewood Studios, six months of extensive special effects and model photography were completed by Boss Film Corporation in Los Angeles under the direction of Richard Edlund. His highly-complex and technical wizardry contributed to many of the breathtaking sequences that took place in space and on the planet surface.

Richard Edlund had always been fascinated with motion pictures and how the "magic" worked. At age nine, he asked his father how the filmmakers had achieved a particular effect in a movie, and the elder Edlund replied "magic"; not satisfied with the answer, Richard began a lifelong quest to learn as much as he could about the "magic" of special effects. After completing school, he started working on commercials and numerous television projects. In the late 1970's, he moved to Marin County, California, with Industrial Light & Magic to begin a long and noteworthy career with Lucasfilm Ltd. Edlund worked alongside John Dykstra, Dennis Muren, Peter Kuran, Phil Tippet and other special effects luminaries on some of the most magical films of the age, including THE EMPIRE STRIKES BACK (1980), RAIDERS OF THE LOST ARK (1981), POLTERGEIST (1982) and RETURN OF THE JEDI (1983).

After a stellar seven-year association with Industrial Light & Magic, which had netted him four Academy Awards for Special Visual Effects, Richard Edlund left to establish his own effects organization at Entertainment Effects Group (formerly owned and operated by Douglas Trumbull and Richard Yuricich). He renamed the facility the Boss Film Corporation, and began taking on projects that ILM was too busy to handle. His first project was GHOSTBUSTERS (1984), the uproarious Ivan Reitman comedy that established a new way to depict ghosts on film. Edlund worked simultaneously on the effects for Peter Hyams' big budget follow-up to the classic 2001, appropriately entitled 2010: THE YEAR WE MAKE CONTACT (1984). Subsequent work on FRIGHT NIGHT (1985), POLTERGEIST II (1986), LEGAL EAGLES (1986), MASTERS OF THEUNIVERSE (1987) and other films very quickly established his company's reputation for excellence. Richard Edlund received another Academy Award-nomination for his incredibly complex special effects in DIE HARD (1988), but lost the coveted statue to his friends at ILM for their work on WHO FRAMED ROGER RABBIT (1988). When the partners at Brandywine Productions called, he was very eager to work on ALIEN 3.

The special effects, provided by Edlund's Boss Film Corporation, worked seamlessly with Fincher's live action sequences, including those that featured an impressive but briefly seen, fast-moving alien. Most of the effects and model work centered around the alien stalking prisoners through the prison complex. Although the creature was supposed to be nine-feet tall, Edlund's crew worked with a rod-puppet approximately a foot in height. With special puppetry techniques, they were able to make the alien move in ways a man-in-a-rubber-suit could not. Multiple exposure shots, composited with a blue screen, were used to give the illusion that the creature was actually crawling up and down walls, moving across ceilings, and scampering through dark corridors. Other visual effects, which include the establishing shots of the prison complex as well as the few scenes in space, were completed with miniatures and motion control photography. Budgetary constraints limited the total number of effects in the film, but Edlund's brilliant artistry combined with the latest technology from his Boss Film Corporation helped to join that fine line between reality and magic.

THE PRODUCTION CREW

Satisfied with his choices for creature effects designers and a special effects supervisor, David Fincher realized that his selection of the right production team was equally critical to the success of the film. Regrettably, Fincher was never extended the same creative autonomy that Scott and Cameron had received with their ALIEN films. The fact that he was working with a much larger budget and that the project had been troubled from the start contributed much to having each of his choices second-guessed. Even though he had proven himself as a director of commercials and music videos, Twentieth Century-Fox and his producers never let him forget that this was his feature film debut. Fincher tried not to let that interfere with his decisions. He made no attempt to achieve a continuity of personnel between the new film and its two highly-praised predecessors. He simply chose those individuals who would help bring his personal vision to the screen.

Based upon the recommendations of Hill and Giler, he selected Norman Reynolds as his production designer. Reynolds had already established himself as one of the most talented production designers in the industry with his visionary work on the STAR WARS trilogy and RAIDERS OF THE LOST ARK (1981). He seemed the perfect choice to transport audiences to the harsh prison planet of Fiorina 161, and was readily approved by the studio executives at Fox. But long before actual set construction began, Reynolds was asked to make elaborate models of the set. His designs combined several architectural styles, including art noveau and a sort of retrofitted science fiction. Since Fincher was not going to have the extensive art departments of the first two films, he was forced to rely on Reynolds to create the overall look of the film. Artists Bill Stallion and Martin Asbury were not only hired to assist Reynolds but also create the hundreds of storyboards which the director would use to shoot ALIEN 3.

For his director of photography, Fincher chose one of his all-time heroes, the cinematographer of BLADE RUNNER (1982), Jordan Cronenweth. "When Cronenweth works, it's like he's playing 3-D chess and the rest of us are playing Chinese checkers," Fincher said. "The tonal range is amazing. It's like Ansel Adams." Jordan Cronenweth began work in the industry as a clapper-loader and a focus puller. His first assignment as a cinematographer was on Robert Altman's BREWSTER MCCLOUD (1970). His stunning and imaginative camera work earned him tremendous critical praise, and eventually led to work on PLAY IT AS IT LAYS (1972), ZANDY'S BRIDE (1974), THE FRONT PAGE (1974), HANDLE WITH CARE (1977) and ROLLING THUNDER (1977). When Ken Russell was looking for a first rate cinematographer to film his science fiction epic ALTERED STATES (1980), he turned to Cronenweth. Cronenweth's ground-breaking work on ALTERED STATES and Ridley Scott's BLADE RUNNER established his reputation as a director of photography throughout the world. The only problem with his work, which Fincher would soon discover, was that he was very slow and exacting in his set-up of each scene.

Less than two weeks into the shoot, Fincher reluctantly replaced Cronenweth with a British cinematographer, Alex Thompson. (His decision to fire his first choice as director of photography came at the bequest of Twentieth Century-Fox. The studio executives were concerned that Fincher would be able to finish in time.) Thompson, who had not worked on feature films in some time, was still highly regarded as a director of photography. His work on HERE WE GO ROUND THE MULBERRY BUSH (1967), THE STRANGE AFFAIR (1968) and ALFRED THE GREAT (1969) was still being studied by students in film school. While lacking the stylish camera work of Cronenweth, Thompson was the perfect choice to keep the production on schedule.

At the urging of Twentieth Century-Fox, Hill and Giler also hired Tim Zinneman to act as the line producer. With the two producers now functioning as writers, they needed someone to carry out the thousand daily details of a producer, as well as serve as a buffer between Fincher and the men who had hired him. Weaver described him as "one of the best line producers" she had ever worked with. But three weeks before the actual shooting began, Fox fired him because he wasn't getting Fincher to compromise his production schedule and budget. The studio had already lost millions with cost overruns on THE ABYSS (1989) and DIE HARD 2 (1991), and they were extremely wary of another runaway film. Zinneman was replaced by Roth's handpicked line producer, Ezra Swerdlow. Swerdlow had worked with Woody Allen, Mel Brooks and Mike Nichols, and knew how to keep the production on track. She was later replaced by Jon Landau.

*****

For economic reasons, Hill and Giler decided to retain Pinewood Studios, at which Vincent Ward had already assembled some of the production staff and sets, for their ambitious sequel. Since Twentieth Century-Fox had already invested nearly $15 million in the project, and would eventually spend another $35-40 million before the film was complete, they knew how important it was to keep additional production costs to a minimum. Unfortunately, the dollar had begun to loose its value against the pound in the United Kingdom, and by the end of the shoot, the cost would have far exceeded their expectations. Carroll and Giler had also pushed Fox for an 18-week shooting schedule with four months for post-production. But the studio executives would only agree to thirteen weeks. "The first ALIEN took sixteen and a half weeks, and the second one took eighteen weeks," Weaver later explained her frustration. "Why they thought we could make the third one in thirteen weeks I'll never understand." With time of the essence, Fincher got down to business with his production staff, while the final casting choices were made.

THE CAST

With Walter Hill and David Giler busy revising the script and Gordon Carroll overseeing the various phases of preproduction at Pinewood Studios in England, casting directors Billy Hopkins (in Los Angeles) and Priscilla John (in England) began looking for the actors who would inhabit the all-male correctional facility of Fiorina 161. They hoped to re-create the casting magic of the two previous films, and looked for performers who would bring much of themselves to the roles. Of course,

two of the lead roles (that of Warrant Officer Ripley and her android companion Bishop) had already been filled by Sigourney Weaver and Lance Henriksen.

Even though movie fans remember her best for the powerful performances as Ripley in the ALIEN trilogy, Sigourney Weaver is one of America's most talented and versatile actresses. She made her motion picture debut in the original ALIEN (1979) and followed it with such films as the mystery EYEWITNESS, the drama THE YEAR OF LIVING DANGEROUSLY, and the comedy GHOSTBUSTERS, proving that there was no genre at which she couldn't excel. Reprising her role as Ripley in ALIENS, she received the first of her three Academy-Award nominations (this one as "Best Actress in a Leading Role"). The unanimous critical acclaim for her performance as Ripley and the high-priced call girl in HALF MOON STREET (1986) put Weaver on the "A" list of leading actresses, as well as providing her with an enormous amount of creative autonomy. She played against type in both GORILLAS IN THE MIST (1988) and WORKING GIRL (1988), and secured two more Academy-Award nominations (for "Best Actress" and "Best Supporting Actress"). She reprised her comic role as Dana Barrett in GHOST-BUSTERS II before agreeing to play Ripley a third time in ALIEN 3. (Weaver's contract also stipulated that she would have some creative control by naming her as co-producer.) Following ALIEN 3, she was featured in Ridley Scott's 1492 (1992, as Queen Isabella of Spain) and the First Lady in DAVE (1993).

Lance Henriksen returned as Bishop in Alien 3 *(photo copyright ©1989 United Artists Pictures)*

Veteran actor Lance Henriksen first heard discussion about his reprising the role of Bishop for a third and possibly a fourth film in the series while he was still filming ALIENS. "I wouldn't agree to anything without knowing what the script was," he admitted, but later agreed to reprise his character at the behest of producer Walter Hill. "Walter called me and said, 'Lance, go to England. Do the role.....'" Since the 1986 blockbuster, Henriksen, the "chameleon," had been busy creating a handful of

new characters in films as diverse as NEAR DARK (1987) and PUMPKINHEAD (1988). His turn as a mercenary hit-man on television's BEAUTY AND THE BEAST (1989, CBS) won him enormous critical praise. His return to the Bishop role, which he credits as a major breakthrough in his career, gave Henriksen the chance to play a dual role as the faithful android and his badass creator.

Charles Dance, threatening Eddie Murphy in The Golden Child, *portrayed prison planet inmate Clemens in* Alien 3 *(photo copyright ©1986 Paramount Pictures)*

British-born Charles Dance, the soft-spoken and distinguished actor of both stage and screen, was cast in the role of the chief medical officer. Having played many classical characters on the British stage, Dance brought a certain charisma to the part of Clemens that projects both sympathetic desperation and lonely introspection. He first came to the attention of American audiences by playing opposite Meryl Streep in Fred Schepisi's PLENTY (1985). Featured roles as the villain in THE GOLDEN CHILD (1986) and as James Bond creator Ian Fleming in GOLDENEYE (1988) helped to further his reputation. Later, as the disfigured and tortured music composer in the 1990 miniseries PHANTOM OF THE OPERA, Charles projected an air of inner tension and vulnerability behind a masked exterior. His strong characterization of the "Phantom" brought him many well-deserved accolades, and the hearts of many love-struck women. Following ALIEN 3, Dance was cast against type as a death-dealing hitman in Schwarzenegger's LAST ACTION HERO (1993).

The role of Andrew, the prison's uptight warden, was awarded to Brian Glover. A former actor on the British Stage, Glover found the character of Andrews very different from the kind of roles he had often played. Prior to ALIEN 3, the Britisher had appeared in dozens of motion pictures, including AN AMERICAN WEREWOLF IN LONDON (1981). Although predominantly known for his serious work in film, Brian Glover appeared in a series of humorous tea-bag commercials which have forever marked him as a comic actor in the eyes of his fellow Britains.

Charles Dutton was hired for the pivotal role of Dillon, the prison's spiritual advisor and leader. A native of Baltimore, Dutton spent the first few years of his adult life in the Maryland correctional facility in Jessup as a prison inmate. He studied theatre while a prisoner, and took part in several noteworthy productions. His first big break came when a Twentieth Century-Fox representative offered him the lead role in a television series about a middle-class African-American family living in Baltimore, named ROC. Dutton made his motion picture debut with ALIEN 3, and that celebrated performance was followed by numerous big screen offers. Following ALIEN 3, he returned to his role as "Roc" on the popular television series for Fox.

The supporting roles of Golic, Aaron and Morse were filled with the three British actors Paul McGann, Ralph Brown and Daniel Webb. Future "Best Supporting Actor" nominee (for IN THE NAME OF THE FATHER, 1993) Pete Postlethwaite has a supporting role as one of the prison inmates. Danielle Edmond was also hired as a stand-in for Newt during the autopsy scene.

PRODUCTION DETAILS

Principal photography on ALIEN 3 was scheduled to begin on January 2, 1991, at Pinewood Studios, but was pushed back to January 14th in order to give Hill and Giler enough time to rewrite several scenes. Throughout the first couple of weeks, with huge sections of the script being vetted by Fox's Jon Landau for budgetary reasons and the producers revising and rewriting those sections, director David Fincher concentrated on the dialogue sequences, saving the action scenes for later. He tried to complete most of the scenes that featured Ripley's introduction to Clemens and the prison complex. On the first day of shooting, however, Fincher nearly lost his star, Sigourney Weaver, when a bug wrangler got carried away with hundreds of cute baby crickets (standing-in as lice). This major sequence, which was later scrapped during the editing process, found Ripley lying naked on the infirmary table, being examined by Clemens. He just barely has time to warn her about the prison's lice problem before she experiences it first hand.

"David [Fincher] said, 'Just sprinkle a few bugs on her forehead,'" Weaver recalled the incident in vivid detail. "And my eyes are open and I'm talking, and all these bugs drop on my face. They went in my ears, and my eyes, and I — who pride myself on having worked with gorillas and everything and being a good trooper — went nuts. You realize what it's like to be naked and blind and have bugs thrown in your face? It was the worst beginning with a director I could imagine."

Many of the scenes that followed were understandably tense and business-like, reflecting uneasy feeling and tension the cast and production crew had towards the novice director. But Fincher was able to win Weaver and the others back completely a few weeks later when they shot the scene in the morgue, in which Clemens must perform an autopsy on Newt to make certain no alien parasite is hidden within her. For the character of Ripley, it was perhaps the most emotionally charged scene of the series, and Weaver was anxious to make it right. David was reportedly very sweet and sensitive to her. He talked her carefully through the sequence, and was supportive through several difficult takes. By day's end, Sigourney was convinced that he was a brilliant director. Then, just as production picked up and Fincher was hitting his stride as a director, the Gulf War exploded across every radio and television broadcast. The outbreak of hostilities in the Middle East cast a dark cloud over the production. When the cast and crew weren't actually shooting, many of them sat huddled around a television screen, watching, waiting, hoping for an end to the bloody conflict.

By late February, they had started shooting several of the big action sequences. Fincher was gradually becoming accustomed to Alex Thompson's rhythms as his new director of photography, but he still could not shake the notion that Jordan Cronenweth might have shot a particular scene in a completely different way. Then, one night after a brutally long day of eighteen-hour filming, an explosive effect backfired. Four crew members were badly burned, and a fifth one seriously enough to go to the hospital. The sequence, in which one prisoner accidentally ignites the toxic waste and sets off a huge explosion, was vitally important to the film. After several lost days rebuilding the set, Fincher had to reshoot the entire scene from the beginning. The studio executives at Fox were not pleased, and wanted to close down the set; but David convinced them to let him keep shooting.

In the midst of shooting, however, Hill and Giler suddenly quit the project, over a dispute regarding the script. The producers had maintained from the beginning their desire for a clear-cut, good guys versus bad guys climax to the picture. Fincher, on the other hand, saw Ripley's sacrifice as a necessary part of the story. "[They] had written an ending where Ripley choked up the fetus, got back into a space vessel and went away," Weaver explained in very simple terms. "I thought that was ridiculous. There was something very depressing about her heading off in a shuttle again. The ending as it stands seemed the correct one. Ripley has survived so many times — but for what? Survival has lost its allure. This was her destiny. She saves the world. She kills the last alien. She makes the right choice." The argument finally reached its climax when Roger Birnbaum agreed to support Fincher instead of the producers. Walter Hill and David Giler walked off the set in protest, and severed all ties with the production.

The scene, in which Ripley plunges to her death, was filmed on Good Friday. Even though the sequence was similar to one in James Cameron's TERMINATOR 2: JUDGMENT DAY (1991), they decided to shoot it exactly as originally planned. When filming wrapped for the afternoon, the production crew took a few well-deserved days off, while Fincher reviewed his shooting schedule. The stalemate had cost him valuable time, and he was already running about ten days behind schedule.

At about the same time, Jon Landau tried to gather some rough footage together for the trailer. When he realized there was very little that was actually usable for a trailer, Landau instructed his technical staff to simply slap one together using the signature from the original. It didn't seem to matter to him, or anyone else at the studio, that they had little idea what the final film was about. So, his technical staff pulled together a composite of the "splitting egg" graphic from ALIEN over a shot of the earth, and superimposed the film title, with a voice over suggestion that the third film in the series would have an earth setting. Tagged onto the front of POINT BREAK (1990), the trailer began running in theatres in June 1990, proudly proclaiming that ALIEN 3 would be in theatres at Christmas. Little did Twentieth Century-Fox know at the time how that simple trailer would later come back to haunt them.

As the production continued into May 1990, Fincher had well exceeded his thirteen-week shooting schedule. Jon Landau replaced Swerdlow as the line producer, and began to make some critical decisions. They were already ten days over budget, and money was scarce, with Fox keeping a very close watch over every penny. Landau cut several scenes at the bequest of the studio. Fincher was very upset with those cuts, but continued to work eighteen-hour days, supervising all four units. By now, his various teams were shooting the climatic scenes, and work was enormously complicated and tense.

After watching David Fincher scramble for two weeks in a futile effort to shoot the last few scenes and save his film, Landau finally closed the production down. Even though the motion picture was still unfinished, they had surpassed all budgetary and timing constraints. Weaver tried phoning Joe Roth personally to get an extension, but he simply wouldn't budge. The sets were put into storage, and everyone was sent home.

*****

During the next few weeks of post-production, David Fincher worked with editor Terry Rawlings, who had worked on the first film, to transform the thousands of feet of raw footage into a rough cut. They trimmed much of the earlier footage which had been shot by

Cronenweth, and concentrated on pulling together a story that made some sense. Like Ridley Scott, Fincher also wisely chose to limit the number of appearances of the Alien, once again proving that the most convincing movie monsters were the ones that appeared on screen the least. The novice director also added a temporary soundtrack using music from the first film. (Ultimately, Elliot Goldenthal would write a musical score which was highly evocative of the one Jerry Goldsmith produced for ALIEN.)

Producers Walter Hill and David Giler returned to the project in post-production, and reviewed Fincher's rough cut with Fox. "Everyone could see there were certain problems," Hill said, but declined to note his specific objections. On the other hand, Joe Roth claimed the film was "too long, lacked pace, and needed to be more like a traditional horror movie."

For the next six months, David Fincher struggled in the editing room to produce a workable film. Finally, in November of 1991, Twentieth Century-Fox gave the novice director an additional $2.5 million for an eight-day reshoot in Los Angeles. The sets were rebuilt on the Fox lot, and Fincher worked quickly to complete the necessary scenes. Jon Landau also helped with the reshoot by working with Alec Gillis and Tom Woodruff at A.D.I. on several new effects shots. Towards the end of the year, Hill and Giler began praising Fincher's film, claiming how unusual and provocative it was. Roger Birnbaum remained cautiously optimistic. "I think the picture will find an audience," the worldwide production president ventured. "The core of the ALIEN fans will go back. I think this movie holds up the integrity of the franchise."

With less than a few months remaining before its theatrical release, the motion picture was screened for test audiences. Most agreed the film was very downbeat and generally depressing, and recommended several changes prior to its cinematic debut. The MPAA also mandated several cuts, including one sequence in which the alien smashes the brain of one inmate, in order to give the film an "R" rating. Under the supervision of his producers, Fincher spent the last few weeks, right up to its May release, recutting and reediting the film.

THE THEATRICAL RELEASE

Originally scheduled for a Christmas 1991 release, then an Easter 1992 opening, Twentieth Century-Fox finally released ALIEN 3 on May 22, 1992 with very little fanfare. David Fincher's feature film debut faced incredibly still competition from Richard Donner's LETHAL WEAPON 3, Ron Howard's historic epic FAR & AWAY, Tim Burton's BATMAN RETURNS, and Robert Zemeckis' DEATH BECOMES HER. Debuting in over a thousand theaters, the motion picture failed to make much of a splash with either critics or moviegoers. By the second week, in fact, business had fallen off so substantially that the industry was calling it a bomb. Following the enormous box-office success of the previous two entries, studio executives were very disappointed to learn that their $40-50 million gamble would end up costing them dearly. If not for a surprisingly high foreign box office gross, ALIEN 3 would have been a complete disaster.

Although audiences found plenty of fault with the motion picture, several critics were impressed by the film's technical brilliance and with Fincher's stylistic direction. Owen Gleiberman in ENTERTAINMENT WEEK-LY wrote that "ALIEN 3 is a grimly seductive end-of-the-world thriller, with pop-tragic overtones that build in resonance as the movie goes on. One of the rare sequels that truly measures up...." Both Siskel and Ebert turned thumbs down on the motion picture, but Roger did cite Fincher's visionary work in reshaping the horror film. David Ansen of NEWSWEEK, Jami Bernard of the NEW YORK POST, Janet Maslin of the NEW YORK TIMES and Richard Schickel of TIME were all highly critical and down-right contemptuous of the second sequel. By the end of the summer, ALIEN 3 had finished well behind the other films, and well on its way to box office obscurity.

In February of 1993, ALIEN 3 was honored with a single award nominations from the Academy of Motion Picture Arts and Sciences for the Best Achievement in Visual Effects (for Richard Edlund, Alec Gillis and Tom Woodruff Jr.). At the actual Academy Awards ceremony, ALIEN 3 lost out to the very imaginative work by Industrial Light & Magic on DEATH BECOMES HER (1992). The film was also nominated for a "Hugo" award from the World Science Fiction community, but lost that coveted award as well.

Even though Kenner Products continued to produce its immensely popular line of "Alien" action figures, no specific figures from ALIEN 3 were licensed for production by the company. Halcyon, the Britain-based model company, released only one original model kit inspired by the movie, and also reissued many of its other popular kits, including the "Alien Warrior," the "Face-Hugger," and the "Alien Queen." Dark Horse Publishing published a three-part comic book adaptation of the movie, and continued with its popular series. But there were no souvenir programs, posters, special books, costumes, merchandise or other promotional items.

CRITICAL COMMENTARY

Lacking the strong visual imagination of Ridley Scott's ALIEN or the tremendous narrative drive of James Cameron's ALIENS, David Fincher's third installment stumbles through the dark corridors of its prison complex on a pathetic quest for some sense of originality. Admittedly, there's plenty of gross-out shocks to satisfy fans of the original, or plenty of action sequences to distract fans of the first sequel; but when it comes to new material or ideas, the third film is very lacking. After all, what is so incredibly unique about an alien monster running around loose on a prison planet? Both Scott and Cameron had already explored every potential angle with their two films. At least, William Gibson's political allegory or Vincent Ward's wooden planetoid would have been far more interesting, and potentially visionary, than the final product. Showing signs of heavy editing, even its one hundred and fifteen minutes of length must have seemed overly boring to its producers as well.

The fault for this lackluster effort probably lies with the film's producers and possibly, to a lesser extent, with the studio itself. Their decision to mount a multimillion dollar production without a completed script or narrative direction was, at best, unwise. Fox was equally negligent for continually pumping money into the project when it was clear that no one knew what they were doing. The multiple rewrites, production delays, hirings and firings, and behind-the-scenes bickering only contributed to the other mounting problems, not the least of

which was the conflict about the ending of the film. Hill and Giler's decision to build a $40-50 million motion picture around a 28 year-old MTV veteran was also questionable, even though Fincher proved that he was a capable director. Then, instead of walking off the set in a dispute over the production, they should have been much more supportive, and simply accepted his vision as the final one. After all, they had trusted both Ridley Scott and James Cameron, two then unproven directors, with their film.

Likewise, Twentieth Century-Fox might have seen a better return on its investment if the studio had left the creative process to the director. When Fincher told them it would take more than thirteen weeks to complete the film, the executives should have extended him the same shooting schedule they had given to Cameron or Scott. Instead the studio sent Jon Landau to cut essential scenes which might have made the contrived plot seem much more believable. Working from a corporate ledger is no way to make a motion picture.

The enduring popularity and success of the ALIEN series can be attributed to many key elements, from the archetypal nature of the story to the visual style of its particular director and, finally, to the contributions of the many artists and technicians. But the franchise's true essence lies in the screen magic that those numerous storytelling and filmmaking techniques combined to create. Burdened with an "idiot plot," in which the narrative is kept in motion solely by virtue of the fact that everyone is an idiot, a limited artistic budget, and few special effects, it is truly a wonder that ALIEN 3 turned out as "good" as it did. Much of that credit belongs solely with the director.

Like Ridley Scott, David Fincher is truly a brilliant visual stylist. He has taken special pains to resurrect the original film's atmosphere of foreboding and imminent danger. His shots of the Alien, actually mere glimpses as the creature skitters through the corridors like some giant spider, contribute much to the feeling of unease. Audience members never know where, or when, the monster will strike. He even manages to get some extra mileage out of the famous shower scene from PSYCHO (1960), by unleashing his monster somewhat unexpectedly. Even though we know the character shouldn't go into the shower, we are still shocked by the Alien's appearance as the curtains are slowly pulled back. His rock video-like style with the camera helps to evoke a much more disjointed portrait of reality, and the scenes focusing on the inmates as they struggle to fight the Alien in their decaying prison complex are highly reminiscent of the Mad Max movies. However, his collection of prisoners are never sentimentalized by his direction; in fact, quite the opposite is true — he creates vivid characters out of each of them with warts and all. He also manages to evoke thoughtful performances from Charles Dance as the mysterious medical officer and Charles S. Dutton as the convicted rapist who "found God at the ass-end of the universe." ALIEN 3 clearly demonstrates his superior ability to transcend his MTV origins in order to make feature films.

Sigourney Weaver turns in another wonderful performance as Lieutenant Ellen Ripley. Shorn of her beautiful hair, she still projects beauty, and gradually reveals — during the course of the film — a sensual side to her character as she turns to Clemens for affection. Ripley's already spent the previous two films proving her metal as both a warrior and surrogate mother. So, her decision to sleep with the chief medical officer helps to extend and expand the believability of her character. She is also particularly effective in portraying Ripley's inner struggle with the demon growing inside her. She progresses from denial to anger to bargaining and depression and finally — in the climatic scene — acceptance. She realizes that Ripley is doomed, and that survival (to potentially face other nightmares) is no longer as appealing to her. Her descent into the pit, while decidedly downbeat, does bring her character full circle.

ALIEN 3 is regrettably a tired remake of the first film set in the claustrophobic interiors of a deep space correctional facility rather than aboard a starship. Whereas the original ALIEN was a triumph of production design, set decoration, special effects, and makeup, and its first sequel was a rousing, rollercoaster descent into hell-and-back, David Fincher's is little more than a grim, nihilistic downer to an otherwise brilliant trilogy. Without any new elements, the classic conflict between man and the unknown forces of nature (as represented by the alien) has simply lost its original luster. ALIEN 3 is currently available on both videocassette and laserdisc from Twentieth Century-Fox home video.

CHAPTER FOUR
"ALIEN 4" AND
THE "ALIENS VS. PREDATOR" CONFRONTATION

Light years away from Fiorina 161, the final resting place of former Warrant Officer Ellen Ripley, a new Alien threat is discovered ....and....a group of Colonial Marines is assembled under orders from the Weyland-Yutani corporation to track the alien menace back to its home world and to destroy the nest once and for all — only they don't realize that a member of the squad has instructions to return a healthy specimen to the bio-weapons division on earth....a race of intergalactic hunters, known as Predators, have been seeding planets with Alien eggs in order to produce a worthy adversary for the hunt, and the human colony on Ryushi is the next target....an esteemed archeologist discovers a pair of fossilized eggs on an expedition to Acheron, and manages to slip them past quarantine procedures on earth....or Ripley awakens from a horrible dream about being trapped on a prison planet with an Alien, and discovers that the nightmare actually pales in comparison to her next encounter.

Rumors of a fourth ALIEN film first began circulating in 1992 after the release of David Fincher's lackluster sequel, and reached a feverpitch eighteen months later. At the 1993 World Science Fiction Convention held in San Francisco, a publicist for the studio would only confirm that a fourth movie was in the early stages of development. Even though ALIEN 3 had been both a critical and box office failure, Twentieth Century-Fox was not about to abandon one of its most popular film series. Stan Winston, who made a special appearance at the annual event to discuss his work on INTERVIEW WITH THE VAMPIRE (1994) and to receive some much-deserved kudos for JURASSIC PARK (1993), would not confirm or deny his future involvement. He simply stated his fondness for the series as a whole, and wished the new production well.

The author who has been given the daunting task of crafting a new story is Joss Whedon. A former story editor for ROSEANNE and the author of BUFFY: THE VAMPIRE SLAYER (1992) ("I'm waiting for the day when BUFFY isn't the film I'm remembered for," he laughed), and "script doctor " of SPEED and WATERWORLD, Whedon reputedly impressed both Walter Hill and David Giler with his grasp of "what the Alien metaphor meant" and collection of ideas.

The failure of ALIEN 3 to engage American movie audiences is not lost on Whedon. "ALIEN 3 made a lot of money overseas," he observed, "but I think even the Fox executives felt something was missing. I've found the studio is mostly interested in ALIENS because of its action-adventure elements. The first film was really a straight horror film, which is not quite as exciting to the studio."

The screenwriter indicated that the oft-cited storyline in which the Aliens make it to Earth is not the scenario for the next film. "First of all," he pointed out, "it would require an enormous budget and gigantic scope. I don't know if the studio is ready to make that commitment yet. Everyone thinks it would be a great idea, but what exactly about their coming to Earth would you want to see? Nobody, including myself, can answer that. We know Earth won't be anything like it is today, so it's not like you'd be afraid Aliens are under your bed."

Planned for a 1996 release, the new production will hopefully employ the same elements which made the first two films so successful, and discard those that caused the innumerable problems on the third. For example, the element that worked best from the original ALIEN was clearly the element of suspense generated by the relentless death-struggle between a small crew and the cosmic creature in the claustrophobic interiors of a spaceship. In ALIENS, the rousing, non-stop action helped distinguish Cameron's as an audience favorite. The third film, while fraught with problems, did introduce a new kind of alien, one which takes on the physical attributes of its host. Among the elements that are easily discardable is the foul language, the gratuitous sex and violence, and the interchangeable cast of anonymous faces who are presented merely to die, in true slasher form, at the hands of the Alien. As to the potential return of Ellen Ripley, anything in the universe is possible.

While Sigourney Weaver had flatly denied (a

position since changed) her future involvement as an actress in the popular series, she did express an interest in seeing the ALIEN movies continue. She also hoped to co-produce a future installment. "I hope they do make more," she said. "There are so many different strands to explore. What is the Alien really doing? Where does it come from? What does it want from the human race? How does it communicate? I'd like to see all these ideas developed. For the Alien image is anything that terrifies each of us on a highly personal level, manifested as the ultimate indestructible nightmare."

"A movie of this size, with this kind of pedigree [and combined grosses in excess of $200 million] needs to pack a huge wallop," said Roger Birnbaum, the president of worldwide production at Fox, who concedes that "action" is at the top of his list; but when asked specifics about the storyline for ALIEN 4, he declined, preferring instead to speak in general terms about the franchise.

Producer David Giler was equally evasive in his responses to questions about a new film. "Part of what makes an ALIEN movie work is they're a reworking of other genres of movies," he explained. "We felt the first was truck drivers in space; the second was marines in space; the third was tough guys in space, so who knows? Keeping genre elements alive that have worked well before — the claustrophobic environment, a lot of people no one cared much about in theory, the flotsam and jetsam of the future — are essential. Simply because Ripley dies at the end of the third film, and it's a trilogy and it's over, is silly. There will be a fourth one. It's science fiction — there are nine million ways to bring Ripley back, or to do other alien stories. You could bring it back to the planet of the aliens, never mind Earth."

Joss Whedon admitted that the idea of Ripley returning "has come up. All they said to me was, 'Ripley may come back.' The idea of doing an ALIEN movie without the anchor makes them a little nervous. I would be interested in bringing Ripley back, just to see how I could do it. There has also been talk of bringing an older Newt back instead of Ripley. Their arcs are different. With Newt you have a blank page, but, with Ripley, that page has been written on so many times that you really have to find something new to say."

Once Joss Whedon was assigned to write **Alien 4**, *an early premise discussed was the Aliens reaching Earth. "But then what?" queries the writer, who decided the idea was unworkable — plus prohibitively expensive.*

Now Whedon, who is like the proverbial kid in the candy store, will be given that opportunity, even though a year and a half passed between his being hired and the commencement of writing.

"We had to work with the producers, we had to make the deal, we had to write a treatment and here we are a year and a half later," he said. "But it's okay. I've been dreaming about this my whole life. I saw ALIEN when I was 14, and there's not another movie that has had as big an impact on me viscerally or aesthetically. ALIEN changed the nature of science fiction as much as STAR WARS did by turning it into a working man's universe. It was a submarine movie. It was like that scene in

STAR WARS where Luke looks at the Millenium Falcon — which is the coolest thing I've ever seen — and says, 'What a piece of a junk!' All of a sudden you're not in robes saying, 'Mars will explode,' but rather science fiction is inhabited by you and me. That's part of the appeal, the fact that they created a monster that was not only genuinely new but also horribly resonant.

"That's what was probably disappointing about the third one for me," he added. "I thought they had the attitude and the feel was great, but people want to see something different. They say, 'We know the alien and we know it intimately. What's new? What's out there that's different?' When James Cameron made ALIENS, he did that in spades just with the title alone. And ALIEN 3 said, 'Yeah, well this one is small and kind of slow.' Ooh, that's scary!"

According to the writer, the previous films in the series were all modeled on specific film genres — specifically a submarine film, an army film and a prison film. "Only ALIEN 3 *wasn't* a prison movie, and that's where it failed," he noted. "A friend of mine said, 'Look at all the bald British guys, you can't tell one from the other.' That's not prison genre. In prison genre films they're all Americans, very specifically. Prison movies carry their own level of terror and it was hard to be scared of these guys. But I think the thing that upset me the most is that they actually had a scene where people we didn't know were killed by the Alien. That's Jason. That's bullshit! That totally betrays these movies, because nothing is more boring than somebody you don't care about being killed."

But audiences most definitely did care about Ripley, and one can't help but have images of Bobby Ewing in his shower in terms of the character's resurrection.

"I've made that joke, actually," smiled Whedon. "Of course Ripley *did* die in ALIEN 3. But if we can clone dinosaurs and get people to buy it, we can certainly clone a thirtysomething actress."

And although Ripley will be back through cloning, she will *not* be the same character that audiences met in the first three films. The Aliens, too, will be genetically different.

"The main thing about these movies is to be more exciting and scary than any other movie that comes out," he emphasized. "It's the ride, and a sci-fi coolness factor that's there as well. The genetics issue is definitely secondary to what are they going to look like, what are they going to do, who are they going to kill?

"We're dealing with Ripley's resurrection responsibly," Whedon elaborated. "We're not just saying, 'Oh, Sigourney's back, let's go make the movie!' It's the central issue of the movie, the fact that we bring her back, and we know that once you do that, everything must be different. If somebody comes back from the dead, especially in a movie where death is the ultimate threat, you can't just say, 'It's okay, anybody can die and come back because we can do this now.' It's very important to me that it be a very torturous, sort of grotesque process so that the audience can viscerally feel what it's like to be sort of horribly reborn in a lab. And Ripley's not too happy about being brought back. She's angry and has to deal with a lot of shit. What's interesting for me is that she can be running a whole gamut of emotions. She can be amused when it's not funny, she can be all kinds of different people at this point rather than just play that same note again. I want to write a juicy role for Sigourney, and I want to have as much fun with it as I can."

One particular question comes to mind: wasn't Ripley already impregnated with the Alien Queen at the time her DNA samples were taken? Whedon gave a hint of a smile in response. "Is she all woman or is there just a little something wrong?" he asked cryptically. "The whole intention is that when she comes back from the dead she has to be larger than life."

As, one would imagine, are the challenges of writing ALIEN 4 and getting the franchise back on track.

"Resurrecting Ripley is a no-brainer," Whedon said pointedly. "Getting the franchise back on track — I'm not going to take on that responsibility. As I said before, each one of these movies had a very specific model, and finding a model is probably my biggest challenge. I have the plot of the movie, the characters, the whole arc, but, visually, I want to find a new feel for it that does not betray the look of the other ones. Again, I think the third one put the nail in dark, grimy corridors. It's hard to find something that people will look at and go,

'Oh, they're doing this and look at this place that we're in.' It should be new and exciting but still feel like an ALIEN movie. I'm no production designer, but I can't work unless I work completely visually; unless I understand exactly the space that everybody is in, especially for an action movie. That, for me, is the hard part."

What's easy is knowing exactly what he *does* want to deliver. "I want every scene to contain something special," he said simply. "I want to do an EVIL DEAD, where it's really menacing and about 20 minutes into it the action starts and *never* stops. *That's* what I want to do. My only qualification for this is that I'm the biggest fan and I demand what the biggest fan wants. I want it all."

The biggest challenge for Whedon and the Fox marketing team may be to get moviegoers back into the theatres, after not only killing Ripley but almost killing the franchise as well in ALIEN 3.

Said Whedon, "If ALIEN 3 had been as great as the first two, I wouldn't go near this film. I would be too frightened. I knew what I wanted from a third ALIEN film, and it wasn't a bunch of bald guys running around and getting eaten. What I liked was that I saw something new, but it was really just a bitter, bleak movie. It's like the sequel to PLANET OF THE APES, in which they nuked the Earth. I didn't feel like ALIEN 3 was a step forward. I wanted to see something that I hadn't seen before, and a smaller, less ferocious alien was not what I had in mind."

Though everyone continues to remain tight-lipped about specifics for the new sequel, several directors have been discussed as leading candidates for the project. Among the front runners are Geoff Murphy, Steven Soderbergh and Mick Garris. Murphy, the New Zealander whose former occupations as a rock-n-roll musician and school teacher eventually led to directing, has produced a number of successful projects, including THE QUIET EARTH (1985), YOUNG GUNS II (1990) and FREEJACK (1992). He is a good action-adventure director who can evoke the fantasy settings (his retrofitted, BLADE RUNNEResque city of the future for his 1992 science fiction epic was particularly effective). Murphy also brings a high level of craftsmanship to each of his projects, and could easily duplicate the success of James Cameron. On the other hand, Soderbergh, the man responsible for the understated, highly praised SEX, LIES AND VIDEOTAPE (1989), demonstrated a darker side similar to Ridley Scott with KAFKA (1991). Whereas his debut feature was a low-budget comedy, his follow-up was a paranoid fantasy about the legendary Franz Kafka with high production values and shadowy camera work recalling the best of the German expressionist period.

The third candidate, Mick Garris, is a veteran of horror films who might restore the element of relentless terror to the series. His first two feature films as a director, CRITTERS 2: THE MAIN COURSE (1988) and PSYCHO IV: A NEW BEGINNING (1990), and as a writer, THE FLY 2 (1988), may well have been sequels to other hit movies, but Mick has clearly established his own style with SLEEPWALKERS (1992) and the massive miniseries THE STAND (1994). Like Ridley Scott and David Fincher, he would certainly bring a macabre sensibility to the sequel. Of course, Birnbaum and Giler should certainly not rule out the possibility of using an experienced director, like Wes Craven, David Cronenberg, John Carpenter or even George Romero for its next ALIEN installment.

Future entries will have to chart an uncertain course between the breathtaking imagination and maelstrom of terror and suspense of the first and the roller-coaster ride of the second in order to satisfy ticket buyers and be critically successful. Thrills, chills, innovative and spectacular special effects notwithstanding, the innovative storyline is ultimately what separates the ALIEN series from its closest competitors.

*****

While David Giler and the other partners at Brandywine Productions continue to explore other avenues and plotlines for its series, Twentieth Century-Fox has also purchased a script for an ALIEN VS. PREDATOR storyline. Written by Peter Briggs, an English screenwriter, the story logically bridges the two diverse universes. For years now, since the first appearance of the galactic hunter in PREDATOR (1987), fans of the ALIEN series have dreamt about the ultimate confrontation between these two races. The 1990 sequel even hinted that the two cosmic creatures had already met, and the Predator emerged victorious by placing an Alien skull in the hunter's trophy case. Dark Horse Publishing has also devoted two limited, comic series to exploring that confrontation. It was really only a matter of time before studio executives realized the potential in their two franchises for a contest.

The first draft screenplay by Peter Briggs, dated September 4, 1991, opens on a desert world — Death Valley on an incredibly grand scale — where five Predators, a race of intergalactic big-game hunters, are closing on their prey. Broken Tusk, the leader whose one mandible has been sheared away, pauses at the entrance of a bio-mechanical structure. Just then, as a face-hugger scrambles by, the hunters are attacked by a horde of Alien warriors. The bloody carnage is swift and terrifying, but the Predators eventually emerge from the sea of bio-mechanical limbs strewn around like a charnel house. Broken Tusk carries his trophy — the head of an Alien warrior — proudly as they transport back to their starship. Once aboard the ship, the Predators pass a captive Alien Queen, its limbs tethered by restraining clamps to prevent movement, and their actions become crystal clear. The Predators are seeding planets with her Alien eggs so that its hatchlings can infest all living creatures, and provide them worthy opponents to stalk as big game.

On the jungle planet of Ryushi, nestled in the lush rain forest where the Yutani-Templin Corporation has constructed a communications relay station, Rob Parsons and Cassie Dollander are tracking two signals on their deep space monitors. The two traffic controllers have never seen signals quite like these, and interrupt the corporate boss, Hiroko Noguchi, who is busy enjoying herself fighting four Ninja swordsmen in a holographic simulation. Noguchi curses the interruption; in the three years since she was first promoted to chief executive, she's had her fill of the assignment. Primarily a colony of freelance ranchers and their families, plus a token staff of corporate overseers, the outpost raises rhino-like herd animals to feed an increasingly hungry Mother Earth and monitors space traffic. Once in a while, corporate executives arrive to hunt big game in the jungle, but rarely does anything out of the ordinary happen. Little does she know that Ryushi has been selected as the site for an unusual contest between two alien races.

Hiroko Noguchi joins Parson and Cassie in the command center, and they watch as the signals gradually approach then land on the surface. Fearing that the signals may be hostiles, Noguchi radios Antarctica Traffic Control for instructions. She then questions Don Kamen, a cowboy trucker who occasionally does freelance scouting work for the Company, where he took the four corporate executives hunting. He tells her Linson's Range....the landing coordinates of the first signal. Meanwhile, at Linson's Range, the four Company executives (York, Ackland, Minh and Beauvais) have dispensed with their big-game hunting to investigate a downed spacecraft. Their curiosity leads to an unfortunate discovery — the ship was carrying Alien eggs, and the eggs have hatched multiple face-huggers. Ackland and several rhinos soon fall victim to the otherworldly creatures, while Minh and Beauvais are killed trying to destroy the face-huggers by an invisible, Predatory force. York somehow manages to evade capture, and escapes on one of the hover-bikes. Other Predators, using their cloaking devices, track York back through the jungle to the colony's uplink tower.

Some hours later, Hiroko and Kamen reach the campsite at Linson's Range. They find two bloodied bodies (Minh and Beauvais) dangling, head-first, from the trees, Ackland (who appears comatose) and a shriveled face-hugger nearby. All around the campsite, there are signs of a tremendous struggle, but no real clues as to who or what may have done this. Hiroko decides to carry Ackland's body back to the command center aboard her hover-bike, and instructs Kamen to warn the other colonists. But since most of them are simple ranchers and their family members, they do not pose a threat or challenge to the Predators, and are essentially left alone throughout the rest of the story. The personnel at the command center — most of them company workers — are in fact fair game to the interstellar hunters. And the group of Predators take great pains to infiltrate the Alien eggs throughout the complex.

Returning to the command center, Hiroko takes Ackland to Dr. Revna in the infirmary. York is there also, raving about the creatures in the jungle, but no one seems to know what he's talking about. Ackland soon recovers, unable to remember anything since the strange "meteor" crashed near their campsite. (When Ackland identifies the signal as a "meteor" and not a spaceship, Hiroko begins to suspect York may have gone crazy, rendered Ackland unconscious and killed the other men. No other explanation makes any sense to them. They certainly don't believe York's wild ravings about invisible monsters.) Annie Urioste, an Italian systems mechanic, interrupts their conjecture with some very bad news. The station's pumps are all failing, and unless something is immediately done to rectify the situation, the command center will sink into the swamp-like terrain of the jungle. Hiroko turns her attention from York and Ackland to the far more pressing concerns of the Yutani-Templin facility. (Urioste and Diller are assigned to descend into the lower depths of the complex, and fix the pump if possible.)

In the infirmary, however, Ackland suddenly starts to act funny, confessing to the others that he doesn't know what's happening to him. But before Revna can get to him, the Company man suddenly doubles over at the waist and begins convulsing. He then grasps at his chest and an alien creature emerges. The Doctor, who has never seen anything like this, panics, striking wildly at the alien chest-burster. He get struck by the creature's acid blood, and falls to the floor. York tries to force the door closed, but the chest-burster escapes into the colony's labyrinthine structure. Hiroko, Kamen and Thomas organize a search party, and send a distress call to the Marines at Fort Powell as a precautionary move. At the same time, Guttierez and DeVries, two shop stewards, investigate the perimeter of the complex when the Company's mascot Brewster refuses to stop barking at movement in the jungle. They find several dead rhinos, whose chests have somehow exploded from within, and discover evidence that someone (or something) has been watching them.

Down in the pump room, Urioste and Diller are attacked and brutally killed by an alien warrior, then suddenly all hell breaks loose. Aliens begin appearing everywhere. From the overhead ducts; over the platform edges; along the overhead cable supports. Having taken on the genetic characteristics of their host, many of the creatures are non-humanoid. All of them are living nightmares as they tear and rend their victims literally limb-from-limb. Kamen, Devries and Guttierez fight the beasts

on the lower level near the auto shop, while Hiroko, Thomas and the others struggle to remain mere steps ahead of the death-dealing, indestructible monsters.

The Predators, under the charge of Broken Tusk, shimmer into view, deactivating their cloaking devices, and join in the battle. At first, Thomas turns his weapons on the newcomers, but Hiroko warns him off, realizing the hunters may be the only chance they have. She then cuts an Alien in two, with one of the Predator's circular "smart weapons" saving Broken Tusk from the fury of the bio-mechanoid beast. The Predator acknowledges her help, and not wasting a moment, leaps from the platform into another gathering of the creatures. And yet, despite their ferocity and weapons, it's clear that the small group of Predators and humans are being overrun by the alien horde. They all continue to fight nobly against them, using whatever resources they can. (In fact, Hiroko lures an Alien into the holographic room, and activates her Ninja swordsmen program. The Alien halts, momentarily confused by the intrusion, bewildered by the lack of contact as its claws through them. Hiroko strikes and destroys the creature with one blow.)

Eventually, Hiroko marshals her forces in the command center, and locks down all the possible entrances in or out of the complex. Outside, the battle is going badly for the Predators. There's only three of them left, and one is Broken Tusk. The Aliens sting and paralyze two of the hunters, for the inevitable implantation process, but the Predator leader gets away.

During the lull in battle, everything electrical in the command center flickers, and the bank of monitors turn to static. They have less than thirty-six hours before all the power fails, and they have no way of knowing if the Colonial Marines will arrive in time. Hiroko entertains options from the remaining survivors. Cassie, York, Driscoll and Parsons seem to think they can get away on the shuttle if the administrative module is lowered into place from outside. (Kamen, DeVries and Guttierez are trapped in the auto shop, and can provide no help at all.) As station chief, Hiroko Noguchi agrees to risk her life for the others and suits up for her adventure.

Descending into the heart of darkness, through a shaft which leads to the Central Reservoir — a long cylindrical concrete tunnel that runs the length of the complex, she encounters a scene from hell. The Aliens have glued, with a secretive resin, the bodies of humans, rhinos and other livestock in the curved wall. Most are dead, their innards blown open; the rest are comatose, twitching occasionally in pain. Every square inch not con-taining bodies is filled with Alien eggs. Apparently, the alien parasite gestates inside a living organism, and then takes on the physical attributes or characteristics of that organism when it finally emerges. Hiroko is sickened by what she has seen, and scrambles down a convenient airduct to avoid becoming a face-huggers' next victim.

Alien 4 *screenwriter Joss Whedon along with the Fox executives decided against* **Aliens vs. Predator,** *feeling that it smacked of something along the lines of* Destroy All Monsters *(photo copyright ©1973 American International Television, Inc.)*

She soon emerges from the tunnel at the central crane, and manages to free the administrative model from the rest of the complex. They can now lift-off to a safe distance in the shuttle, and await the rescue of the Colonial Marines. But Hiroko is suddenly cut off by an advancing horde of Aliens, led by an Alien Queen. She tries to slip back into the tunnel, and runs into Broken Tusk. He has not forgotten that she saved his life. The Predator leader motions her to another exit, and the two escape into another chamber. There, they discover the cocooned body of Kamen and two Predators. Still conscious, Kamen begs his companion to kill him, but she simply cannot do that to him. Broken Tusk obliges him, with a single blow to the head which crushes his skull. The Predator attempts to do the same to his warriors, but one has already "given birth" to a Predator-Alien hybrid. In mere heartbeats, the "Prealion" appears from the shadows, and gives battle. Broken Tusk narrowly defeats the hybrid, with Hiroko's help, and turns to escape.

With their path to the surface cut off, Hiroko and her companion stumble through a reservoir. Explosive fireballs are erupting all around them as the two warriors climb to freedom. Hiroko and the Predator are momentarily separated by the advancing horde of Aliens, but she quickly formulates a plan to save him from the impossible odds. While Broken Tusk battles with the monsters, Hiroko takes the colony's only chopper, and pilots the vehicle in the direction of the remaining livestock. By stampeding the colonist's rhinos, she hopes to disrupt the Alien-Predator battle long enough so that she can save her companion. The plan works beautifully, crushing many of the combatants under the weight of the rhinos; she rescues the alien hunter in the nick of time, then turns to the colony complex for safety. At first, Hiroko thinks they are safe, but an Alien stowaway strikes, fatally wounding Broken Tusk. The Predator leader fights back, and kills his very last opponent before dying.

Finally, the Colonial Marines arrive in several drop ships, and begin fighting off the remaining Alien warriors. In the midst of their mopping-up operation, a Predator shuttlecraft also lands, and offers Hiroko a spear as a token of their gratitude for a fight well fought. She accepts the spear graciously. They then offer her a chance to continue hunting with them, and Hiroko Noguchi agrees to their terms. After all, she has little respect for her current position.

*****

Inspired in part by Randy Stradley's four-part comic series for Dark Horse Comics, ALIEN VERSUS PREDATOR: THE HUNT by Peter Briggs is an exceptional story that captures the spirit of the oft-discussed confrontation between the two alien races — those insatiable interstellar hunters known as the Predators and their death-dealing indestructible prey, the Aliens. The as-yet unproduced script combines many of the more popular elements from the ALIEN series, including the elements of suspense and non-stop action. Briggs was also bright enough to introduce several new kind of aliens, one in fact which takes on the physical attributes of the Predator. His characters are very believable, more so than the ones first created by Dan O'Bannon. In particular, Hiroko Noguchi is a worthy followup to Lt. Ellen Ripley. Kenner's recent line of toys (notably the Alien-rhino and the Predator figures) anticipate the new film. Only time and money will tell if this very worthy successor to the ALIEN series goes into production.

Joss Whedon, assigned screenwriter of ALIEN 4, just doesn't see the scenario a likely one to be brought to life.

"Some of us felt that might have sullied the ALIEN films," he said. "It becomes like DESTROY ALL MONSTERS or Freddy vs. Jason. I think it would be a mistake."

CHAPTER FIVE
ALTERNATE ALIENS
FROM DARK HORSE PUBLISHING

Dark Horse Comics, an Oregon-based publishing company, in cooperation with Twentieth Century-Fox began issuing brand new stories about the Aliens under the direction of publisher Mike Richardson in the summer of 1988. Though fiercely protective of the rights to their series, the creative staff at Fox were apparently very helpful and excited about the directions the writers had taken with the series. In return, the writers and artists at Dark Horse have consistently delivered some of the finest tales of science fiction and horror related to the monsters first conceived by Dan O'Bannon and H.R. Giger. The stories have all been extensions of the films, and with (possibly) one exception have maintained a harmony with the Fox franchise. Whereas Heavy Metal published a fine comics adaptation of the first film with "Alien": the Illustrated Story, written by Archie Goodwin and illustrated by Walt Simonson, Dark Horse has published mostly original stories. In fact, often the originality of the comic books have been far superior to that of the sequels. The popularity and collectability of the comics forced Dark Horse to become international in 1992 with the publication of a U.K. ALIENS magazine. Offering British-produced Aliens comics, photo features, interviews, and reprints of U.S. ALIENS comics, in a slightly larger format, the magazine now threatens to eclipse the work done in the states.

The following series guide should provide the novice with an introduction to the alternative worlds of the Aliens in comics, and the serious collector with an invaluable checklist. Each entry includes the month and date of publication, the number of issues in the series, along with a listing of the creative staff, a short plot synopsis, and review.

July, September, February, March, June and July 1988/89 -ALIENS - Six-Issue Series, Black and White, with color covers. Writer: Mark Verheiden. Artist: Mark A. Nelson. Letterer: Willie Schuben. Editor: Randy Stradley. Cover Colorists: Mark A. Nelson, Randy Stradley and Chris Chalenor.

Writer Mark Verheiden teamed with noted artist Mark A. Nelson to create the first story in the highly-popular ALIENS series from Dark Horse. Although this Black and White shocker owes much to James Cameron's rousing 1986 sequel, the plot's highly-original extension of the film expertly combines elements of science fiction and horror to create a truly memorable comic.

Ten years after the events (in the second movie), Newt is suffering from the same type of delayed stress syndrome Ripley went through after she was first rescued. Confined to a mental institution for the insane, she continues to endure endless hours of psycho-therapy; the teen-aged girl can't really shake the bad dreams, and she fears they may have to lobotomize her. Likewise, Hicks, who is still in the Colonial Marine Corps, has been experiencing the same severe psychological problems since his return to earth. He has a self-destructive behavior, and his sterling record has been tarnished. A simple reference to Ripley: "Well, you know what became of her....." reveals that she, too, may have gone insane.

Hicks learns from his commanding officer that a Coast Guard space-cruiser, while on a routine mission to destroy an abandoned cargo ship, made contact with an Alien, which subsequently attacked and destroyed the ship and all its military crew. James Likowski, pilot of the derelict cargo ship, Junket, survived the explosion, which destroyed both ships, by ejecting in his escape pod. Unluckily for him and the rest of the world, the Bio-National Corporation rescued him from the pod, and brought him to Bio-National's Houston labs for analysis. (The Company is seeking to patent the Alien warrior as a new biological organism, and hope Likowski will "give birth to" a new one.) Hicks also learns that the Government has discovered the location of the homeworld in the salvaged computer log of the cargo ship Junket. (Apparently, the ship stumbled on the location while on a mission for the Bio-National Corporation.) Dr. Waidslaw Orona assigns Hicks to obtain specimens from the homeworld for government study. The Corporal knows that they are crazy to want Alien specimens, but he reluctantly agrees to the assignment. (Newt also insists upon going, in order to face her demons, and Hicks arranges to smuggle her aboard the spaceship Benedict.)

Meanwhile, a tele-evangelist named Salvaje sees the Alien as the true messiah, and begins sending messages over his various cable stations. People all over the world have been experiencing visions of the Alien, and he uses that psychic link to the creature to gather an immense congregation for their salvation. His church of the Immaculate Incubation seeks the ultimate communion with the true messiah.

Bio-National learns that the Government is seeking to retrieve specimens of an alien lifeform for its Weapons Development Program. If they are successful, this could seriously impact Bio-National's claim of sole patent right on the new lifeform technology. Thus, the corporate leaders dispatch a spaceship, the K-014, with a two-fold mission to first follow Benedict to the alien homeworld and gather another lifeform, and, second, to inhibit the Benedict's crew from retrieving a viable test subject. They are ordered to use any means possible to stop the Benedict, and the K-014's captain, Patrick Massey, decides they will take over the Colonial Marine transport, and hold its men hostage.

James Liowski, the captain of the space freighter, gives birth to an alien queen in a quarantined medical facility, and Dr. Ostrow kills one of his own guards in order to save the chest-burster's life. However, the mad, fanatical preacher has other ideas for the creature. He and his followers break into the lab, and release the corporation's captive queen on an unsuspecting earth. His goal: to force mankind into an unholy "communion," but he becomes the creature's first victim. Apparently, the Queen has been using her psychic abilities to trick others into believing it was the messiah, and now the Alien intends to take over the whole world.

Captured by the Bio-National troops, Hicks and his Colonial Marines are forced to land on the Alien homeworld to capture a specimen for them. Newt, who has hidden aboard the ship as a stowaway (under the Corporal's instructions), emerges in the nick of time to save Hicks but not his men. The Marines find conditions on the Alien homeworld to be more than they bargained for, and are quickly out-numbered by its hostile inhabitants. Hicks manages to rescue some of them, but his drop ship falls under attack as well. At the moment everything seems utterly hopeless, a large elephantine creature (similar to the "space jockey" that was fossilized in the original ALIEN) arrives and kills all the Aliens. His interstellar race had been breeding the alien warriors for war when they realized how potentially dangerous they were. They tried shipping the creatures away, but the cargo ship (seen in ALIEN) crashed on Archeron. The "elephant-alien" offers to return to Earth to help. . .

But back on Earth, the Government's attempts to confine the spore infestation to a narrow geographical range have failed, and the Aliens have rapidly taken over the whole planet Civilization crumbles, as evolution allows a new dominant creature to survive. Dr. Waidslaw Orona realizes they failed to stop the creatures because the Aliens were perceived as sentient warriors rather than like a disease. The Aliens overwhelmed earth like a cancer. Hicks and Newt arrive with their alien guest far too late, and watch in horror as the last remnants of the military withdraw from the planet. Earth is doomed.

Mark Verheiden's ALIENS brilliantly captures the characters and the atmosphere of the suspense of the film series in a way that is often hard to do with the printed word. Mark Nelson, a former art teacher who had done other comics work, including CLONEZONE at First Comics, several SKYWOLF at Eclipse and a number of short features for Dark Horse Presents, has managed to reproduce the visual styling of the first film. His art has a "dark" quality that works best in the Black-and-White format. Verheiden's spine-chilling episodes and Nelson's spectacular art combine to form a unique experience that becomes better and better with each reading.

August, December, March and May 1989/1990 - ALIENS, VOLUME TWO - Four-Issue Series, Color. Writer: Mark Verheiden. Artist: Denis Beauvais. Letterers: Bob Pinaha and David Jackson. Editor: Randy Stradley. Cover by Denis Beauvais.

The success of Dark Horse Comics' first ALIENS series, presented in six, black-and-white issues, prompted them to produce a second series. Scripted (again) by Mark Verheiden with artwork by Denis Beauvias, the new series picked up right where the last one had ended. ALIENS, VOLUME TWO, a four-issue series, was also presented in glorious color.

Returning to Earth aboard the military transport American, Hicks tries to re-align the main antenna, but he continues to receive shadowy fragments of the disaster back home. Newt is equally bothered by bad dreams, most notably about her first love, Butler — an android who was torn in half by an Alien. She begins to suspect her dreams have a basis in reality, and convinces Hicks to investigate the spacecraft. Predictably, there are alien warriors on board — hundreds of them, frozen in specimen chambers by the military. General T. Spears plans to study the Aliens for possible mutations brought on by the creatures' exposure to multiple human strains — his own men — with the thoughts of building an army of warriors to reclaim the Earth from their brethren. Hicks and Newt fear that he's gone mad, but they are quickly locked away in the brig, powerless to interfere.

The situation gets much worse for Hicks and Newt as the General decides to start infecting not only his own men but also his prisoners. With the help of Butler, however, they manage to escape confinement, and Hicks rounds up as many Marines as he can find to battle Spears. The Corporal soon discovers the ultimate horror — the mad man has transformed all his men into Aliens. Escaping aboard the cargo vessel McArthur, Hicks and Newt attempt to warn Gateway Station of the General's treachery. But it is far too late! Spears and his squad of alien commandos have already successfully landed on Earth and, not surprisingly, the death-dealing, indestructible creatures have turned on the General. Only human arrogance could have convinced him to attempt such an impossible feat. When Hicks and Newt finally reach the space station, they are greeted by a familiar face, a well-armed Ripley who's ready to kick Alien ass. From the stunning cover paintings by Denis Beauvais, through the great script by Mark Verheiden, the interior illustrations and surprise ending, ALIENS, VOLUME TWO was clearly one of the best comic series published in a long while. The only complaint that many fans expressed about the two series was the long wait between issues.

June, July, September and October 1990 — ALIENS: EARTH WAR — Four-Issue Series, Color. Writer: Mark Verheiden. Artist: Sam Kieth. Letterer: Jim Massara. Colorist: Monika Livingston. Editor: Diana Schutz. Painted Cover by John Bolton.

ALIENS: EARTH WAR, the third and final installment in Mark Verheiden's epic saga, attempted to tie-up all the loose-ends of the series, notably what happened to Ripley. While some of the background story conflicts with details now known from ALIEN 3 (1992), the material offered a much more interesting alternative to the ALIEN chronology of events. Like its predecessors, this final installment was well-plotted, fast-paced and "darkly" fascinating.

With the planet overrun by Alien warriors, the Colonial Marines are planning to return to Earth for one final showdown. They must hurry because the few remaining survivors don't have long to live, hiding out in tunnels and sewer systems, waiting for rescue, and fighting the nightmares of each passing day. But Ripley has a plan — an impossible plan to return to the homeworld in

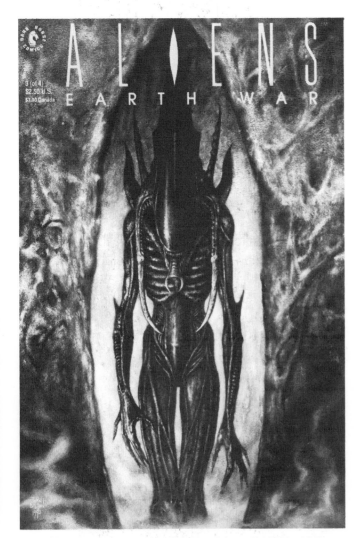

earlier civilization ruled by an Alien Queen Monarch, much like the power structure in insect colonies. Controlling a monarch would mean being able to control the others....at least in theory.

Ripley and her crew of Marines achieve the impossible by capturing the monarch, and race home towards Earth before it's too late. Meanwhile, Dr. Orona's stockpile of atomic bombs is counting down to destruction as the last survivors struggle to stay alive. With moments to spare, they release the Alien Queen, and gather the few remaining humans together in their ship. But then, something extraordinary — something so totally unexpected — happens. The elephantine creature (that race was first introduced as the fossilized "space jockey" in the original ALIEN) arrives to claim Earth as its own. It used Ripley's plan to eradicate the alien scourge

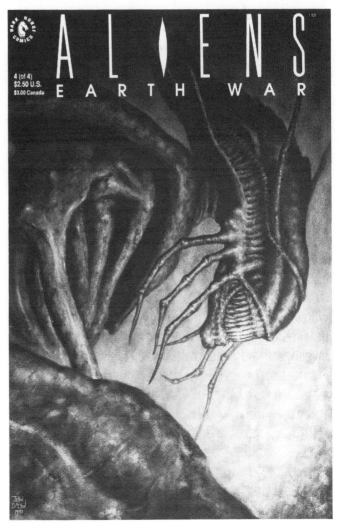

an effort to capture the Queen-ruler of all the Aliens. Then, by using her as a "judas goat," lure the other ones to their death. Hicks and Newt aren't really satisfied with her plan, and ask her specific questions, like how she knows so much about the Alien creatures . .

Apparently, when Ripley and the others were returning from LV-426 aboard the Sulaco, she was awakened from her hypersleep by Marines from another troop carrier that had been monitoring and analyzing their transmissions. Captain Hankerson and his men had been assigned to travel back to Acheron to investigate the derelict space-craft and find out as much as they could about the "space jockey." Ripley was never really given any choice in the matter, and simply pressed into service as their guide. In the hull of the derelict ship, they found evidence of alien infestation that went back thousands of years....to an so that it could terraform the planet for its own purposes.

Arriving safely at Gateway Station, Ripley, Newt, Hicks and his men watch helplessly as their home is reshaped and restructured for the new inhabitants. Perhaps "they" would learn from the human's mistakes.

ALIENS: EARTH WAR brings to conclusion an incredible top-notch epic from Mark Verheiden. He has not only managed to introduce a new cast and bring readers up to date on the story thus far but has also set up an exciting new scenario. The return of Ripley is handled with equal precision; he also gives her a credible reason for her absence from the previous issues. Sam Kieth's artwork in the first issue is somewhat rough, but it gradually improves in the course of the story. His characters change from being somewhat cartoony to being more like graphic representations of real life actors and actresses. In addition to a gripping story and original artwork, each of the stunning covers by John Bolton reminds avid ALIEN fans of H.R. Giger's original paintings from the Necronomicon.

June, August, October and December 1990 - ALIENS VS. PREDATOR - Four-Issue Series, Color. Writer: Randy Stradley. Penciller: Phill Norwood. Inker: Karl Story. Letterer: Pat Brosseau. Colorist: Monika Livingston. Editor: Diana Schutz. Painted Cover by Phill Norwood.

The oft-discussed, much ballyhooed confrontation between the two alien races — those insatiable interstellar hunters known as the Predators and their death-dealing indestructible prey, the Aliens — was finally dramatized in the exceptional, four-part series ALIENS VERSUS PREDATOR. Written by Randy Stradley, whose previous work as an editor on ALIENS was brilliant, and illustrated by Phill Norwood (with inks by Karl Story), the story helped bridge the two disparate universes (both being examined in detail by Dark Horse Comics) in a believable way. The series was also produced in a slick, visually-alluring format, similar to comics being introduced in Europe.

Three years ago, the first humans arrived on the planet Ryushi, at the edge of the Chigusa Corporation's holding in the Beta Cygni System to build the human outpost, Prosperity Wells. Now, primarily a colony of 115 freelance ranchers and their families, plus a token staff of corporate overseers under the command of Machiko

Noguchi, the outpost raises rhino-like herd animals to feed an increasingly hungry Mother Earth. Little do they know that their world has been selected as the site for an unusual battle between two alien races.

In preparation for a cyclical rite-of-passage, known as the "coming of age," the intergalactic race of Predators has "seeded" the planet with Alien eggs. The hatchlings infest all living creatures (including the rhinos) to spawn new breeds of gruesome Aliens. With this well-stocked hunting ground of ghastly Aliens, the Predators are ready to test their young warriors. However, after a chance encounter with Dr. Kesar Revna, the colony's expert on extraterrestrial biology, who causes the destruction of their landing craft, the leaderless young Predators forget about their ritual and go on a rampage of revenge — attacking outlying ranches and indiscriminately killing the defenseless settlers. Many ranchers attempt to escape aboard a visiting star freighter, The Lector, only to discover that it too has become infested with alien warriors and an Alien Queen.

Thinking quickly, Machiko discerns a plan she believes will allow the colonists a chance for escape into the surrounding desert. The plan is risky, but before she can put it into action, she's alerted to a commotion in the Medical Center. Dr. Miriam Revna, who has been carrying for the wounded leader of the Predator, is attacked by one of the marauding young Predators. Intervention by the grizzled, broken-tusked Predator leader saves her. Broken Tusk examines the young Predator's trophies and is enraged to find the skull of a human child among them — an apparent violation of Predator hunting ethics. While the two Predators battle to the death, Machiko and Dr. Revna take the colony's only hovercraft, and put Machiko's plan in effect. By stampeding the colonist's rhinos, they hope to disrupt the Alien-Predator battle long enough so that the colonist's can make good their escape. The plan works beautifully, crushing many of the combatants; but Machiko is torn between joining her fellow colonists, or attempting to help Broken Tusk put an end to the madness.

Predictably, Machiko returns to Prosperity Wells to help her Predator friend. She rescues the alien hunter in the nick of time, then turns to the colony complex for safety. At first, she hopes the Company will send Colonial Marines to their aid; but when Machiko receives word that the Chigusa Corporation wants all specimens preserved, she joins forces with the Predators to wipe the Aliens completely out.

Stradley's storyline makes excellent use of filmmaking techniques by often juxtaposing different art and dialogue captions. The author can then pursue different threads of the story simultaneously, and inject certain scenes with irony and dark humor. His actual story is dark, thrilling and quite profound in its content. Phill Norwood's pencil illustrations and Karl Story's inks provide one of the best combinations of graphic design. The material is elaborately detailed, flowing and graceful, and always very, very menacing. Overall, the work in this series is among the best in the whole line. (Note: the

ALIENS VS. PREDATOR storyline actually began with a series of short vignettes in DARK HORSE PRESENTS that were later gathered in one volume as a prequel, numbered "0.")

November, December, January and February 1991/1992 — ALIENS: GENOCIDE — Four-Issue Series, Color. Writer: John Arcudi. Based on a story by Mike Richardson. Penciller: Damon Willis. Inker: Karl Story. Letterer: Jim Massara. Colorist: Arthur Suydam. Painted Cover by Arthur Suydam.

"More Aliens action than all of the other series combined" was the hype behind the story, and in this particular case the comic series actually lived up to the hype. Mike Richardson's ALIENS: GENOCIDE, scripted by John Arcudi, proposed yet another reason why earth scientists might be interested in the death-dealing, indestructible creatures. Rather than utilize the Alien warriors for the bio-weapons division, they had produced a highly-addictive drug from the Queen's birthing sack. Daniel Grant, a wealthy Donald Trump-like developer, has authorized his company, Neo-Pharm, to begin mass-producing the wonder drug "Xeno-zip" for distribution. Now that the Earth has been reclaimed from the Aliens, even though small pockets of Alien infestation remain, he hopes that his corporation will profit from the sale to builders, construction workers and their families on the new planet. The only problem in his plan: corporate scientists cannot synthesize the "royal jelly"; it must come directly from an Alien Queen, and there are no more Queens.

At the bidding (and bribery) of Daniel Grant, the Government launches a military expedition to the Alien homeworld to capture a Queen. When the U.S.S. Razzia arrives, however, they discover that hundreds of thousands of the alien creatures (some red and some blue-green) are fighting one another for dominance and territorial control. The interspecies war is frightening and deadly, and costs the lives of many Colonial Marines as they attempt to carry out their mission. Ultimately, they decide to turn the tide of battle by dropping tactical nukes in an effort to destroy the red Aliens.

On board the military transport, Grant learns that an android named Henriksen has been programmed to not only sabotage the mission but also kill him. Their deadly confrontation as well as the fate of thousands of Alien warriors come to a dramatic climax in the thrilling conclusion of the series.

Even though the story is fraught with many technical problems (not the least of which is how a radioactive Earth was rebuilt in such a short period of time), the artwork is superb. Damon Willis' dynamic drawings provide a moody, atmospheric feeling of doom and hopelessness throughout the piece. The artistry on the homeworld is also very detailed and bring to life a brilliantly realized world.

April 1992 — ALIENS: TRIBES - One-shot, Color, Squarebound in Hardcover format. Writer: Steve Bissette. Artist: Dave Dorman. Painted Cover by Dave Dorman.

ALIENS: TRIBES was the first in a series of graphic story albums from Dark Horse Comics. Written by today's master of horror comics, Steve Bissette, whose illustrations for SWAMP THING were considered the high point of the series in the Eighties, the story takes place on board an orbiting medical facility infested with the Alien scourge. When the Aliens are first detected, a crack extermination team is sent to the space station to wipe them out. But the success of their mission is jeopardized by a sinister man in a lethal exoskeleton who has gone right over the edge of sanity.

Truly, a stunning book, ALIENS: TRIBES is presented in novel-length format (in a deluxe hardcover edition), accompanied by twenty-four full-color paintings by Dave Dorman, one of the most sought-after painters working in the field of comics. Well worth the $24.95 investment. (Note: ALIENS: TRIBES won the 1992 Bram Stoker Award as the best novelette from the Horror Writers of America.)

February, March, April and May 1992 — ALIENS: HIVE — Four-Issue Series, Color. Writer: Jerry Prossner. Artist: Kelley Jones. Letterer: Clem Robins. Colorist: Les Dorscheid. Painted Cover by Kelley Jones.

ALIENS: HIVE by Jerry Prossner was conceived as a semi-sequel to Mike Richardson's ALIENS: GENOCIDE, but the four-issue series easily eclipses the first work in terms of both story and artwork. Dr. Stanislaw Mayakovski knows that the Alien Queen's "royal jelly" is the most sought-after consciousness-altering substance in existence, and he intends to corner the market with a very interesting plan. Conceived by his associate and lover, Julian Lish (who is really a small-time thief), they plan to infiltrate an artificially-created Alien android in the Alien society. Mayakovski has been studying ants (in particular, one ant named Ari) for years, and he is convinced the Aliens function like ants in a hive. Unfortunately, their plan doesn't have a chance in hell of working, and it may even cost them their lives.

Darker than ALIENS: GENOCIDE, with a sense of impending gloom and doom, the bold artwork of Kelley Jones has never been more superb and chilling. In fact, several of the large-paneled pages in the series have a relatively sparse use of description and dialogue that add to the intensity of the story. Prossner's tale is equally riveting, offering a unique twist on the drug-theme that was introduced in the previous book.

May 1992 — ALIENS: CYBERANTICS — One-shot, Black and White, Squarebound in Hardcover format. Writer: Jerry Prossner. Artist: Kelley Jones. Painted Cover by Kelley Jones.

A companion book to ALIENS: HIVE, the one-shot ALIENS: CYBERANTICS offered readers a chance to more fully understand the ant's role in Dr. Stanislaw Mayakovsky's experiments. The story is about how Ari, an artificially created Ant android, was created to go into an ant colony and retrieve information. The parallels between ants and Aliens are never more clearly drawn than in this thoroughly delightful book. ALIENS completists and Prossner's fans will want to own this one!

May 1992 — DARK HORSE PRESENTS: ALIENS — One-Shot, Color, Squarebound. Assorted writers, illustrators and stories. Editor: Randy Stradley. Painted Cover by Simon Bisley.

DARK HORSE PRESENTS: ALIENS was a one-shot anthology featuring some of the finest ALIENS stories in color for the first time from the leading book in the line. "THEORY OF ALIEN PROPAGATION" by Mark Verheiden, art by Mark Nelson and colors by Chris Chalenor was originally published in DARK HORSE PRESENTS #24. The story, more an excerpt from the work of Dr. Waidslaw Orona — the civilian advisor to the Colonial Marine Corps, details all known information about the Aliens species. "ADVENT (1)" and "TERMINUS (2)" by Paul Guinan and Anina Bennett with lettering by Willie Schubert and colors by Rachelle Menashe were originally published in DARK HORSE PRESENTS #42 and #43. Archeologists investigate a strange pyramid on another planet and discover the remains of both human and Alien life. "REAPERS" by John Arcudi, art by Simon Bisley and colors by Chris Chalenor, was originally published in DARK HORSE PRESENTS FIFTH ANNIVERSARY SPECIAL. The short tale presents a strange confrontation between another human-like race and the Aliens. And "THE ALIEN" by John Arcudi with pencils by Tony Akins, layouts and colors by Paul Guinan was first published in DARK HORSE PRESENTS #56. At long last, readers are introduced to the race of creatures first responsible for the Aliens.

June-July 1992 — ALIENS: NEWT'S TALE — Two Issues, Color, Squarebound. Writer: Mike Richardson. Based on the screenplay by James Cameron. Penciller: Jim Somerville. Inker: Brian Garvey. Letterer: Ellie De Ville. Colorist: Gregory Wright. Painted Cover by John Bolton.

ALIENS: NEWT'S TALE was a two-issue series that basically retold the screen story of ALIENS (1986) from the point of view of the colony's little survivor. As the military transport Sulaco returns to earth, Newt slumbers in hypersleep, recalling the terrible events at Hadley's Hope on LV-426. Part one of the story details how her parents, Ann and Russ Jorden, first discovered the derelict craft, and returned to the colony with a face-hugger implanted on her father's head. Predictably, the colonists further investigate the Jorden's claim, and the complex is overrun with alien warriors. Newt concludes her memories in part one with her rescue by Ellen Ripley and the Colonial Marines.

Part two of the story follows the Marines through their first encounter with the beasts, the destruction of the drop ship and their battle in the colony complex. Towards the end, Newt is separated from Ripley and Hicks, and taken by an alien warrior for cocooning. She is soon rescued from the marauding face-huggers by Ripley. Unfortunately, Newt's story ends on a down note. After having been tucked safely away in hypersleep, a face-hugger mysteriously appears, and crawls atop her solitary hibernation chamber. The horrible implication is clear: the little girl must die to set up the action in ALIEN 3.

Mike Richardson takes the discarded material from Cameron's film, and weaves a spellbinding tale of horror that is both familiar and at the same time terrifying. Those fans of the series who already own the laserdisc version of ALIENS, with the restored footage, will no doubt find the Richardson connecting scenes interesting. Others who have not seen the final director's cut of the film will find this series a must addition to their collection of comic books.

June-August 1992 - ALIEN 3 - Three-Issue Series, Color. Writer: Steven Grant. Based on the screenplay by David Giler, Walter Hill and Larry Ferguson. Penciller: Christopher Taylor. Inker: Rick Magyar. Letterer: Jim Massara. Colorist: Matt Webb. Cover by Arthur Swydam.

The three-issue series of ALIEN 3, scripted by Steven Grant from the screenplay by David Giler, Walter

Hill and Larry Ferguson, was very faithful to the film, and gave readers a chance to experience the conclusion with their eyes open this time. With interior illustrations penciled by Christopher Taylor and inked by Rick Magyar, the series also boasted three outstanding covers by Arthur Swydam. In many ways, this comic adaptation was far better than David Fincher's dark, nihilistic film.

April-July, 1993 — ALIENS: COUNTDOWN — Serialized in Dark Horse INSIDER. Writer: Mike Richardson. Artist: Denis Beauvais.

ALIENS: COUNTDOWN was a collection of thrilling fan favorites from Dark Horse INSIDER by Mike Richardson and Denis Beauvais.

May 1993 — ALIENS: SACRIFICE — One-Shot, Color, Squarebound. Writer: Peter Milligan. Artist: Paul Johnson. Letterer: Ellie De Ville. Editor: Dick Hansom. Painted Cover by Paul Johnson.

Originally serialized in Dark Horse U.K.'s ALIENS title, ALIENS: SACRIFICE was a one-shot issue which may have presented the most disturbing and emotionally powerful story in the series. Stranded on a remote planet when her Missionary drop ship crashes, Ann McKay takes shelter in an isolated village that is being terrorized by an Alien. She soon discovers that its inhabitants are harboring an appalling secret. They have been creating test-tube babies, created genetically in the lab, to feed to the alien menace. But in order to save the souls of the villagers and destroy the monster, she must face her own innermost demons. Writer Peter Milligan, who scripted several BATMAN stories, and artist Paul Johnson, of BOOKS OF MAGIC fame, weave an exciting and complex tale of mystery and terror that goes right to the heart of the ALIENS mythology.

April-July, 1993 — ALIENS: ROGUE — 4-Part Series, Color. Writer: Ian Edginton. Artist: Will Simpson. Letterer: John Costanza. Editors: Anina Bennet and Ryder Windham Colorist: Robbie Busch. Painted Cover by Will Simpson.

Ian Edginton's ALIENS: ROGUE, a four-part series illustrated by Will Simpson, offered readers a startling glimpse into the heart of madness, both of the individual and society. On an isolated asteroid colony, known as Charon Base, Professor Ernst Kleist has been experimenting with the indigenous alien life-forms. His research

into the D.N.A. reflex, identified as Project Chimera, shows that an Alien exhibits certain physical characteristics "inherited" from its host. He has cloned a set of human "dummies" to test his theories with the hope that the Alien might, one day, become man's tool instead of adversary. Kleist has also developed a "kind of dog whistle," which disrupts the impulses of the Alien's central nervous system, to keep the creature in check. His work, though very radical and morally wrong, is apparently sanctioned by the Z.T.C. corporation.

Despite the angry protests of the colony's military commander, most of the Marines stationed there are secretly being "executed" by the Company. The remaining "grunts" are being sent to their deaths in a nasty new kind of bug-hunt. Kray, who may be a company spy, and Captain Palmer investigate those charges, and discover Kleist has been harvesting Aliens by numerous methods that are both unethical and illegal. Since Kleist's attempts to breed a tame Alien Queen have failed, the mad doctor tries a new approach — one that involves using Kray's DNA, with or without his consent.

The genetically engineered Alien King, mutated from Kray's cells, emerges but then refrains from attacking the injured Kray. Kleist's attempts to breed a "tame" Alien seem to have finally paid off; unfortunately, his latest creation proves to be dangerously unpredictable, and attacks the other specimens. On another part of the station, the elite Sci-Tech patrol, under Company orders, attempt to hunt down and kill Palmer before he reveals what he's seen. The Marine captain evades capture, and enlists the aid of Deegan and some of his remaining men to rescue Kray from the mad scientist.

In the heart-pounding conclusion, Kleist's Alien King wreaks havoc upon Charon base, while Kray, Palmer and the every-resourceful Deegan escape in the last shuttlecraft from the Aliens and Sci-Tech forces. Will Simpson's art brings all the visual style and excitement that had made the films so appealing, and Edginton, who previously scripted the excellent TERMINATOR: THE ENEMY WITHIN series, turns in a complex and compelling work. Ian's work in the series allows you to glance into the heart of madness, while at the same time contemplating man's place in the cosmos and the role science has to play.

January, February, March, April, May, August, September 1993, February 1992 (Cont.) — ALIENS: COLONIAL MARINES — 12-Part Series, Color. Writers: Chris Warner and Kelley Puckett. Pencillers: Tony Akins and Allen Nunis. Inker: Paul Guinan. Letterer: Clem Robins. Editors: Dan Thorsland and Randy Stradley. Colorist: Matt Hollinsworth. Painted Cover by Roger Mentor and Joe Phillips.

The life of a "grunt" in the Colonial Marine Corps was the focus of a twelve-issue maxi-series titled ALIENS: COLONIAL MARINES. While the action was still unfolding at the time of this writing, the central focus seem to be centered around Carmen Vasquez. Still angry about the death of her sister (as depicted in James Cameron's ALIENS, 1986), Vasquez has enlisted as a private to fight "bugs." She gets very little respect from her fellow soldiers or her tough-as-nails drill sergeant. After a very close encounter with Aliens aboard an orbiting space station, Vasquez and her fellow Marines are sent to the only major city on Bracken's World to fight an Alien infestation problem. Beliveau, a high-powered Company man, accompanies them on the journey to the remote planet to oversee several clandestine research projects. (Chief among these projects is the bizarre attempt to create an Alien-human hybrid — a Bug-Man.)

Their first battle with the Aliens ends in disaster as the Colonial Marines are forced to fight the death-dealing, indestructible monsters on two fronts. Vastly outnumbered, Lt. Henry attempts to rally the local colonists against the approaching Alien army. (Beliveau, in the meantime, has met with his hybrid creations, and planned several well-organized attacks.) The series comes to a climatic showdown as the Marines and colonists go toe-to-toe with the forces of the maniacal Bug-Men. ALIENS: COLONIAL MARINES comes from several highly-talented members of the comic book community, including the author of numerous BATMAN ADVENTURES and the illustrator of the CLASSIC STAR WARS series. Intrigue, suspense and mind-blowing action are the hallmarks of this series.

July, September, November 1993, January, March, May 1994 (cont.) — ALIENS-PREDATOR: DEADLIEST OF THE SPECIES — 12-Part Series, Color. Writer: Chris Claremont. Penciller: Jackson Guice. Inkers: John Beatty and Eduardo Barreto. Letterer: Tom Orzechowski. Editor: Diana Schutz. Colorist: Gregory Wright. Painted Cover by John Bolton.

The second confrontation between those insatiable interstellar hunters, known as the Predators, and their death-dealing indestructible prey, the Aliens was explored in Chris Claremont's well-scripted ALIENS-PREDATOR: DEADLIEST OF THE SPECIES.

In a skyliner high above the Alien-contaminated Earth, Caryn Delacroix can't seem to sleep. Terrifying images of pursuit, disfigurement, and bloody death have invaded not only her peaceful dreams but also her safe and privileged world. She can't distinguish whether the dreams are only nightmares or reflections of some other life. Soon the beautiful trophy-consort of corporate magnate Lucien Delacroix discovers that her dreams and ultimate fate are in the hands of a Predator, who whispers cryptically "Ash....Parnall." Though unfinished at the time of this writing, the twelve-issue maxi-series from the renowned writer of the X-MEN was a chilling mix of classic science fiction and traditional horror. Claremont's Caryn Delacroix emerges as a highly resourceful figure, much like Ellen Ripley, as her story twists and turns through a labyrinth of nightmare and reality. Jackson Guice and John Beatty, co-workers on THE TERMINATOR: ENDGAME, deliver some of the best work of their careers, and the cover paintings by John Bolton are simply stunning.

September-December 1993 — ALIENS: LABYRINTH — 4-Part Series, Color. Writer: Jim Woodring. Artist: Kilian Plunkett. Letterer: Ellie De Ville. Editor: Ryder Windham. Colorist: Matt Hollinsworth. Painted Cover by Kilian Plunkett.

Dark Horse Comics returns to familiar ground with Jim Woodring's ALIENS: LABYRINTH. Illustrated by newcomer Kilian Plunkett, who won the assignment after sending unsolicited copies of his layouts to the publishers, the story details yet-another mad scientist's work with the Alien. Colonel Dr. Anthony Crespi has been sent to Innominata station to investigate the clandestine research of Colonel Dr. Church. At first, he is given only limited access to the mad doctor's work — something to do with a telephantine drug which helps to immobilize Alien warriors by making humans appear invulnerable. However, Sharon McGuinness, a research technician who lost her boyfriend recently to one of Church's experiments, is convinced that the doctor is up to no good, and informs Crespi of her suspicions. The Colonel can't really take action based on accusation; he needs physical proof.

Eventually, McGuinness produces evidence that shows all the crew's medical records have been altered for the past five years. Many military members have died, but no one seems to know what happened to their bodies. Together with Crespi, she infiltrates Church's secret chamber beyond K-lab and discovers the horrible truth. He has been using the dead bodies, in conjunction with his five Alien specimens, for Frankenstein-like research. Unfortunately, before they can reveal the horrible truth, Church locks them in a labyrinthine structure, and unleashes his pet Alien warriors.

Even though the story is a familiar one, with humans trying to domesticate Aliens for their own purposes, the writing is still dark and disturbing — particularly the last frame of the series. Kilian Plunkett strikes a chilling balance in his artwork between the hideousness and bizarre kind of beauty of the Aliens. Jim's writing and Kilian's art combine to create a sense of tension and dread that carries readers from one end of this tremendous series to the other.

November 1993 — ALIENS: SALVATION — One-Shot, Color, Squarebound. Writer: Daniel Gibbons. Penciller: Mike Mignola. Inker: Kevin Nowlan. Letterer: Clem Robins. Editors: Anina Bennett and Ryder Windham. Colorist: Matt Hollingsworth. Designer: Scott Tice. Painted Cover by Mike Mignola.

ALIENS: SALVATION was a one-shot comic conceived by Daniel Gibbons. Three survivors of the Nova Maru, a Company ship which has been recruiting humans from backworld colonies to serve its unusual cargo, find themselves trapped on a hostile, jungle world with their cargo, a horde of alien warriors. Selkirk, the ship's religious cook, is bothered by dreams about dying at the hands of the death-dealing, indestructible monsters, and prays for some type of salvation. First Officer Dean fears the dark and for her own sanity. Captain Foss, who's gone completely mad, soon dies, and provides sustenance for the other two. Ultimately, surrounded by the Aliens, they are forced to destroy their ship, in order to kill as many creatures as possible. Dark and nihilistic, Gibbons' story was a tremendous departure from others being published by Dark Horse. Credit Mike Mignola, Kevin Nowlan, Matt Hollingsworth and Scott Tice for some outstanding artistry and design work.

January-April 1994 — ALIENS: MUSIC OF THE SPEARS 4-Part —Series, Color. Writer: Chet Williamson. Penciller: Tim Hamilton.. Inker: Timothy Bradstreet. Letterer: Clem Robins.. Editors: Bob Cooper and Jerry Prosser. Colorist: Matt Webb.. Painted Cover by Timothy Bradstreet and Guy Burwell.

ALIENS: MUSIC OF THE SPEARS, the most recent (but certainly not the last) series from Dark Horse Comics, offered quite an unusual variation. Written with Chet Williamson, with pencils by Tim Hamilton and inks by Timothy Bradstreet, the story introduced Damon Eddington to its growing collection of madmen. Damon, the most popular musical entertainer represented by the multicorporation SynSound, wants an Alien for his next recording. He is convinced the sound of hatred, rage and fury are exactly what he needs for his new "sound." Predictably, Damon becomes so obsessed with his new possession that he must continue to feed the Alien with new victims in order to feed his own sick, twisted desires. He calls upon his Ninja assistant Ahiro to first procure drugged-out vagrants, then cultists, and sound technicians. Finally, Damon realizes the only "sound" he doesn't possess is the sound of his own screams, and he sacrifices himself. In the dramatic conclusion, the Alien escapes captivity, and terrorizes the punked-out rockers at Presley Hall. Chet's story is a profound metaphor for the excesses of drugs and rock-n-roll in contemporary society. The illustrations are first rate, including a series of wonderfully realized covers by Timothy Bradstreet and Guy Burwell.

1993 — ALIENS: ASSORTED STORIES 1-10 Ten-Part Series, in association with Kenner Toys, Color. Various writers and artists.

In addition to the various comics and graphic novels, Dark Horse Comics also produced a series of children's mini-comics to be included with the Kenner line of action figures. These comics, numbered 1-10, told stories about the individual characters, from Lt. Ripley and Hicks to Sgt. Apone and the Mantis alien. Sometime in the future, when humans have begun to explore space, Colonial Marines guard the frontier, and protect colonists from the dreaded Alien warriors. The stories are somewhat simplistic, but the artwork is quite sensational.

CHAPTER SIX
PARODIES, PASTICHES AND RIP-OFFS

The box office success of Ridley Scott's ALIEN (1979) and James Cameron's ALIENS (1986) spawned a host of clones, parodies and pastiches. In fact, no sooner had one completed its run at the local multi-plex, another was waiting to take its place. But just as ALIEN and its two high-powered sequels had been influenced by the low budget science fiction films of the Fifties and Sixties, the critically-acclaimed series inspired its own collection of imitators, including INSEMINOID (1980), THE CREATURE WASN'T NICE (1981), GALAXINA (1981), GALAXY OF TERROR (1981), THE THING (1982), CREATURE (1983) and many others. Most of those productions failed to generate any popular enthusiasm, and quickly died at the box office. Others that received the favor of audiences seemingly generated their own host of sequels and imitators. ALIEN was no longer just a Twentieth Century-Fox franchise but a whole industry unto itself. Similarly, H.R. Giger's distinctive bio-mechanical designs began appearing in numerous films with the same regularity. Hollywood had apparently discovered an idea source for inspiration.

1980 — SATURN THREE — Transcontinental Film Productions, 87 min. Director and Producer: Stanley Donen Screenwriter: Martin Amis. Based upon ideas by John Barry. Starring: Farrah Fawcett, Kirk Douglas, Harvey Keitel, Douglas Lambert, and Ed Bishop.

A dark thriller reminiscent of Ridley Scott's ALIEN (1979), SATURN THREE (1980) effectively combined elements from Gothic horror classics with traditional science fiction themes. Released less than one year after Twentieth Century-Fox's classic, this misunderstood motion picture was not very well-received by critics or audience goers; but over the years, it has gained a certain cult status among the Cyberpunk crowd for its gritty portrayal of a film noir future.

Farrah Fawcett and Kirk Douglas play two research scientists who are studying advance techniques of food production on the third moon of Saturn. When a deranged scientist (Harvey Keitel), who dreams of creat-

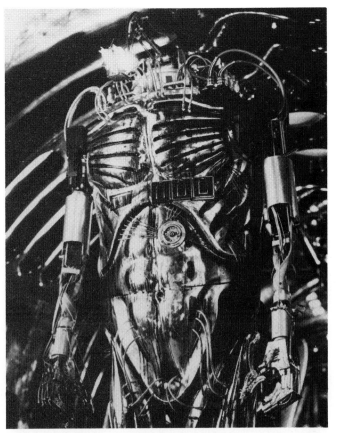

Saturn 3 *brought some of the basic design concepts of* **Alien** *to the world of robotics (photo copyright ©1979 AFD)*

ing a super-race of robots, arrives, their innocent little paradise is threatened. He creates the first of his robot race, an eight-foot tall Hector, and imprints his brainwave patterns on its memory bank. But since Keitel is imperfect, his creation shares his imperfections. Hector destroys its creator, then lustfully chases Fawcett through the dark, claustrophobic corridors of the space station. Ultimately, Douglas must sacrifice his life in order to destroy Hector, so that she can survive and safely deliver their work to a dying mother earth.

The film was first started by set designer John Barry, who had worked on SUPERMAN (1978), then later completed by Stanley Donen when Barry took ill and died. Their collaborative effort is a dark, cynical feature that combines elements from Mary Shelley's Frankenstein with Ridley Scott's thriller. The mad doctor's creation (Hector) is a blank tablet, neither good nor evil; but when it receives the deranged scientist's lustful or destructive personality, it becomes lustful and destructive. Like Frankenstein's benign creature, science and technology have much to offer humanity; they are neither good nor evil. But when science and technology are perverted by madness, they become instruments to be feared. Stuart Craig's designs for the eight-foot tall robots are clearly inspired by the bio-mechanical world of Hans Rudi Giger. SATURN THREE's dark, nihilistic tone also evokes David Fincher's dismal ALIEN 3, and is certainly worth another look.

1980 — GALAXINA — Marimar/Crown International, 95 min. Director and Screenwriter: William Sachs. Producer: Marilyn J. Tenser. Starring: Stephen Macht, Dorothy Stratten, James David Hinton, and Avery Schreiber.

GALAXINA (1980) was an intergalactic spoof of STAR WARS (1977), ALIEN (1979) and dozens of other science fiction pictures. Galaxina (Dorothy Stratten) is the perfect female android — sexy, attractive and very subservient to male partners. There's just one problem that keeps her from being totally equipped as a female, and that makes consummating a relationship with her human lover (Stephen Macht) difficult. After retrieving the all-powerful "Blue Star" from Altar I, the two potential lovers agree to review the mail-order catalog for the correct android part. The film's American opening was regrettably marred by the death of the former Playmate model Dorothy Stratten by her estranged husband. (Those unfortunate incidents were recorded in DEATH OF A CENTERFOLD: THE DOROTHY STRATTEN STORY, 1981, and STAR '80, 1983.)

Part parody and part pastiche, GALAXINA not only pokes fun at ALIEN but also pays worthy homage by introducing its own "chest-buster" which is choked up by Captain Avery Schreiber. The cute little creature, designed by Chris Walas, easily manages to evade capture, but appears at the most inappropriate times. Walas who would later create Gremlins for Joe Dante and the Oscar-winning makeup for THE FLY (1986), depicts the chest-buster with loving eyes, a winning smile, and a single snaggle-tooth. Cute and humorously effective.

1980 — INSEMINOID (a.k.a. HORROR PLANET) — Jupiter Film Productions, 92 min. Director: Norman J. Warren. Producers: Richard Gordon and David Speechley. Screenwriters: Nick Maley and Gloria Maley. Starring: Robin Clark, Jennifer Ashley, Stephanie Beacham, Judy Geeson, Steven Grives, and Barry Houghton.

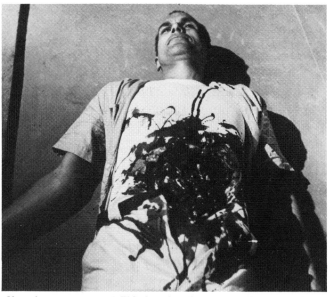

Chest-busters anyone? This is a familiar moment from Inseminoid *(photo copyright ©1980 Jupiter Film Productions, Inc.)*

This low-low budget retelling of ALIEN deposits a group of male and female astronauts on a forbidden world where they discover the remains of some lost civilization. The crew's archaeologist (Judy Geeson), determined to uncover the secret of the ruins, decides to remain behind, and is subsequently raped by a long-dormant monster. She later gives birth to its mutant offspring. Her fellow astronauts attempt to destroy the crawling terror, but it quickly grows to full-size. Relentlessly, the creature stalks and murders the members of the crew. (As usual in films like this, the crew behaves rather stupidly, and make easy prey for the creature.) The captain and remaining survivors attempt to contain the monster, but it soon breaks free and pursues them right to the dismal end.

Conceived by director Norman Warren and his writers as an attempt to combine elements of science fiction and horror, the plotline is an almost scene by scene remake of ALIEN, beginning with the first discovery of the alien civilization and climaxing with the destruction of the monster. Those analogous scenes are complimented by similarities in the make-up of the crew and the set design of the space ships. Even the alien creatures share a common link. Both are bio-mechanical in form, and follow a similar life-cycle, by first gestating within a human host, then emerging and maturing into a nearly indestructible monster. However, the film's special effects are remarkably unsophisticated, and the rubber-suited monster is less than credible.

The British motion picture, whose original title was HORROR PLANET, was ultimately cut for release in the United States, thus eliminating about six minutes worth of excessive gore and grue.

1981 — ALIEN CONTAINMENT — Cannon Films/Italian Pictures, 85 min. Director and Screenwriter: Lewis Coates. Producer: Claudio Mancini. Starring: Ian McCulloch, Louis Monroe, Sigfried Rauch, Martin Mase, and Lisa Hahn.

Like INSEMINOID, ALIEN CONTAINMENT (1981) was another attempt to profit from the enormous popularity of Ridley Scott's thriller. A cyclopian creature from Mars tricks a former astronaut (Siegfried Rauch) into helping spread its alien eggs all over the earth. (Apparently, the Martian menace has plans to take over the world by hatching its own army of monsters.) When a ship laden with the eggs finally lands in New York City (with every member of its crew dead), the alien threat is discovered. The astronaut's mission commander (Ian McCulloch) teams with a Brooklyn cop (Martin Mase) and a government agent (Louis Monroe) to track the eggs back to their source. Writer/Director Lewis Coates guides audiences through a very familiar landscape to a predictable conclusion. The premise appears to be borrowed from creative musings about the eventual introduction of Aliens (from the movie ALIEN) to earth, and even the title suggests a connection to the popular Fox franchise.

1981 — THE CREATURE WASN'T NICE (a.k.a. SPACESHIP) — Creature Feature Productions, 88 min. Director and Screenwriter: Bruce Kimmel. Producer: Mark Haggard. Starring: Cindy Williams, Bruce Kimmel, Leslie Nielsen, Gerrit Graham, Patrick MacNee and Ron Kurowski.

A good-natured parody of ALIEN, THE CREATURE WASN'T NICE (1981) attempted to not only pay homage to the traditions of science fiction and horror but also capture the scattershot humor of AIRPLANE! (1980) in its comic send-up of genres. The loony crew of Spaceship, led by stalwart captain Leslie Nielsen (poking fun at this role in FORBIDDEN PLANET, 1956) and mad doctor Patrick MacNee, take aboard an alien life-form that quickly transmutes into a monster (Ron Kurowski). MacNee

Leslie Nielsen parodied his Forbidden Planet *role in* The Creature Wasn't Nice

attempts to control the creature through his highly-advanced computer; but the alien breaks away and begins performing a song-and-dance number entitled "I Want to Eat Your Face" moments before eating the doctor. Cindy Williams, as the token female member of the crew, tracks the monster through the claustrophobic interiors of her ship, and eventually confronts it. Predictably, all the creature wanted was love. Writer/Director Bruce Kimmel attempts to work miracles with his limited budget, and some of the time the humor actually works.

1981 — GALAXY OF TERROR (a.k.a. MINDWARP: AN INFINITY OF TERROR and PLANET OF HORRORS) — New World Pictures, 80 min. Director: B. D. Clark. Producers: Roger Corman and Marc Siegler. Screenwriters: Clark and Siegler. Starring: Edward Albert, Erin Moran, Ray Walston, Zalman Kind, Robert Englund, Sid Haig, Bernard Behrens and Taaffe O'Connell.

GALAXY OF TERROR (1981), Roger Corman's low-budget rip-off of ALIEN, owes as much to FORBIDDEN PLANET (1956) and George Orwell's novel 1984 as the Ridley Scott thriller. Handsomely produced, with superior set designs and special effects by James Cameron and Robert Skotak, this was clearly the best of the imitators that followed in the wake of ALIEN's success.

After traveling for more than a year in hyperspace, Captain Edward Albert and his crew arrive at a forbidden world. Dispatched by Earth base to investigate

Cool Alien-esque art utilized in the promotion of **Galaxy of Terror**

tures, and they must surrender their primitive fears in order to survive.

The evil monsters in GALAXY OF TERROR are the synthesis of all their petty jealousies and unspeakable desires transformed into bio-mechanical nightmares. Like the "id" monster in FORBIDDEN PLANET (1956) and its lineal descendant in ALIEN, the invisible forces grow and mutate, becoming larger and more terrible, with each attack. Despite the best efforts of the crew, they are unable to destroy the alien menace until they begin thinking on the same instinctual levels. Though derivative of many different sources, the motion picture still remains very thought-provoking. The alien pyramid and bio-mechanical landscape, credited to Cameron, appear to be "borrowed" from Giger's discarded ALIEN material. [Note: the film was released under a number of different titles, including MINDWARP: AN INFINITY OF TERROR and PLANET OF HORRORS, by New World Pictures.]

1981 — THE INTRUDER WITHIN — ABC/Circle Films, 100 min. Director: Peter Carter. Starring: Chad Everett, Joseph Bottoms, Jennifer Warren, Rockne Tarkington, and Lynda Mason Green.

ABC attempted to rip off the Alien films in their TV movie **The Intruder Within** *(photo copyright © ABC)*

the fate of a lost spaceship, which was supposed to have crashed there years before, they discover an alien pyramid and its bio-mechanical interior. Later that night, a crew member is murdered by some strange invisible force, which literally rends and tears the astronaut apart. The ship's doctor (Ray Walston) suspects the pyramid may hold the answers to his death, and they venture inside the structure in search parties of two. Eventually, they discover the remains of a buried civilization, abandoned millions of years before by its builders, and a whole array of monsters from their subconscious id. The lone female (Erin Moran, of HAPPY DAYS fame) is raped by a giant worm, and several others are gruesomely killed. The Captain soon learns that the pyramid has the power to convert their worst fears into monstrous crea-

THE INTRUDER WITHIN (1981), a made-for-television movie for ABC, simply moved the action aboard the Nostromo (from ALIEN) to an isolated, oil-drilling rig in the North Atlantic. When a primeval creature is roused from its million-year slumber in the ocean depths, it climbs aboard the rig and impregnates Linda Mason Green. She eventually gives birth to its hideous off-spring, a slithering chest burster-like thing, that matures rapidly into a full-grown beastie. The blood-thirsty creature pursues Oil-rig workers (commanded by heroic Chad Everett) through the claustrophobic interiors of the drilling platform, killing them one by one. It is soon cornered, and forced to return to the ocean depths. Directed with top-notch precision by Peter Carter and featuring some winning performances by Everett and Bottoms, the real star of the picture is the hideous sea-creature. The strange cross between a lizard and a bio-mechanoid designed by James Cummins and Henry Golas is some-how very familiar.

Fangs for the memories! Roger Corman takes on Alien *in* Forbidden World *(photo copyright ©1982 New World Pictures)*

1981 — SCARED TO DEATH (a.k.a. SYNGENOR) — Lone Star Films, 90 min. Director and Screenwriter: William Malone. Producer: Bill Dunn. Starring: John Stinson, Diana Davidson, David Moses and Toni Janotta.

The creature in William Malone's SCARED TO DEATH (1981) was a synthetically-created genetic organism (or Syngenor) that sucked the spinal fluid from its victims (with the help of a forked tongue). Released into the sewer systems of suburban Los Angeles by a mad scientist who has been experimenting with volatile chemicals, the Syngenor strikes randomly throughout the metropolis. Eventually, the film's nominal hero must venture into the subterranean depths to find and destroy the creature. Featuring lines, like "I do not intend to just sit here and let my face get ripped off," the motion picture was simply a low-low budget attempt to capitalize on ALIEN. However, unlike the other blatant rip-offs, Malone does acknowledge his source material, and credit Giger with the inspiration for his bio-mechanical monster (built by Jim Suthors). [Note: the film has recently appeared on the Sci-Fi Channel under the name SYNGENOR.]

1982 — FORBIDDEN WORLD (a.k.a. MUTANT) — New World Pictures, 86 min. Director: Allan Holzman. Producer: Roger Corman. Screenwriter: Tim Curren. Starring: Jesse Vint, June Chadwick, Dawn Dunlap, Linden Chiles, Fox Harris and Raymond Oliver.

The second of Roger Corman's ALIEN rip-offs, FORBIDDEN WORLD was regrettably an exercise in recycling rather than a legitimate filmmaking. Produced to make use of the sets built for GALAXY OF TERROR (1981) as well as unused battle footage from BATTLE BEYOND THE STARS (1980) — both a product of James Cameron's skillful design talents — the film told a very familiar story. Scientists discover and unwittingly release an alien parasite that grows and mutates into a bio-mechanoid. Investigative troubleshooter Jesse Vint arrives, in the nick of time, and feeds the monster the cancerous liver of one of the scientists. The creature promptly dies. Designed by Steve Neil and John Carl Buechler and sculpted by Robert and Dennis Skotak, the alien creature bears a striking resemblance to Giger's original conception for the Alien. Both are man-like in form, though inhumanly strong and nearly indestructible; both have razor-sharp teeth and claws for rending and tearing victims, and both seem to follow a similar life-cycle. Surprisingly, neither the Swiss surrealist nor Twentieth Century-Fox contemplated filing charges of design and copyright infringement.

1982 — PARASITE — Charles Band Productions, 85 min. Director and Producer: Charles Band. Screenwriters: Alan J. Adler, Michael Shoob and Frank Levering. Starring: Robert Glaudini, Demi Moore, James Davidson, Al Fann, Luca Bercovici and Cherie Currie.

Director Charles Band's PARASITE (1982) combined horror elements from ALIEN, MAD MAX (1979) and David Cronenberg's THE PARASITE MURDERS (1974) to produce this gimmick-laden quickie for the 3-D renaissance that never really came. In the repressive, post-holocaust world of the near future, a government research scientist (Robert Glaudini) produces a species of human-symbiont that will help solve many of the world's problems. His totalitarian government, however, wants the parasitic creature, which takes root in the human host, trained to turn monstrous in order to destroy mutant punks which threaten society. In an attempt to protect his creation, the scientist implants the parasite inside himself and races into the California desert. The organism soon devours the insides of its human host, and emerges to continue its eating frenzy. Eventually, the parasite finds itself caught between the government forces, on one side, and the mutant survivors, on the other. It chooses to chase Demi Moore instead through the claustrophobic interiors of an isolated complex before facing its own annihilation. Charles Band's foray into the field of low budget genre films has all the visual pace and styling of a classic horror film, even though the narrative logic is somewhat strained and the plot is derivative of half a dozen other films.

1982 - THE THING - Universal Pictures, 109 min. Director: John Carpenter. Producers: Davis Foster and Lawrence Turman. Screenwriter: Bill Lancaster. Based on the novella "Who Goes There?" by John W. Campbell. Starring: Kurt Russell, A. Wilford Brimley, T.K. Carter, David Clennon, Keith David, Richard Dysart and Charles Hallahan.

Though supposedly based on the 1938 novella "Who Goes There?" by John W. Campbell rather than the Howard Hawks' classic, John Carpenter's THE THING (1982) was, in fact, an inspired pastiche of ALIEN. But Carpenter does more than simply redress the story with a new locale and a different collection of characters. He dispenses with many of the tired, overworked conventions of the science fiction genre, and plunges his audience into a Gothic horror tale of spine-tingling terror, dismemberment, mutilation, paranoia and betrayal.

The discovery of a flying saucer embedded in the snow near an Antarctic research station makes the civilian and military personnel (including Kurt Russell, A. Wilford Brimley, T.K. Carter, David Clennon, Keith David, Richard Dysart and Charles Hallahan) suspicious of one another's intentions. Predictably, they recover the only

Make-up maestro Rob Bottin and friend on the set of John Carpenter's remake of The Thing *(photo copyright ©1982 Universal City Studios)*

survivor of its crew — a carnivorous, shape-changing creature — and bring its frozen body to the safety of their encampment. Once the creature thaws, it begins to take on the identity and physical make-up of each person it encounters, killing and draining the very essence of life. The station's resident mad doctor (Dysart) urges the others to capture the "thing" alive, while the rebellious Russell simply wants to destroy it as long as he can determine which person the monster has replaced. Eventually, he figures out an ingenious way to find out the truth, but by then, the alien creature has already burned half the research station to the ground. Knowing that they will soon be frozen to death, Russell sits quietly with a fellow survivor (David), and asks him if he is friend or foe.

Even though the action in John Carpenter's remake of THE THING takes place entirely on earth, the structure and general plotting of the film recalls elements of ALIEN by former collaborator Dan O'Bannon. Both films open with a small, isolated group of explorers discovering the remains of an alien spacecraft. By accident, they introduce an alien lifeform into their environment, which matures and later destroys their fellow members. Each creature undergoes an unusual transformation which changes its cellular structure and form. Though ultimately man-like in shape, the aliens are essentially bio-mechanical in design, and virtually invulnerable to conventional means of attack. Both groups try every means possible to destroy the creature, and are eventually reduced down in numbers to one or two survivors. The claustrophobic environments of the research station in the Antarctic — with its collection of cramped underground passageways, control center and convenient airducts — are also strangely reminiscent of the twisting corridors of the Nostromo's three levels. In fact, the alien creature instinctively knows the best routes through the maze of corridors, and times each attack appropriately when only one human is present. The plots, though similar in nature, are like most murder mysteries, exercises in mounting terror, beginning with the initial discovery and moving carefully through each murder to the bitter end.

THE THING was not very well-received in its day, having debuted just weeks after Steven Spielberg's cute and cuddly E.T.-THE EXTRATERRESTRIAL. Critics who praised the motion picture for returning to the original source material were nonetheless offended by its non-stop violence and gruesome special effects. Over the years, the film has developed a cult following, like Carpenter's DARK STAR (1974) and ESCAPE FROM NEW YORK (1981), and continues to delight new fans nearly a dozen years later in spite of its derivative origins.

1985 — LIFEFORCE—THE SPACE VAMPIRES — MGM/United Artists, in association with Cannon Films, 100 min. Director: Tobe Hooper. Producers: Golan and Globus. Screenwriters: Dan O'Bannon and Don Jakoby. Based on the novel The Space Vampires by Colin Wilson. Starring: Steve Railsback, Frank Finlay, Peter Firth, Michael Gothard, Nicholas Ball, Patrick Stewart and Mathilda May.

Like ALIEN, LIFEFORCE—THE SPACE VAMPIRES (1985) from director Tobe Hooper was yet another attempt to combine the traditional elements of science fiction with horror. The vampire is depicted as something very alien, threatening human existence, certainly not an ordinary force with which common people can come to terms. Based on the popular science fiction novel by Colin Wilson, the vampire is also an astral force which must return to earth every seventy-seven years to replenish its "life force." Like Dracula and all his predecessors, these beings survive on human vitality, but instead of blood, they must drain the very essence, or soul, of their victims.

An exploration of the space vampires' space craft results in a realm very similar to the one established in the first Alien (photo copyright ©1985 Tri-Star Pictures)

The story, set in the near future, begins in deep space as seven astronauts, aboard a British-American spaceshuttle rendezvous with Halley's Comet. They discover in the comet's corona a strange, derelict spacecraft which appears to be centuries old. The mission commander, Captain Carlsen (Steve Railsback), unable to contact earth, decides to investigate the craft. Exploring the otherworldly environment, the landing party finds amazing architecture, huge organic formations, and creatures that resemble giant bats. Farther into the craft, they discover three comatose bodies — one woman and two men — that appear humanoid. Carlsen becomes telepathically linked to the woman and orders his men to bring them aboard the ship. But in doing so, the space vampires consume the entire crew except the captain. The female wants him, but he resists her charms and sabotages the shuttle. Unfortunately, a rescue ship returns them all safely to earth.

Once on earth, the vampires escape their confinement at a London scientific installation and begin to ravage the country. Hans Fallada (Frank Finlay), a criminologist known as "the Sherlock Holmes of psychology," suspects the true nature of the vampires and enlists Carlsen's aide in tracking them down. But the space vampires can leave their original bodies to possess other beings as "mind parasites," and the hunt becomes an impossible one. Eventually, the vampires and their victims consume most of Britain and threaten to spread the terror to Europe and American. Carlsen fights his way through the destructive chaos and offers himself to the female in exchange for the safety of the world. She accepts, and though he betrays his word by impaling her on a stake, she teleports the two of them aboard her "revived" spacecraft, and pilots the ship into deep space.

Although LIFEFORCE—THE SPACE VAMPIRES owes much of its plot and visual style to films like PLAN-ET OF THE VAMPIRES (1965), QUEEN OF BLOOD (1966) and HORROR OF THE BLOOD CREATURES (1971), its most direct link is to Ridley Scott's ALIEN. Scripted by Dan O'Bannon (with Dan Jakoby), the plotline is strongly reminiscent of his original treatment for ALIEN. Interstellar vampires have simply replaced his indestructible juggernaut as the central menace, but his collection of astronauts are not all that different from the courageous, one-dimensional crew. The production design, from the bio-mechanical interiors of the craft to the look of the creatures, by John Graysmark derives much from H.R. Giger's original ideas as well.

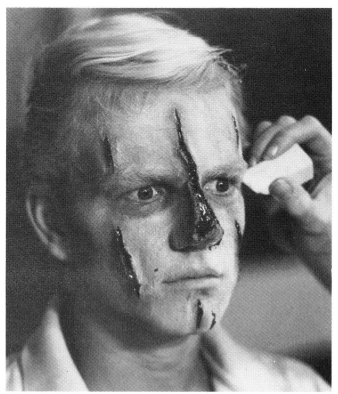

This behind the scenes photo from **Creature** *shows a victim being prepared for his death by a xenomorph*

1986 — THE TITAN FIND (a.k.a. CREATURE) — Trans-World Entertainment, 100 min. Director: William Malone. Producer: Bill Dunn. Based on an original story by William Malone. Starring: Klaus Kinski, Stan Ivar, Wendy Schaal and Diane Salinger.

Dark, expertly photographed in shadowy interiors that recall the claustrophobic paranoia of Howard Hawks' THE THING (FROM ANOTHER WORLD) and reminding audiences of Ridley Scott's ALIEN, THE TITAN FIND (a.k.a. CREATURE, 1985) was clearly more a remake of PLANET OF THE VAMPIRES. William Malone, the thirty-seven year-old director of SCARED TO DEATH (1981), returned to familiar territory for his second feature, but his $4.2 million production does manage to transcend those threadbare plotlines to be a compellingly atmospheric piece of horror fantasy, thanks in part to the film's outstanding production design.

On the surface of Titan, the largest moon of Saturn, a research ship has discovered the remains of an ancient alien laboratory and its collection of seemingly "dead" specimens. One of the specimens, however, is still very much alive, and kills all but one of the crew. The survivor lives long enough to make it back to earth, setting off a race between two competing multi-national firms for possession of whatever they can salvage, both

unaware of just how deadly the alien creature is. Even though the American ship Shenendoah reaches the moon first, it falls through the surface of Titan into the caverns below upon landing. Their discovery of the German ship Richter Dynamics and its mad scientist (Klaus Kinski) leads ultimately to the creature. Its shape-changing abilities confuse and confound the crew with images (such as a naked woman walking on the moon's harsh surface) that cannot possibly be real, then it strikes. Trapped in their small spaceship, with nowhere else to run, the crew is forced to electrocute the alien monster.

The film's rudimentary plot aside, THE TITAN FIND was an effective thriller. Even though audiences have been led down these same narrow, claustrophobic corridors before, Malone still manages to generate a real sense of terror with his expert direction. The outstanding special effects work from the L.A. Effects Group (notably Robert and Dennis Skotak) add immensely to the film's chilling premise and believability. While some moviegoers were quick to dismiss the film as a blatant ALIEN rip-off, Malone defended his creation in a 1985 interview. "I guess it depends on whether you consider ALIEN an original story," he said. "I don't look at that many films as real originals. I know ALIEN had elements of several films in it that I could name, but beyond that, most genre films are pretty derivative. I think that THE TITAN FIND has got some unusual and interesting things in it. Certainly the film is going to be compared to other films, but I don't think you can help that. I actually think there's a lot more of 1950's science fiction in it than anything else, and that it resembles ALIEN because Dan O'Bannon and myself were probably inspired by the same pictures."

Similarities certainly abound between THE TITAN FIND and its direct, lineal descendant PLANET OF THE VAMPIRES. The crew's discovery of a derelict ship and their ultimate conflict with some alien, predatory force, determined to possess them, are played out in much the same way from the opening frames of the film to its conclusion. Other elements in the film are strangely familiar, not the least of which is the alien landscape (while easily attributable to H.R. Giger's designs for the storm-swept planetoid in ALIEN) is drawn from dozens of other films, like THE THING (FROM ANOTHER WORLD, 1951), FORBIDDEN PLANET (1956) and IT! THE TERROR FROM BEYOND SPACE (1958). But then the same thing can be said of a number of other horror fantasies from the Fifties and Sixties. [Note: The title of William Malone's THE TITAN FIND was ultimately changed to CREATURE by its distributor to take advantage of the audiences' continued fascination with ALIEN.]

1986 — INVADERS FROM MARS — Cannon Films, 100 min. Director: Tobe Hooper. Producers: Golan and Globus. Based on the original film by William Cameron Menzies. Starring: Karen Black, Hunter Carson, Timothy Bottoms, Laraine Newman, James Karen, Louise Fletcher, Bud Cort and Jimmy Hunt.

On the surface, INVADERS FROM MARS (1986) by director Tobe Hooper seems like an honest attempt to recapture the magic of the original 1953 feature, but the film was in fact a deliberate ploy by Cannon Films to exploit the popularity of ALIEN's unique designs. Like the original, a youngster (Hunter Carson) is awakened by the sound of a flying saucer in his backyard. When his parents (Timothy Bottoms and Laraine Newman) disappear (while investigating his claim) and return as

changed people, he seeks out the professional help of a psychologist (Karen Black). Soon, as each of his friends, neighbors and even the police begin to display grossly altered personalities, the boy realizes that he is embroiled in a struggle by tentacled Martian creatures to take over the world. Stan Winston made the Martian creatures, and Les Dilley, who worked with Giger on the original ALIEN, designed the bio-mechanical look of the production. At first glance even the Martian vessel appeared Giger-esque in concept, vaguely reminiscent of the derelict spacecraft in ALIEN, although concept illustrator William Stout still maintains (to this day) that the ship was actually inspired by the work of Spanish architect Antonio Gaudi. Simply rent the film on videotape, and judge for yourself.

1987 — PREDATOR (a.k.a. HUNTER) — Twentieth Century Fox, 107 min. Director: John McTiernan. Producers: Joel Silver, Lawrence Gordon, and John Davis. Executive Producers: Laurence Pereira and Jim Thomas. Screenwriters: Jim Thomas and John Thomas. Music Composer: Alan Silvestri. Starring: Arnold Schwarzenegger, Carl Weathers, Elpidia Carrillo, Bill Duke, Jesse Ventura, Shane Black, Sonny Landham, Richard Chaves, R.G. Armstrong, and Kevin Peter Hall.

John McTiernan's PREDATOR (1987) combined elements from RAMBO (1985), COMMANDO (1985), and ALIENS (1986) — which were themselves aggregates of other cinematic productions — to create the perfect hybrid of special effects, science fiction, horror, and action-adventure. Produced by Joel Silver (with the help of Lawrence Gordon and John Davis) and written by Jim and John Thomas, the motion picture also provided Arnold Schwarzenegger with his best starring vehicle since THE TERMINATOR (1984). Although many critics were apt to dismiss the feature as simply another retelling of THE MOST DANGEROUS GAME, it does manage to succeed on almost every level. Packed with spectacular effects, gut-wrenching combat scenes and the best alien bio-mechanoid since ALIEN (1979), PREDATOR went onto become the successor to James Cameron's ALIENS as the box office champion of the year.

In a haunting pre-credits sequence, an unknown space ship rockets toward the earth before depositing a small, one-man craft. The inhabitant of the interstellar craft is an armor-clad, reptilian bio-mechanoid capable of

This **Predator** *comic book, published by Dark Horse, showcases a very different spin on the idea of* **Alien**

near invisibility through a unique "cloaking device." It is a predator, a monster that comes from another planet to hunt other predators for sport. It has been returning to earth for centuries (because of the violent species there known as man), and it has chosen the jungles of Central American for its latest hunt.

Recruited by General Phillips (R.G. Armstrong) and a devious CIA operative named Dillon (Carl Weathers) to rescue hostages held by guerilla fighters in the same Central American jungle (as the predator), Major "Dutch" Schaefer (Arnold Schwarzenegger) and his men embark on a what they believe will be a simple one-day operation. However, as they penetrate the enemy border, the special forces unit becomes the target of the Predator. Through the unique camouflage, the alien

hunter begins stalking the group of soldiers. One by one, the members of the unit are murdered in a mysterious and bloody fashion by an unseen killer. With their roles now revered — the hunters are now the hunted — the men join forces against their common enemy, and attempt to fortify their position with traps and land mines. But since the Predator travels invisibly through the trees, their jungle fortress is quickly penetrated by the foe. Ultimately, Dutch Schaefer must deal with the monster himself.

Stripped of his combat weapons, except a knife and some flares, the career soldier relies upon primitive survival skills to fight the creature. By combining brains and brawn, he sets a series of deadly traps to ensnare the Predator. Then, he lures it onto his battleground. An action-packed final battle between the two ensues, with Schaefer getting the upper hand. Fatally wounded, the alien cynically snarls at Dutch, "I am what you are," and sets off a delayed, self-destruct weapon. Dutch runs for cover, and manages to survive the nuclear explosion that lays waste to the jungle. Hours later, the bruised and badly injured warrior is rescued by General Phillips, and taken to safety.

Written by Jim Thomas and John Thomas, a pair of novice screenwriters, the tale of PREDATOR (then called HUNTER) was immediately snapped up by Twentieth Century-Fox in 1985 as a big-budget follow-up to ALIENS. Critical reaction to the film was generally favorable, with reviewers crediting McTiernan for its breathtaking pace and nonstop action that was not unlike its predecessor. Most fans did not seem to mind that the film was derivative of Jim Cameron's rousing action-adventure. Not surprisingly, Cameron was called upon by the producers to provide his valuable insight when the production stalled due to technical problems with Richard Edlund's creature. Stan Winston eventually redesigned the intergalactic predator as an armor-clad reptilian humanoid with turquoise eyes, toothy mandibles, and Rastafarian hair. Packed with state-of-the-art special effects, plenty of action, a wonderfully realized monster, and a handful of winning performances, PREDATOR was the perfect summer movie extravaganza.

1990 — PREDATOR 2 — Twentieth Century Fox, 108 min. Director: Stephen Hopkins. Producers: Joel Silver, Lawrence Gordon, and John Davis. Screenwriters: Jim Thomas and John Thomas. Music Composer: Alan Silvestri. Starring: Danny Glover, Gary Busey, Ruben Blades, Maria Conchita Alonso, Bill Paxton, Kevin Peter Hall, Robert Davi, Kent McCord, Calvin Lockhart, Adam Baldwin, and Morton Downy Jr.

Director Stephen Hopkins teamed with producers Joel Silver, Lawrence Gordon and John Davis to create the first action-packed sequel to Twentieth Century-Fox's 1987 box office hit. Although PREDATOR 2 (1990) owed much to its high voltage predecessor, the plotline was yet another reworking of ALIENS, this time set in the violence-torn Los Angeles of the future.

Again scripted by Jim Thomas and John Thomas, the new story finds police lieutenant Mike Harrigan (Danny Glover) investigating a series of gang-land murders between rival drug dealers. Enter the Predator, who is drawn by the heat and conflict of the 1997 drug-war, and a mysterious government agent (Gary Busey) who is searching for the extraterrestrial. As the body count increases, Harrigan begins to suspect that there is another force at work in his gang-land battle. He soon learns about Major Schaefer's battle with the Predator in Central America (from the government spook), and must confront the alien creature on its own turf. While aboard the Predator's interstellar craft, Harrigan sees the trophies of its former hunts (including the skull of an Alien), but the investigation is quickly cut short by the appearance of his opponent. Lured onto a final battleground, the two warriors fight to the death, with Harrigan eventually getting the upper hand.

Released in November of 1990, while Fox was still struggling with a third entry in its ALIEN franchise, PREDATOR 2 did not fare as well as its predecessor even though it had the same electrifying special effects and climatic confrontation between man and Predator. The sequel did provide a tantalizing connection to the ALIEN series by revealing the skull of that now-famous, death-dealing indestructible juggernaut in the Predator's trophy case. Perhaps, future entries in either one of the series will explore how that skull got there in the first place . . .

APPENDIX A.

CHECKLIST OF ALIEN MERCHANDISE

ACTION FIGURES

❑ 12" tall Alien Warrior (from ALIEN) (released in 1979)

❑ Alien Figures (first set released in 1992): Gorilla Alien, Scorpion Alien, Bull Alien and Alien Queen

❑ Alien Figures (second set released in 1993): Panther Alien, Snake Alien, Rhino Alien, Killer-Crab Alien, Mantis Alien. Flying Queen and Queen Face-Hugger.

❑ Aliens Versus the Predator set (released in 1994)

❑ Colonial Marines (first set released in 1992): Sgt. Apone, Corporal Hicks, Drake, Bishop, and Ripley

❑ Colonial Marines (second set released in 1993): Private Hudson, Vasquez, Atax, and O'Malley

❑ Armored Vehicles: Power Loader, Hovertread vehicle, Evac Fighter, and Mini Drop-Ship (released in 1992/93)

❑ Alien Warrior Punch Bag (released in 1992) [Each of these toys were released by Kenner Toys]

BOOKS AND PORTFOLIOS

❑ Alien novelization by Alan Dean Foster (Warner Books, 1979)

❑ "Alien" Movie Novel edited by Richard J. Anobile (Avon Books, 1979.

❑ Aliens novelization by Alan Dean Foster (Warner Books, 1986)

❑ Alien 3 novelization by Alan Dean Foster (Warner Books, 1992)

❑ "Aliens" Art Portfolio (Dark Horse Comics Art by Mark A. Nelson, 1989)

❑ The Book of "Alien" by Paul Scanlon and Michael Gross (Heavy Metal, 1979)

❑ The Comical Alien Art Portfolio by Kevin Davies (1979)

❑ Giger's "Alien" (from Morpheus International, 1979)

❑ H.R. Giger's Necronomicon (from Morpheus International, 1992)

❑ H.R. Giger's Bio-mechanics (from Morpheus International. 1992)

BUBBLE-GUM CARDS

❑ "Alien" (Set of 87 cards, one checklist and eleven stickers released by Topps in 1979)

❑ "Alien 3" (Set of 79 cards, one checklist released by Star Picks in 1992)

COMICS

❑ "Alien": the Illustrated Story, written by Archie Goodwin and illustrated by Walt Simonson (Heavy Metal, 1979)

❑ Aliens - Six-Issue Series (Dark Horse Comics, 1988-89)

❑ Aliens Volume Two- Four-Issue Series (Dark Horse Comics, 1989-90)

❑ Aliens: Earth War - Four-Issue Series (Dark Horse Comics, 1990)

❑ Aliens Versus Predator - Four-Issue Series (Dark Horse Comics, 1990)

❑ Aliens: Genocide - Four-Issue Series (Dark Horse Comics, 1991-92)

❑ Aliens: Hive - Four-Issue Series (Dark Horse Comics, 1992)

❑ Dark Horse Presents: Aliens — One Shot (Dark Horse Comics, 1992)

❑ Aliens: Newt's Tale — Two-Issue Series (Dark Horse Comics, 1992)

❑ Alien 3 - Three Issue Series (Dark Horse Comics, 1992)

❑ Aliens: Countdown — One-Shot (Dark Horse Comics, 1993)

❑ Aliens: Sacrifice — One-Shot (Dark Horse Comics, 1993)

❑ Aliens: Rogue — Four-Issue Series (Dark Horse Comics, 1993)

❑ Aliens: Labyrinth — Four-Issue Series (Dark Horse Comics, 1993)

❑ Aliens: Colonial Marines — Twelve-Issue Series (Dark Horse Comics, 1993-94)

❑ Aliens Versus Predator: Deadliest of Species — Twelve-Issue Series (Dark Horse Comics, 1994)

❑ Aliens: Music of the Spears — Four-Issue Series (Dark Horse Comics, 1994)

ALIENS™

DRAKE™

Specialty: Never defeated in hand to hand combat
Home Planet: Detention Planet 27, Requist system
Background: Born in captivity, he fought his way out to join the Space Marines at 21.
Quote: "Stay Frosty, Marines...and LET IT ROCK!"

TO SAVE: CUT ON DOTTED LINE.

Dark. Empty. Silent. This is deep space...and vicious Aliens are attacking. One force has the guns and the guts to face these ugly monsters. Send in the heavy metal...Send in the Space Marines!
THE INVASION IS ON!

BULL ALIEN™
power-rams a Marine!

CORP. HICKS™
launches Alienator™ missile attack!

BISHOP™
fires punishing Gatling Gun!

CAUTION: NOT RECOMMENDED FOR CHILDREN WHO STILL PUT OBJECTS IN THEIR MOUTHS. CONTAINS SMALL PARTS.

DRAKE™
blasts away with his Smart Gun™!

SGT. APONE™
tosses Mega Grenades!

POWER LOADER™
battle suit with missile and capture claws!
(Figure Sold Separately)

ALIEN QUEEN™
with attacking double jaws and whipping spiked tail!

GORILLA ALIEN™
grabs and squirts "acid" venom!

LT. RIPLEY™
Turbo Torches an Alien!

SCORPION ALIEN™
explodes when hit!

FILMS AND VIDEO TAPES

☐ 8mm reel of "Alien" (from Ken Films, 1980)
☐ "Alien" (1979) (Twentieth Century-Fox Home Video)
☐ "Alien" (1979) Special Laserdisc Edition (Twentieth Century-Fox Home Video)
☐ "Alien" (1979) Laserdisc (Pan & Scan) (Twentieth Century-Fox Home Video)
☐ "Aliens" (1986) (Twentieth Century-Fox Home Video)
☐ "Aliens" (1986) Special Laserdisc Edition (Twentieth Century-Fox Home Video)
☐ "Aliens" (1986) Laserdisc (Pan & Scan) (Twentieth Century-Fox Home Video)
☐ "Alien 3" (1992) (Twentieth Century-Fox Home Video)
☐ "Alien 3" (1992) (Twentieth Century-Fox Home Video) Videos and Laserdiscs

GAMES

☐ "Alien" Board game (from Kenner, 1979)
☐ "Aliens" Board game (from Leading Edge, 1988)
☐ "Aliens" Role-playing Game (from Leading Edge, 1990)
☐ "Alien 3" for Nintendo and Sega-Genesis (1992)

LEAD MINIATURES

first Collection:

☐ B Squad (Hicks, Drake, Frost and Dietrich), Alien Warrior "A," and a 54mm Armored Personnel Carrier
☐ A. Squad (Apone, Vasquez, Wiersbowski, Crowe and Hudson), APC interior, Asst. of four eyes, face-huggers, chest-burster and Alien Warrior "B"
☐ Command and Control (Gorman, Spunkmeyer and Ferro), Alien Warrior "C," and the Narcissus
☐ Civilians, Nostromo, Sulaco, Dropship, Alien Queen with Egg-sac, assorted lower torso seated figures, 54mm Power Loader and Alien Warrior "D" [Each of these Limited Edition Lead Miniature Sets were released by AEF Designs, Inc. in 1989.]

second Collection:

☐ Colonial Marines Boxed Set #1: Features Wierzbowski, Hicks, Ferro, Ripley, Gorman, Newt, Drake and Frost.
☐ Colonial Marines Boxed Set #2: Features Vasquez, Hudson, Apone, Bishop, Spunkmeyer, and Carter Burke.
☐ Power Loader Boxed Set: Features Ripley in Power Loader suit and four "smart" machine guns
☐ Alien Queen Boxed Set: Features the Queen, 2 eggs and 2

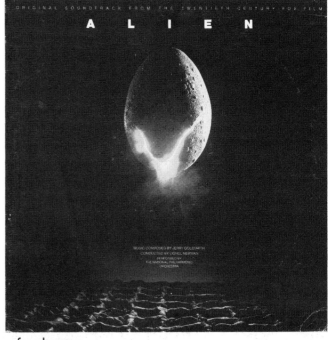

face-huggers
☐ Alien Warrior Boxed Set #1: Features six alien warriors in various poses.
☐ Alien Warrior Boxed Set #2: Features six alien warriors in various poses.
☐ LV-426 Colonists 25mm Lead Miniature Sets were sculpted by Bob Ridolfi and released by Leading Edge Games of Pasadena, California in 1992.]

MASKS AND COSTUMES

☐ "Alien" children's costume (from Ben Cooper, Inc, 1979)
☐ Limited Edition, custom-designed Face-Hugger (from Don Post Studios, 1979)
☐ Collector's Set of Patches (from "Alien" 1979)

PLASTIC MODEL KITS

☐ Alien Chest-Burster (Halcyon, 1992)
☐ Alien Dog-Burster (Halcyon, 1992)
☐ Alien Face-Hugger (Halcyon, 1992)
☐ Alien Face-Hugger (1:1 scale) (Halcyon, 1992)
☐ Alien Queen (Halcyon, 1992)
☐ Alien Warrior (Fundimentions, 1979)
☐ Alien Warrior Porcelain-cast (Dark Horse Comics, 1991 sculpted by Randy Bowen)
☐ Alien Warrior and Eggs (Halcyon, 1992)
☐ Alien 3 Warrior (Halcyon, 1992)
☐ Armored Personnel Carrier (A.P.C.) (Halcyon, 1992)

❏ Drop-Ship (Halcyon, 1992)
❏ "The Narcissus" (Halcyon, 1992)
❏ Power Loader (Halcyon, 1992)
❏ "The Space Jockey" (Halcyon, 1992)
❏ "The Sulaco" (Halcyon, 1992)
❏ Pulse-rifle (from Japanese corporation, 1987)

PINS AND BUTTONS

❏ "Alien" (promotional button from studio)
❏ "Aliens" (promotional button from studio)
❏ "Aliens" and "The Fly" double-feature (promotional button from studio)
❏ "Alien 3" (promotional button from studio)
❏ Alien Warrior #1 (Dark Horse, 1989)
❏ Alien Warrior #2 (Dark Horse, 1989)

❏ Alien Queen (Dark Horse, 1989)
❏ Chest-Burster (Dark Horse, 1989)

POSTERS

❏ "Alien" (1979) movie poster (studio, 1979)
❏ "Alien" Assorted posters (Dargis & Associates)
❏ "Aliens" (1986) movie posters (studio, 1986)
❏ "Alien 3" (1992) movie poster (studio, 1992)
❏ "Aliens Don't Knock" Door-Size Poster (1987)

T-SHIRTS

❏ "Alien" 3-D Chest-burster T-Shirt (Distortions, 1979)
❏ "Aliens" (movie tie-in released in 1986)
❏ "Alien 3" (movie tie-in released in 1992)
❏ Aliens Front-and-Back T-Shirt (Dark Horse Comics, 1989)

AGES 4 AND UP ™

ALIENS ™

SPACE MARINE
**POWER
LOADER** ™
WITH ALIENATOR™ MISSILE
AND GRABBING CLAWS

Figure sold separately

SELECTED BIBLIOGRAPHY

Aldiss, Brian W. Billion Year Spree: The True History of Science Fiction. New York: Schocken Books, 1973.

Andrews, Nigel. Horror Films. New York: Gallery Books, 1985. Anobile, Richard J., editor. "Alien" Movie Novel. New York: Avon Books, 1979.

Aylesworth, Thomas G. Monsters from the Movies. New York: Bantam Skylark Books, 1972.

Baxter, John. Science Fiction in the Cinema. New York: Paperback Library, 1970.

Butler, Ivan. Horror in the Cinema. New York: Paperback Library, 1971.

Clarens, Carlos. Horror Movies. London: Secker and Warburg, 1968.

Cohen, Daniel. Horror in the Movies. New York: Houghton Mifflin Company, Inc., 1982.

Di Franco, J. Philip, ed. The Movie World of Roger Corman. New York: Chelsea House, 1979.

Doherty, Thomas. "James Cameron's 'Aliens.'" Cinefantastique (October 1986). Oak Park, Illinois: CFQ Press.

Edelson, Edward. GREAT MONSTERS OF THE MOVIES. New York: Doubleday and Company, 1973.

FAMOUS MONSTERS OF FILMLAND Magazine. Forrest J. Ackerman, editor. Philadelphia: Warren Publishing, 1958.

Flynn, John L. Cinematic Vampires: The Living Dead on Film and Television. Jefferson, North Carolina: McFarland & Company, Publishers, 1992.

Films of Arnold Schwarzenegger, The. New York: Citadel Books, 1993.

Halliwell, Leslie. Halliwell's Film Guide. New York: Scribner's, 1984.

Huss, Roy Gerard. Focus on the Horror Film. New York: Prentice-Hall, 1972.

King, Stephen. Danse Macabre. New York: Berkeley, 1982. McDonnell, Dave, editor. "Aliens": The Official Movie Book. New York: Starlog Publications, 1986.

Maltin, Leonard. Leonard Maltin's Movie and Video Guide. New York: Signet Publishers, 1994.

Monsterland magazine, nos. 1-6. Forrest J. Ackerman, ed. Los Angeles, California: New Media Publishing.

Phantoms of the Opera: The Face Behind the Mask. New York: Image Publishing, 1993.

Pohl, Frederick. Science Fiction Studies in Film. New York: Ace Books, 1981.

Scanlon, Paul and Michael Gross. The Book of "Alien." New York: Simon and Schuster, 1979.

Shay, Don. "Making ALIENS" from Cinefex 27 (August 1986). Riverside, California: Don Shay Productions.

Stanley, John. The Creature Features Movie Guide. New York: Warner Books, 1981.

ABOUT THE AUTHOR

John L. Flynn was born in Chicago, Illinois, in 1954. He started writing his own *Star Trek* and other science fiction adventures when he was fifteen, and published his earliest fiction in fanzines at the age of nineteen.

While pursuing a Bachelor and Master's Degree in English and Journalism (as well as working two jobs to pay for his education), he became involved in The Florida Suncoast Writer's Conference (1972-77). That involvement led to workshops with John Barth, Michael Shaara, Damon Knight, Kate Wilhelm, and others, and culminated in his first professional sale in 1977 to *Churchman* magazine. He graduated with honors from the University of South Florida also in 1977, and went to work as a high school English teacher. Finding opportunities somewhat limited in Florida, John moved to Baltimore, Maryland, in 1978, and opened one of the area's first science fiction bookstores.

He also continued to write, and has sold more than fifty articles, reviews, essays, and stories, beginning in 1983. His work has appeared in *Starlog, Not of This Earth, Media History Digest, Monsterland, SF Movieland, SFTV, Enterprise, The Annapolis Review, The Daily Planet, Collector's Corner, Sci-Fi Universe, The Antique Reporter* and *Cinescape* He sold his first book, *Future Threads* in 1985, and began teaching courses on writing at Anne Arundel Community College that fall. John became a member of the Science Fiction Writers of America in 1986, and was asked in 1987 to serve as the educational consultant on *The Dictionary of Essential English*. He was listed in 1987 and 1988 in *The Who's Who Men of Achievement*. He has subsequently published three other books, including *Cinematic Vampires: The Living Dead on Film and Television* (McFarland & Company, 1992), *Phantoms of the Opera: Behind the Mask* (Image Publishing, 1993) and *The Films of Arnold Schwarzenegger* (Citadel Press, 1993). He has appeared on television and spoken on the radio about writing and horror films.

Today, John lives in Woodlawn, Maryland, and works for Towson State University.